Flora White

Flora White

In the Vanguard of Gender Equity

Linda C. Morice

LEXINGTON BOOKS
Lanham • Boulder • New York • London

Published by Lexington Books
An imprint of The Rowman & Littlefield Publishing Group, Inc.
4501 Forbes Boulevard, Suite 200, Lanham, Maryland 20706
www.rowman.com

Unit A, Whitacre Mews, 26-34 Stannary Street, London SE11 4AB

British Library Cataloguing in Publication Information Available

Library of Congress Cataloging-in-Publication Data

Library of Congress Cataloging-in-Publication Data Available

ISBN 978-1-4985-4238-8 (cloth : alk. paper)
ISBN 978-1-4985-4239-5 (electronic)

∞™ The paper used in this publication meets the minimum requirements of American National Standard for Information Sciences Permanence of Paper for Printed Library Materials, ANSI/NISO Z39.48-1992.

Printed in the United States of America

To my husband Jim and daughter Sarah,
who provided perspective and support
for the telling of Flora White's story—
from our initial visit to Heath
through the publication of this book.

Contents

Introduction

In 1937, residents of Fargo, Oklahoma, sat in their high school gymnasium, watching a girls' basketball game while enjoying a respite from the harsh realities of the Dust Bowl. One spectator—a seventy-seven-year-old woman seated next to the aisle—attracted attention by enthusiastically clapping and yelling "Bravo! Bravo!" as though she were in a concert hall in New York or Boston. When, at half time, the referee walked down the aisle to the dressing room, the woman took his arm and asked in a New England accent, "How long are the girls supposed to hold the ball?" He answered, "Three seconds." She replied, "Just as I thought, and they have been holding it much longer."[1]

The spectator, Flora White of Massachusetts, was referring to one of several rules adopted for women's basketball to make it less strenuous than the men's game. The rules reflected prevailing attitudes about women's alleged frailty. Unlike men's basketball, the women's court was divided into three zones, and players were required to remain within their designated area throughout the game. They could not hold the ball for more than three seconds, bounce it more than three times, or grab it from another player's hand. However, White was not concerned with rules enforcement per se. She would later observe, "When one is 70, one may laugh at all the rules and do precisely as one pleases."[2] What she *did* care about was increasing the speed of the game to better reflect the physical capabilities of the female players.

Later the referee asked Grace Moyer, a Fargo teacher seated with Flora White, about her companion's identity. The short answer was that she was the sister of Grace's grandfather Joseph ("Uncle Joe") White, a "pioneer citizen" who had settled in the new state of Oklahoma after spending most of his adult life in the Midwest.[3] A longer answer, while more complicated, would have explained Flora's behavior. Although her name was never a household word, Flora White had a distinguished career promoting the physi-

1

cal and intellectual achievements of girls and women. She spent her child-hood in poverty but, as an adult, gave lectures in Boston that alternated with those of Harvard professor William James. Early in her career White rebelled against the industrial model that characterized U.S. public education and in 1897 founded her own private school in Concord, Massachusetts. The school—an early effort in child-centered, progressive education—counted among its students the direct descendents of three U.S. presidents, as well as the daughters of a Cabinet secretary, eminent educators, attorneys, industrial-ists, and financiers. White's alumnae included the dean of Wellesley College, noted artists, and women who were prominent in civic affairs. The school was a forerunner of Concord Academy, today considered one of the top secondary schools in the United States.

Flora White's career was not confined to her school, however. Through her work in kinesiology, White challenged widely held assumptions about women's physical limitations. She taught *physical culture* classes in health and bodily movement and collaborated with Dr. Grace Wolcott, a pioneering physician in women's healthcare. White was also instrumental in establish-ing a summer colony of social progressives and intellectuals at her birthplace of Heath, Massachusetts. There, in the company of such luminaries as jurist Felix Frankfurter and theologian Reinhold Niebuhr—as well as lesser-known women and men, many with first-rate minds—White debated, spoke, and wrote for wider audiences on the important issues of the day.

In part because of her accomplishments in a society that marginalized women, Flora White defied easy categorization. She had the race privilege of being white, but her social class fluctuated throughout her life, depending on the immediate circumstances. She was poor during her childhood, as well as in her later years. Since White was unmarried, she had to earn a living. She lacked the financial resources for higher education and was able to attend two years of normal school only through the generosity of a minister who remembered the fatherless young woman in his will. On the other hand, she used her professional contacts and writing ability to travel the globe when few women could do so. White taught in the Cape Colony in southern Africa and studied in Sweden. She published in *Harper's New Monthly Magazine* and in a book edited by William Dean Howells and Henry Mills Alden. Knowing that she could experience privilege or oppression at any moment, White sought *agency*, or the capacity to act autonomously in an environment of possibility and constraint. She frequently quoted Tennyson's poem, "Two Voices," which describes the individual's essential choice between Life and Death. Like Tennyson, White wanted "More life, and fuller," a goal that would direct her actions throughout her eighty-seven years.[4]

While biographies have long focused on subjects whose political, social, intellectual, or literary contributions were sufficiently important to *entitle* them to a recorded life story, White's experience fits a newer biographical form. Historian Barbara Caine writes of a recent "biographical turn" in the humanities and social sciences involving a "preoccupation with individual lives . . . as a way of understanding contemporary societies and the whole process of social and historical change."[5] She argues that especially in women's history, it is not the most powerful people who offer the best insights but, rather, those who are "less-exalted." Caine suggests such biographical subjects provide "extraordinary" perceptions in their understanding of particular institutions and of major social, economic and/or political events they experienced.[6]

Flora White's value as a biographical subject is further enhanced by primary and secondary sources that have only recently become the subject of scholarly research. The story of their retrieval is interesting in itself. White left instructions that, following her death, the extensive collection of her personal papers should go to her brother Joseph and his progeny. When she died the executor of her will, Alice Whiteman, found White's correspondence from the Cape Colony in 1885–1887 to be especially interesting. Whiteman sent the letters to New York to Flora's longtime friend and editor, John Haynes Holmes. A Unitarian minister and editor of *Unity* magazine, Holmes was a prominent leader of liberal causes and a founder of both the National Association for the Advancement of Colored People (NAACP) and American Civil Liberties Union (ACLU). His receipt of the letters evoked concern in Margaret Malone, a member of the Heath summer colony. On January 19, 1949, Malone typed a letter to Whiteman, requesting that she ask Holmes to return the correspondence so it could be sent to Flora's relatives who loved her. Malone argued that the original letters were best placed with White's only surviving sibling—her ninety-two-year-old brother Joseph, who was mentally alert and in good health, and living with his daughter in Oklahoma. In making the request, Malone added that abridged versions of a dozen or so letters might also be kept in the back of the White family genealogy in the Heath Historical Society.[7]

Joseph White died eleven days later. While there is no record of Whiteman's response to Malone, the letters from the Cape Colony were shipped to Oklahoma and held by his daughter Catherine—my grandmother—until her death in 1964. For the next four decades White's papers remained in Oklahoma in the custody of my grandmother's oldest son, and then his widow. In 2005, they came unexpectedly to me, Joseph White's great-granddaughter. Given the difficulty of finding sources on the lives of women (who were often silenced in historical writing) the collection of White's letters, speeches, newspaper clippings, published articles, books, photographs, and brochures was an important find.[8] They have been supplemented by census data, school booklets and catalogues, advertisements, and local and institutional histories, as well as by written reminiscences and photographs that White's great-niece Grace maintained in her Nebraska home until 2003.

Additionally, I have consulted archival material in the Health Historical Society, tapes and transcripts of interviews of White's former Concord students (conducted in the 1970s), and secondary sources that contextualize White's actions and achievements. Although I never knew Flora White, the final segment of this book is an Appendix on Sources and Methodology in which I discuss my family relationship and how the connection affected my portrayal of her.

As I began the book, I viewed my task as one of identifying sources, synthesizing pertinent information on White's life, and presenting my biographical subject to readers with a minimum of bias. I hoped that, through my findings, I might offer new facts and interpretations to influence scholars of educational history and women's history. Specifically, I wanted to foster a better understanding of women's contributions to the progressive education movement, as well as explore how gender, race, and class intersected in one woman's life. From the outset, I recognized a need for secondary sources to contextualize my archival finds. Accordingly, I began to gather seminal works on major social and cultural trends during White's life, including such titles as Michael B. Katz, *The Irony of School Reform*;[9] David B. Tyack, *The One Best System*;[10] Alan R. Sadovnik and Susan F Semel, eds., *Founding Mothers and Others: Women Educational Leaders during the Progressive Era*;[11] and Sara Alpern et al., *The Challenge of Feminist Biography: Writing the Lives of Modern American Women.*[12]

While working with primary and secondary sources, I also came to appreciate what Louis M. Smith calls the "adventuring" experiences of a biographer.[13] In the early stages of his research on Nora Barlow (Charles Darwin's granddaughter), Smith embarked on a ten-day visit to England to seek information about a school she had attended. As Smith made contacts and pursued leads in London, Cambridge, and other English towns, he learned the value of "constant browsing." (In Smith's words, he "poked around" and was rewarded with important research finds.)[14] Following his example, I went to Massachusetts as a researcher where I visited Flora and Mary White's house at Heath, walked the bucolic paths, toured historic buildings in the town center, and spoke to a mentally alert woman over one hundred years of age who recalled her experiences with my biographical subject. I also journeyed to northwest Oklahoma where I visited the farm homes of White's relatives, retraced her steps, and spoke to family members who directed me to a tree Flora had sent long ago to mitigate her loved ones' exposure to heat and drought. These experiences helped to humanize Flora White, thereby supplementing the other sources I had acquired.

As I "poked around" Heath for information on White's parents, I discovered my most important primary source: a notebook titled "Life Facts of Flora White and Family Recorded Mar. 18, 1939."[15] White penned this narrative, apparently influenced by two factors. The first was the 1938 death of

Mary White, Flora's housemate and confidante and the last of her sisters. A second factor was that Flora had passed the age of seventy, which, in her mind, gave her the freedom to disclose details of her own life as she wished. "Life Facts" contains many important details of Flora White's experiences— her close friends and family, professional activities, publications, religious involvement, travel, and real estate dealings. In writing the document, White seemingly wanted to leave a record of events that she alone remembered. Although she might not have anticipated developments in women's history and biography that would prompt scholarly interest in her life story seven decades later, White clearly believed that someone would find her personal story—or her family's—interesting or useful.

Flora White: In the Vanguard of Gender Equity seeks to achieve several goals. First, it presents White as a biographical subject. Her contributions are little known in the annals of history, like a majority of nineteenth- and twentieth-century women. However, while White was marginalized due to her gender (and sometimes her class), she nevertheless influenced, and was influenced by, the social and cultural developments of her day. Through her efforts to promote women's intellectual and physical well-being, she helped to form the social and cultural landscape of the United States in the twenty-first century.

Second, the book makes a scholarly contribution by placing Flora White in the context of progressive education's formative period. White's documents, coupled with other primary and secondary sources, show the historical record is fraught with inaccuracies and omissions, especially as regards John Dewey's role in the reform known as Organic Education. This book seeks to correct the record while suggesting new directions for educational research to create a better understanding of the development of progressive education and the role women played in it.

Third, the book introduces evidence of Flora White's critique of another well-known leader in educational history, G. Stanley Hall, who drew on evolutionary theory to propose a sexist view of educated women who were childless. White's critique of Hall appears in an unlikely form and location (in verse, in a published poetry collection). It exemplifies the work of Joan N. Radner and Susan S. Lanser, who contend that marginalized women express their thoughts in code in order to gain protection from people who might find their ideas disturbing.[16] White's critique of Hall points the way to possible new sources of information on women's history.

Finally, the book builds on the work of Diana Moyer, Petra Munro Hendry, and Lucy E. Bailey in bringing a gendered lens to educational history. Like Moyer's research, White's biography negates the long-held view of progressive education that cast men in the role of theorists and women as practitioners. (Throughout her teaching career, Flora White informed theory while also being influenced by it.)[17] Her reaction to G. Stanley Hall reveals a woman who was not—in Hendry's words—simply a "dutiful" daughter who implemented the father's ideas without being "generative in her own right."[18] It is important to note that White sometimes advanced her views by using code in writing poetry (as well as a male pen name in fiction writing). This suggests a fertile ground for Bailey, her co-researcher Karen Graves, and others who seek not only new sources but also new methodologies for interpreting historical events. Bailey acknowledges that such work in "engendering" educational history involves "stretching" and "expand[ing] in new directions"—an endeavor that would have suited Flora White nicely![19]

Flora White: In the Vanguard of Gender Equity presents her life chronologically. Its first chapter ("A Good Name") establishes the context for White's quest for agency. She was born in Heath, Massachusetts, into a respected family in a society that privileged white Anglo-Americans over all other groups. The early death of White's father forced the family into poverty, and her only brother (Joseph) was "bound out" in a condition resembling indentured servitude. However, the kindness of a retired minister allowed Flora, her mother, and sister Mary to live in his home in Amherst—thereby providing Flora with a superior education, a bequest to attend Westfield Normal School, and social capital that would prove useful for the remainder of her life. The chapter argues that it was the combination of privilege and marginalization during her early years that encouraged White's quest for agency.

Chapter 2 ("Nature Weeps") reveals how Flora White's marginalized status as a female public school teacher led to her revolt against the prevailing industrial model of U.S. public education. The chapter documents how public schools were organized like factories—with men overseeing adults and older students, and women being relegated to nurturing small children. Gender discrimination was evident in stark wage inequities between male and female teachers. Exercising a sense of agency, White resigned her elementary teaching position at a public school in Springfield, Massachusetts, to teach English to adolescent boys at a preparatory school in the Cape Colony in southern Africa.

The major focus of chapter 3 ("Finding Her Voice") is the growth White experienced in the Cape Colony, where she refined her identity in terms of gender, race, class, and nationality. Drawing on White's letters to her mother and sister (and on scholarship showing how trans-Atlantic travel benefited nineteenth-century women), the chapter reveals the process by which White clarified her personal and professional goals and returned home with a resolve to found a new type of private school with her sister Mary. The chapter also shows White's emergence as a writer, resulting in the publication in *Harper's New Monthly Magazine* of a sympathetic short story about a Bantu-speaking girl in the Cape Colony. Despite the fact that White was sharing her views with a national audience, she faced limitations as a woman writer: the story was written in the voice of a male narrator, and was published under a man's pen name.

The fourth chapter ("The New Education") explores the small private school White established in Springfield—a very early example of the formative period of the progressive education movement—and, more specifically, the *child-centered* strand of progressive education. The chapter details how White returned from the Cape Colony with a desire to incorporate *motor training* (fine and gross-motor development) into her instruction. During the summer of 1891 she enrolled at the Seminarium for Teachers in Nääs, Sweden, where she studied educational theory and the use of woodcraft to enhance students' physical and cognitive development. (She also studied Ling gymnastics, a regular part of the curriculum.) At the time woodworking was widely regarded as a "masculine" craft as opposed to "feminine" crafts like sewing or embroidery. White demonstrated a willingness to test convention in her formal studies, as well as in her "dreadfully romantic and scandalous" romance with a male teacher with the common Swedish first name of Nils. [20] The chapter contends that—like other educated white women described by Sara Evans—White apparently chose to return to the United States without Nils, foregoing marriage and immersing herself in her career. [21]

Chapter 5 ("Visionary Women") shows how Flora White and other Massachusetts women collaborated to improve the education of people in an environment of rapid industrialization and urbanization. Amid widespread beliefs about female frailty, they also taught about women's bodies and physical potential while making pioneering advances in physical development and healthcare delivery. The focus is on several key women (including Boston philanthropist Pauline Agassiz Shaw and Dr. Grace Wolcott, a pioneer in women's health) with whom White had close professional or personal contact. The chapter details how, in 1893—at the invitation of the Secretary of the Massachusetts State Board of Education—White closed her small Springfield school and joined the faculty of her alma mater, Westfield Normal School, where she taught gymnastics, physiology theory, and teaching methodology to an overwhelmingly female student body. Two years later White became associate principal at the Boston gymnasium of Nils Posse, an important figure in the history of kinesiology. After his sudden death, White made a career change, in part occasioned by her own extended bed rest following an appendectomy. In 1897 she founded a new private school in the nonconformist community of Concord, Massachusetts. She would regard the school as the pinnacle of her career.

Chapter 6 ("A Redeemer") presents Miss White's Home School in Concord through the eyes of former students whom Renee Garrelick interviewed in the 1970s. The chapter also depicts the rivalry among male theorists in the early progressive education movement, and shows that competition affects current understandings of women's contributions to school reform. Focusing on C. Hanford Henderson—a rival of John Dewey and an endorser of White's school—the chapter shows how Dewey failed to give Henderson appropriate credit for his work in Organic Education, thereby diminishing the presence of New England women school founders (like White) in the current historical narrative. Additionally, chapter 6 discusses Flora White's difficulty with another school endorser—psychologist G. Stanley Hall—who wanted to severely limit the education of women. White continued her program according to her beliefs; she also distanced herself from Hall without losing the endorsement of this powerful man.

Chapter 7 ("Doing 'Precisely What One Pleases'") describes White's quest for agency after she sold her Concord school in 1914 and became a full-time resident of Heath. In retirement, White accepted for herself the same prerogative she held for students: to test, do, and dare. Over time, she and her sister Mary networked with other women to create at Heath a summer colony of social progressives and intellectuals, some of whom had national prominence. It was a congenial environment in which Flora experimented with agriculture, composed music and poetry, wrote and presented an outdoor drama, and published her writing in Massachusetts newspapers as well as *Unity* magazine in New York. In 1925 Flora and Mary White invited their niece Catherine Moyer (Joseph's daughter and a former student at Miss White's Home School), her husband, and five children to live with them at Heath, where Catherine's husband was schoolmaster at the town's Center School. The Moyers returned to their home in northwest Oklahoma at the end of the school year. The reminiscences of Catherine and her children provide important insights on White's personality and daily life.

Chapter 8 ("The Best of Her Generation") shows Flora White's sense of déjà vu when the Moyers experienced the human destruction of their Oklahoma ecosystem, as she had known environmental depletion during her Massachusetts girlhood. The Moyer family lived in an especially hard-hit area of the Dust Bowl, deemed the worst environmental disaster in U.S. history. With a characteristic sense of agency, White provided her relatives with trees to be planted on the windswept plains, as well as clothing and advice—particularly on the education of the Moyer children who had reached college age. She took a special interest in Catherine's oldest daughter Grace, encouraging her to come East and earn a PhD. Beginning in 1938, White made yearly trips to Oklahoma to spend the winters with her brother Joseph. Eventually Flora White lost her ability to enjoy a vigorous life. In 1948 she broke her hip in a fall and died. Her marginalization was evident in the news report of her death in the local paper. Despite a career promoting the development of girls and women, the obituary complimented White by stating that her work had been praised by "men of note throughout the educational world."[22]

As the epilogue makes clear, Flora White exhibited a lifelong desire to obtain "more life, and fuller" for her students, her relatives, and herself. Her final act of agency was to leave documents that would tell her story, specifying they be entrusted to her brother and his progeny. Although White's death occurred when there was little interest in women's lives, time proved her right. White's documents set the record straight on her own accomplishments, and those of other women.

NOTES

1. Grace Moyer Share, "Notes on the Lives of Mary Abby and Flora White" (written in 1986). Flora White Papers, private collection, 3.
2. Miss Pickwick, "Girl about Town," *Daily Oklahoman*, February 9, 1941, C5.
3. Joseph and Jennie White Obituaries, private collection.
4. White quoted Alfred Lord Tennyson, who in the poem, "The Two Voices," juxtaposes Life and Death and notes that it is "More life, and fuller, that I want." See Flora J. White, "Physical Effects of Sloyd," *Sloyd Bulletin* 2 (1899): 9.
5. Barbara Caine, *Biography and History* (New York: Palgrave, 2010), 1.
6. Ibid.
7. Margaret Malone to Alice K. Whiteman, 19 January 1949. Heath (MA) Historical Society.
8. The shortage of sources on women's lives has been documented by a number of scholars. See, for example, Geraldine Joncich Clifford, "The Historical Recovery of Edyth Astrid Ferris," in *Writing Educational Biography: Explorations in Qualitative Research,* ed. Craig Kridel (New York and London: Garland, 1998), 147–155; and Elisabeth Israels Perry, "From Belle Moskowitz to Women's History," in *The Challenge of Feminist Biography: Writing the Lives of Modern American Women,* ed. Sara Alpern et al. (Urbana and Chicago: University of Illinois Press, 1992).
9. Michael B. Katz, *The Irony of School Reform: Educational Innovations in Mid-Nineteenth-Century Massachusetts* (New York: Teachers College, Columbia University, 2001).
10. David B. Tyack, *The One Best System: A History of American Urban Education* (Cambridge, MA: Harvard University Press, 1992).
11. Alan R. Sadovnik and Susan F. Semel, eds., *Founding Mothers and Others: Women Educational Leaders during the Progressive Era* (New York: Palgrave, 2002).
12. Sara Alpern et al., *The Challenge of Feminist Biography: Writing the Lives of Modern American Women* (Urbana and Chicago: University of Illinois Press, 1992).
13. Louis M. Smith, "Adventuring as Biographers: A Chronicle of a Difficult Ten-Day Week," *Vitae Scholasticae* 31 (2014): 5.
14. Ibid., 19.
15. Flora White, "Life Facts of Flora White and Family Recorded Mar. 18, 1939," Heath (MA) Historical Society.
16. Joan N. Radner and Susan S. Lanser, "Strategies of Coding in Women's Cultures," in *Feminist Messages: Coding in Women's Folk Cultures,* ed. Joan Newton Radler (Champaign, IL: University of Illinois Press, 1993), 1–30.
17. Diana Moyer, "The Gendered Boundaries of Child-Centred Education: Elsie-Ripley Clapp and the History of U.S. Progressive Education" *Gender and Education,* 21 (2009): 531–547.
18. Petra Munro Hendry, *Engendering Curriculum History* (New York and London: Routledge, 2011), 19.
19. Lucy E. Bailey, "Engendering Educational History: Some Methodological Musings," *Journal of Philosophy and History of Education* 65 (2015): xv–xxx.
20. Flora White to Mary A. White, 2 August, 1891, Flora White Papers, private collection.
21. Sara Evans, *Born For Liberty* (New York: The Free Press, 1989).
22. "Writer, Educator Miss White Dies," *Greenfield Gazette and Courier* (Greenfield, MA), February 16, 1948, 2.

Chapter One

A Good Name

In 1947, a journalist from the *Greenfield Gazette and Courier* visited the blue and white bedroom of Flora White, an eighty-seven-year-old resident of the Parks Convalescent Home. "Of Gertrude Stein appearance, with clipped grey locks," the "colorful" woman was "almost blind." Although a cane leaned against the door, White's appearance was "still far from feeble and more that of a woman in her late sixties."[1] The journalist noted that until White was eighty, she "was considered the most athletic woman in the country."[2] After the visit, the Massachusetts newspaper ran a feature story describing White's reminiscences on her long life as an educator, writer, and world traveler. Making special mention of the "many notables" who were "among her relatives and ancestors,"[3] the story demonstrated an understanding of an important aspect of Flora White's character: her family played a major role in how she viewed herself.

Six years before the interview, Catherine White Moyer—struggling to care for the needs of her large family in the aftermath of the Oklahoma Dust Bowl—made an observation about her aunt, Flora White: "Aunt Flora . . . pointed out that we have such wonderful ancestors dating back to [the time of] Columbus. Perhaps so—but in the west people are what they are and ancestors are not considered."[4] White was proud of her family heritage. Although it did not prevent her from falling into poverty when her father died in 1861—or shield her Oklahoma relatives from the dire effects of a man-made, ecological disaster seventy years later—the status afforded by her "good name" shaped her self-perception. It allowed White to imagine she could gain agency and achieve "more life, and fuller."[5]

Florence Oetken also noticed Flora White's emphasis on family ancestry. In 1941, Oetken—newly engaged to Catherine's oldest son and White's great nephew—accompanied her fiancé to the Kansas City rail terminal to meet his

Aunt Flora for the first time. The couple entered White's railroad car during the train layover and, following introductions, the two women had tea alone. White told Oetken, "I want you to know about the family into which you are marrying." She then recited her family genealogy over three hundred years. As White's description neared a conclusion, her great nephew returned to announce that the train would soon depart. Oetken was very relieved at their hasty exit because she had feared White would soon inquire of *her* ancestry, a subject about which the Kansas City woman had, by comparison, limited information.[6] In the years following White's death, both Catherine White Moyer and Florence Oetken Moyer would faithfully maintain White's extensive archive that included family histories going back to the Puritan migration—Catherine from 1949 to 1964, and Florence from 2001 to 2005, following her husband's death.

A FAMILY MATTER

Flora White was born into a patriarchy she both celebrated and resisted. Her roots were deep in the rocky soil of her native Massachusetts—specifically in the Berkshire town of Heath, where her family had resided for four generations. White's ancestors had settled in the "howling wilderness" of western Massachusetts after a long journey that began with the Great Migration of Puritans in the 1630s. It was a voluntary relocation of approximately twenty-one thousand men, women, and children from England to North America that began and ended abruptly, shaping the physical and social environment in which the White family lived.[7]

Puritans—members of the Church of England, who sought to reform it—began in 1630 to settle in Massachusetts Bay, a colony established under a joint-stock company of the same name. The Puritans' hope was to create a "City upon a Hill" that would serve as a beacon of righteousness to the rest of the world.[8] Their migration to the New World began when Charles I dissolved Parliament in 1629, thereby depriving the Puritan gentry of a means of protesting royal policies through legitimate political channels. By 1640, when the king was forced to reopen Parliament, its members demanded sweeping reforms that Charles I opposed. He took up arms against his enemies, sparking the English Civil War that brought Oliver Cromwell, a Puritan, to power. Due to changed circumstances in England, no significant Puritan migration occurred after the early 1640s. The New England towns the Puritans established remained ethnically and religiously homogeneous for two hundred years until a large-scale immigration from Ireland altered their demographics.

Flora White's family histories show that her direct ancestor, John White of South Petherton, Somerset, emigrated to Massachusetts Bay Colony in

1638–1639. In August 1639, he was received as an inhabitant of Salem where he was granted sixty acres of land. John White and his wife, the former Joane West, fit the profile of Puritan emigrants of this period. Virginia De John Anderson notes that, unlike people who settled the Chesapeake (primarily single men seeking to improve their lot), nearly nine out of ten participants in the Great Migration traveled in family groups, and three out of four came in nuclear family units. Almost half of New England's settlers during this period were female. Like the Whites, Puritan emigrant couples typically journeyed to North America with three or more children; they had additional offspring after settling there, fueling New England's phenomenal population growth.[9]

Joane White was admitted to the first church in Salem in 1642–1643 where three of her eight children were baptized. (John's name does not appear on the church rolls, and the children were baptized in their mother's name.) That Joane White joined the church without her spouse was not unusual. Although a Puritan husband was unquestionably regarded as master of his family in seventeenth-century New England, a majority of church members—called the "visible saints"—were women.[10]

New England Puritans believed an omnipotent God had predestined some people to salvation and others to damnation. Therefore, persons seeking church membership had to demonstrate a saving faith through an account of their conversion experience. Joane White reported having been "brought up in a poore Ignorant place" and having sinned by breaking the Sabbath and "taking . . . gods name in vayne." She was "drawne towards New England because good people came hither." After reaching Massachusetts Bay "by providence" and being "shut up for a long space of time liveing far remote in ye woods from ye meanes, (of grace)" she received inspiration by reading Romans 10:17: "So then faith *cometh* by hearing and hearing by the word of God."[11]

Francis J. Bremer cites several factors such as the number of female visible saints, a growing emphasis on companionship in marriage, and an idea of family relationships based on love as indications that the status of women was improving in seventeenth-century New England.[12] While John White did not join the church at Salem, he received additional land grants at the nearby town of Wenham and by 1653 had relocated with his family to Lancaster, some sixty miles to the west, where he built a corn mill and was "the wealthiest man in town at that time."[13]

Although local histories detail the accomplishments of John White's male progeny, his female descendants receive scant attention. They had large families, kept house, and managed the barnyards, gardens, and orchards in their families' home lots. One White woman, however, is featured prominently in local histories and elsewhere. She was John and Joane White's daughter Mary, who was born in England and married the Reverend Joseph Rowlandson, the first settled minister of the church at Lancaster. On February 10, 1676, Mary Rowlandson's life changed dramatically when the Nipmucs, Narragansetts, and Wampanoags attacked Lancaster in a united action of Algonquin tribes called Metacom's War—or King Philip's War—that began in Plymouth in 1675. (Metacom was a Wampanoag sachem known to colonists as King Philip.) Mary Rowlandson was taken captive along with her three children, one of whom died in her arms nine days later from injuries sustained in the attack. Her husband was in Boston at the time, seeking military protection from the colonial authorities.

According to Daniel R. Mandell, the war was a result of decades of colonial expansion in which the Puritans' concept of the land and its ownership came into direct conflict with the attitudes of indigenous peoples in the region. Puritans had the European notion of discovery, which awarded sovereignty and territorial rights to the (European) nation that first claimed a particular part of the New World. They also embraced the legal doctrine of *vacuum domicilium,* which held that those who "improved" land by growing crops or raising cattle on it had the right to it. A few colonists (including Roger Williams) pointed out that the Wampanoags and other natives did far more for the land than "wander after the chase;" however, most Puritans incorrectly believed the indigenous people were hunters rather than farmers and could ethically be displaced as long as sufficient land was left for their use. [14] Native landholding was communal—and, in fact, many colonial villages also managed land resources communally throughout the seventeenth century. Nevertheless, English landholding had been moving toward ownership "in severalty, with titles vested in individuals supported by the courts." [15] The difference between the two groups was even more marked in their understanding of the land itself. While natives saw land in terms of its uses and resources, colonists viewed it as a commodity. When natives signed deeds and treaties with the English, they frequently maintained the right to share one or more resources on the land. The colonists, on the other hand, expected a transfer of full possession.

Despite these differences, Mandell notes there was an important similarity in the natives' and settlers' view of landholding. Both groups saw land as sovereign territory. English settlers conceived of sovereignty as "the ultimate power over a given area." [16] The natives' views of sovereignty were similar, although they saw landholding in terms of community use rather than individual ownership. [17] This shared value, Mandell contends, fueled the war in which Metacom and colonial leaders understood their territory in terms of its political, economic, and social significance.

War erupted in July of 1675 after years of growing tension between settlers at Plymouth and Metacom. His warriors attacked nearby Swansea, and within months fighting had spread to other parts of southern New England. Native forces drove the colonists back toward Boston, but by late spring of 1676, the tide had turned. The colonists enlisted indigenous allies in the east, while the formidable Mohawks attacked Metacom's forces in the west. By the war's end, over 10 percent of the region's population had been killed—one-third of the casualties being English and two-thirds native.[18] For indigenous people, the consequences were most catastrophic. Thousands starved, left the region, surrendered (often to be executed or sold as slaves)— or, like Metacom, were hunted down and killed.

Mary Rowlandson was taken captive before the tide turned in the colonists' favor. She was forced to accompany her captors northward one hundred fifty miles, until she was ransomed and returned to her husband in May. The surviving Rowlandson children were released shortly after their mother; however, the family faced additional trials when Rev. Joseph Rowlandson died two years later. The surviving widow, who had never before written for a wider audience, published a book in 1682 titled *The Sovereignty and Goodness of God: Being a Narrative of the Captivity and Restoration of Mrs. Mary Rowlandson.* The narrative recounted the stages of her captivity through twenty distinct "removes," or journeys, in which she repeatedly sought guidance from a Bible one of her captors gave her after obtaining it as plunder from a raid.[19] Rowlandson described how, with each remove, she was further separated from her former life as the wife of a Puritan minister and forced to confront the world of the Algonquins. Throughout her ordeal, Rowlandson was not physically attacked and demonstrated an endurance and adaptability she herself did not anticipate. She ate raw horse liver and bear meat, and she sewed for her captors. She even met Metacom, who asked her to make a shirt for his son. When she obliged, he paid her with a shilling. (Rowlandson offered it to her "mistress" and, after being told to keep it, used it to buy a piece of horse flesh.)[20] In time, Mary Rowlandson learned to acknowledge her captors' humanity as she bargained and negotiated with them. Upon her return, Rowlandson began to recognize how much the experience had changed her, and she wrote her story as a means of gaining emotional release, grace, and public acceptance. Rowlandson's book was published in Cambridge and London and read on both sides of the Atlantic, undergoing four printings in the first year and fifteen editions thereafter. It is one of the earliest autobiographical works published by an Anglo-American woman and the first Native American captivity narrative, a genre that remained popular until the nineteenth century.[21]

Flora White was proud of Mary Rowlandson's recognition as a writer and frequently cited her achievement to female family members. Interestingly, the war that made Rowlandson famous also marked an unfortunate turn in relations between natives and Anglo-American settlers. During the course of her life, Flora White pursued writing for publication, eventually criticizing the "dishonorable" treatment Native Americans received in U.S. history in the aftermath of such deteriorated relations.[22]

Mandell writes that King Philip's—or Metacom's—War was the most devastating armed conflict in American history in terms of its effect on a region. The first war to be driven by an "irresolvable clash between Native and colonial claims to sovereignty," it was a "turning point" in relations between the two groups. Although the war produced unspeakable acts of brutality on both sides, colonists began afterward to depict natives as "subhuman demons"—eventually leading to occasional nineteenth-century efforts to exterminate them.[23] Aside from destroying most of the indigenous population in southern New England and leaving the survivors subordinate to colonial authority, the war also left the settlers deeply in debt, uncertain of their future, and more dependent on the English Crown. In 1684 the Court of the Chancery—sitting in London and acting on a petition from the King—annulled the charter of Massachusetts Bay Company. This decision made it apparent to Puritans that they were not a "City upon a Hill," but rather, a part of an empire run by people who did not share their religious vision.

THE WHITES OF HEATH

The growth of large families in colonial Massachusetts resulted in the further encroachment of Anglo-American settlers in the hunting grounds of indigenous people. The settlers initially regarded the hills to the west of the Connecticut River Valley as suitable only for hunting and grazing; however, as other land filled up they traveled along the valley of the Deerfield River, climbed the hills, and established farms. Among this group was the White family, who would remain in western Massachusetts until Flora's death in 1948. Prior to their arrival, the colonial government set territorial boundaries in the region and established an orderly procedure for supporting local institutions. However, order was subsumed by a larger reality: western Massachusetts was torn by conflict as two European nations and indigenous peoples engaged in a life-and-death struggle over the future of the North American continent. It was a struggle in which the White family fully participated.

As early as 1735, the General Court of Massachusetts granted three townships in the western part of the colony to the town of Boston, "in consideration of the payment by Boston of about one-fifth of the colony tax and large sums for the support of schools and the poor."[24] One of the townships, encompassing what later became the town of Charlemont and part of the town of Buckland, was named Boston Plantation No. 1. Five hundred of its acres were reserved for the first minister, five hundred acres for the support of the ministry, and five hundred acres for the support of schools. After 1737, Boston Plantation No. 1 was named Charlemont, and the part that became the town of Heath was called Charlemont Hill.

By 1744, the General Court felt a need to fortify the region and began construction of Fort Shirley in the eastern part of Charlemont Hill. It was one of a line of forts (from the Connecticut River valley to the New York border) built to guard the colony's northern boundary against raids from Quebec in New France. This action reflected Quebec's proximity to Massachusetts and the fact that France was a long-standing enemy.

Beginning in 1689 and over a period of seventy-four years, England and France engaged in four wars of empire fought in Europe and North America. Over the course of these conflicts North America became, according to John Keegan, "one of the most fortified regions of the world."[25] Many Massachusetts men fought in support of England and became highly proficient in forest warfare. The last war of empire—a global conflict that Europeans called the Seven Years' War (1756–1763)—was known to English colonists in North America as the French and Indian War. The name referred to the enemies the colonists fought: the royal French forces and the indigenous people allied with them, including the Algonquins. (The Iroquois tribes—including the Mohawks—sided with the English.) In French-speaking Canada the war was called La Guerre de la Conquête, since England emerged victorious and France lost its land east of the Mississippi River as a result.[26]

Even after the town of Heath was incorporated in 1785 (and named for a general of the American Revolution), accounts of these early conflicts remained prominent in local lore. One source noted that Charlemont, existing "under the shadow of the forts, . . . directly felt and fanned the martial sentiment."[27] Although Flora White became a pacifist in her later years, she was interested in restoration activities at the Fort Shirley site as well as in her family members' participation in the French and Indian War, and later the American Revolution. White pursued these interests during adulthood as a founding member of the Heath Historical Society.

The first member of the White family to live in Heath was Flora's great-great grandfather, Jonathan White (1709–1788), who was born in Lancaster and built a house in nearby Leominster (once considered a part of Lancaster) where he was "the largest landholder, a man of wealth and education—a gentleman of the old school."[28] Jonathan White arrived in Charlemont in 1752 and, at a meeting of the proprietors the following January, was chosen one of the officers. During 1752–1753 he cleared a few acres on Charlemont Hill, planted an orchard, and built a house on a parcel of land that became known as the White-Wilder tract (Wilder being the name of his wife's family, who also developed the land). After serving in the French and Indian War and receiving a commission as Colonel, White spent most of his time at Lancaster, but went "back and forth" to Charlemont Hill.[29] In 1771, he gave Charlemont a burying ground, which later became Heath's South Cemetery where the Colonel is interred beside other members of the White family (including Flora, her parents, and two of her sisters). Jonathan White also bequeathed his youngest son, Asaph, the title to the Heath farm he had cleared years earlier.

A local history suggests that Jonathan White had an independent frame of mind. On one occasion, he was traveling between Lancaster and Heath when he arrived at Deerfield. Realizing he could not reach his destination without encroaching on the Sabbath (which he considered unacceptable), White remained at Deerfield and attended worship there. Wearing his "homespun frock," he entered the church and walked up the aisle, which was flanked by pews with tall doors. No one recognized Colonel White or offered him a seat. He turned around, walked quietly outside, and picked up a block of wood from a woodpile. White returned, situated himself in front of the pulpit, and sat on the block of wood during the service. By the start of the afternoon worship, the Deerfield townspeople had made his acquaintance and discovered his station in life was not as humble as his clothing would suggest. Every pew door was thrown open to accommodate him. The "stalwart Colonel" took the same block of wood he occupied in the morning and sat through afternoon service.[30]

Asaph White (1747–1828)—Flora's great-grandfather—gained recognition as "a man of remarkable executive and business ability . . . [who] was connected with almost every enterprise of a public nature" in western Massachusetts.[31] As an adolescent, he was a soldier in the French and Indian War and later fought in the American Revolution, first serving as a Minuteman in 1775, then as a First Lieutenant of the Fifth Hampshire Regiment, and finally in the state militia where he received the title of Colonel. After the war's end he engaged in real estate speculation and was one of the incorporators of the Second Massachusetts Turnpike Corporation, which built a toll road across Hoosac Mountain, known for many years as Colonel White's Turnpike. He was also one of the incorporators of the Fifth Massachusetts Turnpike Corporation, which built a toll road from Athol to Boston. Asaph White, along with four other men, oversaw the construction of the first church at Heath in 1789–1790 in which pews were "laid out with the greatest conveniency" and sold to the highest bidder.[32] (Although this practice might seem unusual today, it reflected a Puritan value that economic success was a sign of being in good standing with God.) In 1801, Asaph White was the first settler in the town of Erving, Massachusetts, where he built a dam, sawmill, and later a public house. His oldest son, David White (1777–1851)—Flora's paternal grandfather—inherited the family homestead at Heath and served as a church deacon.

On November 13, 1849, Flora's parents—David's son Joseph II and Harriet Mayhew White, a distant cousin—were married. Since Heath's once healthy church had been without a settled minister since 1845, the ceremony was performed in nearby Vermont. The minister created a certificate of marriage by scrawling on a small piece of paper that the couple had appeared before him and were duly joined as husband and wife.

The newlyweds appeared to be a good match, intellectually and socially. Harriet's grandfather, Benjamin White (1746–1817), was a successful farmer in Heath who, at age sixty-six, turned over his farm and personal estate to his son David (Harriet's father). Family records indicate that David's children were all well-educated, and during her youth Harriet studied Latin and Greek with the local Congregational minister to prepare for the Troy Female Seminary in New York, founded in 1821 by women's rights advocate Emma Willard. There is no record, however, that Harriet White actually attended the Troy Female Seminary, and it is likely that circumstances intervened to prevent her from doing so.[33] Joseph White II, a handsome man with a high forehead, steady gaze, and set jaw, was known in the town as a person of considerable intellect who tried to make the most of every opportunity. His calculus book can still be found in the collection of the Heath Historical Society. As an adult, Flora White wrote of her father, "He was an able mathematician in close touch with all the great mathematicians in the country."[34] In this case, her concept of "country" was considerably smaller than the United States, and certainly no larger than New England.

Twelve months after their wedding Harriet and Joseph White II, welcomed their first child, Emma. She would be followed by Harriet F. White ("Hattie") in 1852, Charles in 1853 (who died shortly after his second birthday), Joseph David in 1856, Mary Abby in 1858, and Flora Jane in 1860. By all accounts it was a loving family. Correspondence sent to Joseph II in Boston from his father David in Heath illustrates both the ties that bound the family together and the small margin of profit on which they operated.

In a brief note, signed "Your Affectionate Father," David White, then seventy-four years of age, recounted:

> After spending the most of the last night in diging [sic] Salt out of the tubs with a Crow Bar, Shovel & Chisel, saving about 3 or 4 bushels of Salt & the Cheese tubs full of brine, we found Pickels [sic] to fill 2 tubs, sent to Greenfield this day, & ordered to Fitchburg Depot Boston—Probably will arrive as soon as you receive this. We are all as well as when you left.[35]

When David White wrote the letter in 1851, Joseph II was 118 miles away, representing Heath for one term in the House of Representatives of the Massachusetts legislature, or General Court, in Boston. This public service required a sacrifice since his wife and infant daughter remained at Heath. There is little doubt that the pickles were intended for sale rather than for Joseph II's enjoyment, and that the funds would be a welcome addition to the family income. It is also clear that the division of labor in this family required the presence of an adult male to continue operating the farm during Joseph II's absence.

A LEGACY OF REFORM

During his short legislative service, Joseph White II became involved in reform initiatives that foreshadowed Flora's reform activities throughout her adult life. He was in the House of Representatives to represent the views of rural townspeople when elite men in Boston dominated the state's economy. Even more important, the issue of slavery defined political discourse in mid-nineteenth-century Massachusetts, and small towns like Heath had a narrow window of time in which to affect the debate.

Based on their population, Massachusetts towns were assigned the number of representatives to which they were entitled as well as the number of terms in a decade their representative(s) could be sent to Boston. All towns with at least twelve hundred inhabitants had a right to annual representation in the House. Towns with fewer than twelve hundred inhabitants (like Heath) were only "entitled to elect a representative as many times within ten years, as the number one hundred sixty is contained in the number of inhabitants of said town."[36] Each partially represented town could also send a representative in the valuation year beginning each decade. For Joseph White II, this was the legislative term immediately following his 1850 election.

In 1851, Joseph White II became involved in antislavery efforts by participating in a coalition of Free Soilers and Democrats in the Massachusetts House of Representatives that elected abolitionist Charles Sumner to the U.S. Senate. (Since the U.S. Constitution had not yet been amended to provide for the direct election of senators, they were chosen by the state legislature.) The coalition upset the power of the Whig establishment—largely based in Boston—who "went hand-in-hand with trade, commerce, manufacturing and banking."[37] Although Joseph White II's political party is not clearly designated in state records, his support of Sumner provides a good indication of his views.

Sumner was a "conscience Whig" leader who had long condemned the political alliance between the northern cotton manufacturers and merchants and the southern planters.[38] In 1848 the Conscience faction separated from the establishment Whigs in hopes of converting the Whig party into a "distinctly national anti-slavery party."[39] Sumner, the leader of antislavery forces in Massachusetts, claimed several different party affiliations during his political career. After initially aligning with the Whigs, he entered the U.S. Senate as a Free Soil Democrat (who opposed the spread of slavery into U.S. territories through popular sovereignty). Sumner later joined the newly established

Republican Party. He was, according to Flora White, Joseph White II's "personal friend."[40]

The coalition that elected Charles Sumner was pragmatic in nature. Democrats, out of favor nationally and in Massachusetts, were eager for office. Free Soilers, weary of "petrified whiggery," were anxious to join forces to achieve practical ends.[41] What resulted was, in the words of one historian, "something of a social and political revolution in Massachusetts" in which the "proud, aristocratic Whigs were no longer the proprietors of power in the state."[42] Free Soilers had already captured a number of Whig strongholds in 1848. In the 1850 election, candidates supporting the Free Soil/Democratic coalition won a total of eighty-three seats in the towns like Heath that were entitled to partial representation, while the Whigs carried only forty-one.

After a protracted process of negotiations and balloting, the coalition elected Free Soil Democrat Robert Rantoul Jr. to serve in the U.S. Senate from February 1 to March 14, 1851. Rantoul filled the position vacated by the Whig Senator Daniel Webster, who resigned to become Secretary of State. (Before resigning, Webster was roundly criticized by his constituents for supporting the Compromise of 1850, which included a Fugitive Slave Law.) The coalition also elected Charles Sumner to fill a regular, six-year Senate term. After being elected by a one-vote majority on April 24, 1851, Sumner assumed office and continued to denounce the spread of slavery into the territories.

In 1856, Sumner delivered a fiery address in the U.S. Senate, attacking popular sovereignty and southern efforts to extend slavery to Kansas Territory. The speech included an insulting reference to an absent, elderly senator, Andrew Butler of South Carolina.[43] Butler's relative, Congressman Preston Brooks, sought to defend the family honor by caning Sumner on the Senate floor, nearly killing him. Each man was immediately hailed as a hero in his respective region. Although Sumner's injuries prevented him from returning to the Senate floor for three years, Massachusetts reelected him in 1857 and kept his Senate seat vacant as a pointed reminder of southern brutality. Brooks's beating of Sumner was highly publicized and served as one of the polarizing events that led the country to civil war in 1861. Four years later Charles Sumner would introduce the Thirteenth Amendment to the U.S. Constitution to abolish slavery.

Although most of Joseph White II's time in the Massachusetts House of Representatives was spent on the U.S. Senate election and his support of Charles Sumner, White also wanted to improve the local economy. He voted on state aid to the Troy and Greenfield Railroad to construct a tunnel through Hoosac Mountain—the same mountain over which his grandfather had built a turnpike. In 1851, work began on the project, which was intended to open up trade between Massachusetts and Upstate New York and (through the Erie

Canal) the Midwest. While supporters were in the minority in 1851, state aid
was allocated years later for construction of the Hoosac Tunnel. When it was
completed in 1875, the tunnel was the longest in the Western Hemisphere
and the second longest in the world.

A CHANGING ECONOMY

Even though Joseph White II was inclined to make the most of opportunities,
they presented themselves with decreasing frequency during his adult life in
Heath. The situation was largely due to dramatic economic changes in
1830–1860 as Massachusetts underwent the First Industrial Revolution and
Heath became more marginalized. This situation was complicated by the fact
that, during the same period, New England faced agricultural competition
from the Midwest after transportation improvements and new farm machinery facilitated large-scale production.

Prior to the transformation, Massachusetts' economy was based on
shipping and agriculture. Embargos—in 1807 and during the War of 1812—
stimulated a demand for local industry when prohibitions on importing
foreign-made products created a shortage of manufactured goods. The embargos also reduced the opportunity for investment in foreign trade.

As early as 1811, Boston merchant Francis Cabot Lowell returned from a
trip to England where he had memorized the construction of a power loom, a
closely guarded industrial secret at the time. Lowell joined with two partners
to acquire a water site at Waltham, Massachusetts, and obtained a corporate
charter for textile manufacturing on a large scale. The three men began
operation in 1813 under the name of Boston Manufacturing Company. Their
success at Waltham led to larger and even more lucrative mills at the Massachusetts towns of Lowell (1822) and Chicopee (1823), where workforces of
unmarried young women from rural areas lived in supervised dormitories.
Other mills sprang up throughout New England, which became the first
important manufacturing region in the United States. By the 1830s, woolen
manufacturing had become concentrated in single production units (with a
supervised workforce gathered in one place), and by 1860 the largest textile
mills in the country were producing wool cloth. Manufacturing was fueled by
a growing supply of Irish immigrants escaping the potato famine who took
jobs at low wages and brought customs and religious practices that seemed
strange to Yankees. Unwilling to work with the Irish, many New England
women left the mills or moved west with their families, and by the 1860s
unskilled factory work was mainly performed by immigrants. The population
of Massachusetts had grown dramatically, from less than half a million people in 1810 to nearly a million and a quarter residents in 1860. While people
throughout Massachusetts and the nation had assumed the state's economy

would continue to rest on commerce and agriculture, it became apparent that manufacturing was the dominant economic sector. In the words of historian Michael B. Katz, "the homogeneous land of Yankees disappeared forever."[44]

Manufacturing was not the only sector of the economy to be transformed by technological change. Agriculture felt the impact as well, through innovations such as Cyrus McCormick's mechanical reaper (patented in 1834) and John Deere's steel plow (invented in 1837 and mass produced in the 1850s). New developments in transportation—including the opening of the Erie Canal in 1825 and the construction of railroads in the 1840s—meant that some products (such as wool and cattle) could be obtained less expensively in the Midwest than in New England. In the face of these macro-economic forces, Massachusetts farm women (who previously had produced clothing in their homes) looked for new means of supplementing their incomes. They tried teaching or raising silk worms (a "brief but abortive fad" that was pursued at the farm of Flora White's maternal grandfather, David).[45] Nevertheless, the societal changes occasioned by economic growth were substantial.

Michael Katz describes the scope and pace of change by referencing the life of Horace Mann (1796–1850), first Secretary of the Massachusetts State Board of Education and father of the common school movement. Katz writes that when Mann was born, "almost no one" would have guessed that within one lifetime the landscape of the state would become "spotted by Irish slums, scarred by iron tracks, disfigured by mills and factories." Neither did "[e]ven the most farsighted" anticipate that by 1859 more Massachusetts children would be growing up in urban areas than rural ones, or that women and children would operate factory machinery that displaced men and "destroyed the traditional crafts of the home." Katz contends that during Horace Mann's life, a "new society" was created—one that "smashed old expectations with the force of steam, that ripped apart and restitched the web of relationships composing the experience of men."[46]

Heath did not share the benefits of the new economy. Although New England's early factories were largely run by water power, Heath's high elevation prohibited the development of water power except for small operations. The town's strongest attribute was its uncommon physical beauty. An essay in its centennial book described Heath as follows:

> Beautiful for situation is this town. At an elevation of about 1500 feet above the sea, and extending on the southeast to the top of Pocumptuck, the highest point but one in the State, it commands in all directions wide and varied views of valley, hill and mountain. On the west, rise the Green Mountains with the giant Greylock towering above its neighbors. A way to the northward, Monadnock stands in serene majesty; far away to the east, may be seen Wachusett; on the south, looking across the fair valley of the Deerfield, the eye roams over and beyond the billowy Buckland hills and away down the Connecticut Valley, over scenes so beautiful that one might exclaim almost in the words of the

pious old angler, "Lord, what glory hast thou prepared for the saints in Heaven, since thou affordest bad men on earth such sights as these!"[47]

Flora White was very conscious of these beautiful physical surroundings. As an adult, she extolled the beauty of the "Heath Hills," describing this natural setting as the place where people might dream they had seen God "face to face."[48] However, much of the terrain is steep and stony, winters are long and severe, and the growing season is short. With the establishment of farms, the original humus was quickly used up, topsoil washed away, and—notwithstanding a brief period in the 1830s when Heath boasted a flock of 2,312 sheep—there were increasingly fewer animals to fertilize the soil.[49] Once the land was cleared and populated, decline set in after only three generations of Anglo-American settlement. Just as earlier generations of Whites moved west to accommodate their growing numbers, Heath residents moved out of Massachusetts into New York State and the Midwest. Ironically, Heath's decline began just as the last farm in the town had been "taken up and improved."[50]

Christopher Clark, in studying economic developments in western Massachusetts between the American Revolution and the Civil War, writes that pressures of agricultural competition from Midwestern markets were felt first in the hill towns.[51] Those with the largest flocks experienced stagnation in sheep raising during the 1830s and a precipitous decline during the 1840s. Seeking to replace their lost income—and mindful of a great demand for building materials and firewood—hill farmers turned to lumber as their most valuable resource. The frequency and extent of land clearances increased. This proved to be only a temporary solution because trees were stripped faster than they could replenish themselves. Timber cutting laid bare much of the natural hill landscape, which was a fragile ecosystem to begin with.

Ignoring the ecosystem for short-term benefits would prove disastrous a century later as Americans continued to move west and created the environmental catastrophe known as the Dust Bowl. However, even in New England in the early nineteenth century, the numbers tell the story. According to Heath's sesquicentennial history, the town "attained its highest prosperity" around 1832—twenty-eight years before Flora White's birth—when the population was about 1,200, the Congregational church had 316 members, and the Sabbath School had 500 people,[52] reportedly the largest enrollment outside Boston.[53] By the 1840 census, Heath's population had dropped to 895, and by the 1850 census it was 803."[54] As an adult, Flora White would attempt to help the town by promoting experimentation with farming methods, founding an agricultural fair, and looking for ways to draw summer residents to enjoy Heath's beauty and tranquility.

ANOTHER JOSEPH WHITE

Useful perspective on factors that affected Joseph White II and his family—and reshaped Massachusetts—can be seen in the experience of his cousin, also named Joseph. Both men were born in the same locale, within two years of each other. Moreover, both were Asaph White's grandsons but—in part because of birth order customs—each lived a life that was very different from the other, and not in a way that would have been predicted at the time of their birth.

Joseph II's father was Asaph White's oldest son David, and his cousin was the son of David's younger brother, Captain John White. Whereas Joseph II inherited from his father the White ancestral farm—long the basis of the family's financial security and social status—his cousin Joseph (1811–1891) was bequeathed what appeared to be a lesser prize, the sword Colonel Jonathan White used at the Battle of Lake George in the French and Indian War. Joseph and his wife, the former Hannah Danforth of Williamstown, had no children, so he later donated the sword to Williams College for display in its history museum.

However, in addition to bequeathing his son a sword, Captain White also brought himself and his family into closer alignment with evolving economic trends by seeking his fortune in textiles. The captain settled his family in Charlemont (described as "a secluded village in the middle of bold, beautiful scenery") and became a "cloth dresser" who served customers over "a very wide circuit."[55] As a young man, Captain White's son prepared himself for Williams College, attending the Academy of Bennington (Vermont) to successfully shore up his sparse academic background. After graduating from Williams he taught for several months and then began to study law in Troy, New York. However, upon entering the practice of law in Troy, the Captain's son found he disliked the "quibbles and quarrels of the bar" and in 1848 moved to Lowell, Massachusetts, where he "took charge of the Massachusetts Cotton Mills, one of the largest manufacturing corporations in New England."[56]

In 1857, his horizons broadened further when he was elected as a Whig to the Massachusetts Senate, chairing two standing committees and a special committee on retrenchment and reform. He was appointed a bank commissioner, resigning the office in 1860, and was appointed the fourth Secretary of the Massachusetts State Board of Education, a position he held for seventeen years. As such, he became the third person to hold the post formerly occupied by Horace Mann, and in 1875 White received an honorary Doctor of Laws degree from Yale.

According to one contemporary, Secretary White "took much more than the ordinary gentleman's pains with his personal appearance. He dressed expensively, but never extravagantly."[57] Even though the Secretary lived much longer than his first cousin, Flora White's father, the disparity of the paths they had taken was already clear by 1860 when the Secretary had attained a major state office with strong business connections, and Joseph White II had personal property worth six hundred dollars.[58]

Flora White was very aware of her father's cousin and proud of his prominence in Massachusetts. She highlighted information in family histories about the positions he held, which included serving as treasurer and trustee of Williams College and trustee of Smith College. She clearly knew the Secretary, who willed Flora and Mary White the writing desk of their great-grandfather, Asaph. However, Flora and the Secretary were not close. When, in 1939, she recorded the "facts" of her life, she named several distant relatives and family friends who assisted her widowed mother and enhanced her own development, but she did not mention the Secretary.[59]

THE FAMILY FRAGMENTS

In the years following his return to Heath from Boston in 1851, Joseph White II's attempts to keep his family afloat financially were complicated by a lengthy illness that sapped his "vigorous" frame and ultimately led to his death on October 17, 1861, only eighteen months after Flora's birth.[60]

A short narrative written by Flora's brother Joseph titled "Reminiscent" paints a poignant portrait of those final years in the life of his father. In it, Joseph describes happy domestic scenes that occurred in 1859–1860 in the White family farmhouse "just north of the old red school in south Heath." Their mother had "just finished paring a pan of apples," and young Joseph crawled up on her lap. She "hugged and kissed him" and explained that she had a "little baby" in her stomach (Flora). Months later, young Joseph found a monkey wrench that had been lost. His mother took the boy to "where . . . [his] father was sick" to explain what had been found. Mr. White "smiled and put his arm around" his son and kissed him, telling young Joseph he was "a good boy," adding "That wrench is worth $1.00."[61] To put the value of the monkey wrench in perspective, Joseph White II's entire estate was valued, upon his death, at $3,091.85.[62]

On October 18, 1861, Joseph White II was laid to rest in Heath's South Cemetery. The burial was preceded by a funeral service at Heath's white-frame Congregational Church. Erected twenty-eight years earlier in the town center, it was Heath's "finest building," completed at what some townspeople considered their "finest hour." Heath's subsequent decline made this an apt description, although townspeople "did not know it at the time."[63]

Just three months after the first major battle of the U.S. Civil War, Joseph White II had left a wife and five children ranging in age from eighteen months to ten years. Standing before a group of family and friends who gathered to mourn the loss, the minister delivered a eulogy that focused on Mr. White's personal traits, as well as the divine message that could be understood from his suffering. The minister acknowledged that Joseph White II, a farmer, was an independent thinker ("Our brother was a Christian. None of us doubted this, however much we may have differed from him in opinion on minor questions of Christian doctrine and duty").[64] He noted that White's unconventional views were an obstacle to his church membership ("We would gladly have welcomed him to membership in the visible Church if he could have accepted such membership consistently with his own convictions").[65] Nevertheless, he added, Joseph White II possessed a superior and disciplined intellect and diligently tried to improve himself at every opportunity. The minister concluded by telling the family that White had left them an important legacy:

> Though industrious and strictly economical, he had not acquired the riches of this world. . . . Our departed friend has enriched you . . . by his godly influence, by his loving heart, and by his good name, and now that he has departed he has bequeathed you a good name, an influence that may never cease to be a power for good to you, and a treasure of prayer and grateful recollections which you would not exchange for anybody's riches.[66]

Joseph White II had inherited a respected family name from his forebears and passed it on to his survivors. Their immediate focus, however, was not other people's riches. Although Heath had long raised "good men and women" on "rough hills" that provided few creature comforts, the death of this father posed a significant threat to his young family, who would soon be very poor.[67]

Seven weeks after the funeral, the probate court named Harriet White administrator of her husband's estate. However, it was only on October 6, 1863—nearly two years after his death—that the probate court appointed Harriet White as the *guardian* of her five minor children. This delay reflects the state of U.S. family law in the antebellum period when, according to Michael Grossberg, guardianship decisions moved from the domain of the father to the domain of the courts. After her husband died, a mother had to request guardianship of her children and prove herself worthy of the responsibility. Grossberg notes that widows had diminished social status, being "viewed as objects of pity and feared as potential drains on community resources."[68]

In the period following her husband's death, Harriet White and her children relocated to nearby Shelburne Falls, Massachusetts, the family farm was sold, and the Whites existed on meager funds. (The importance Flora placed on the loss of the farm became apparent when, over thirty years later, she returned to Heath and tried unsuccessfully to buy it back.) The sole surviving

son, Joseph, later recalled that after the father's death, his mother "was practically an invalid for several years."[69]

An 1871 map of Heath shows that Harriet White, a widowed mother of
five, had returned to the town and was living in a home that later became a
parsonage.[70] Young Joseph did not reside with his mother and sisters, having
been "bound out" to another farm family on his eighth birthday in 1864.[71]
This placement of Harriet White's son is an indication of the dire straits in
which she and her children found themselves.

THE TIE THAT BINDS

Binding children was a widespread practice in the English colonies and in the
United States well into the nineteenth century, and often involved those who
were illegitimate or orphaned, or whose families were unable to take care of
them. In Massachusetts, the practice was rooted in a desire to maintain social
order within the town. From the inception of Puritan settlement, the town
was the center of public life, and the result of a covenant in which members
agreed to live by accepted rules. The community built a meetinghouse for
religious services and town meetings, passed regulations for farming practices, and disciplined people who refused to accept local ordinances. Each
head of household received an allotment of free land that was sufficient to
build a house and raise a family. In return, townsmen were expected to
contribute to the minister's salary, pay taxes, and serve in the local militia.

The first Massachusetts Bay general laws in 1642 required parents to train
their children in an "honest lawful calling, labour or employment."[72] This
was to occur either by the parent's own teaching, or by apprenticing the child
to another master for training. If parents failed to do this, selectmen (town
officials) and justices of the peace could place them with masters who would
"force them to submit unto government."[73]

Under the binding agreement, the master provided the child with food,
clothing, schooling, and preparation for a trade. After the American Revolution, attitudes toward children began to change as courts paid more attention
to the nurturing role of the mother and viewed children less as the father's
property. Still, during the late eighteenth and early nineteenth centuries the
master acted *in loco parentis* under the assumption that the rights of one
superior party (the parent) were transferred to the other (the master). By
1850, 80 percent of the U.S. population lived in rural areas where the labor of
children—indeed, of the entire family—continued to be a necessity.[74]

Charles Loring Brace, founder of the New York Children's Aid Society,
is credited with introducing in 1853 the "placing out" system in the United
States, which required no indenture contract. Brace argued that since there
was "unlimited" demand for children's labor on family farms, and the cost of

a child's food was "of little amount," thousands of "children of the unfortunate" could be placed in this manner as an act of benevolence. Brace also added that, since children were highly valued and "every man's affairs are known to all his neighbors," the chance of mistreatment would be unlikely.[75] In its first twenty-five years, the Society placed some forty thousand homeless or destitute children from New York City in farm homes. Other associations placed thousands of children as well.

Originally hailed as a less expensive alternative to the asylum, poor house, or house of correction, the system had many critics. In 1885, Lyman P. Alden, former superintendent of the state public school in Coldwater, Michigan, reported that it is "well known" among people responsible for binding out children that the "great majority" of adults seeking children over age nine were "looking for cheap help." Alden added that although many adults were fair to their apprentices, "a much larger number . . . expect to make a handsome profit" on children's service by providing "poor food [and] shoddy clothing," working them beyond their capacity, sending then to school only a few months, "and that irregularly," and sometimes treating them "with personal cruelty."[76] Because there was no indenture contract, the courts rarely got involved in disputes between parties in the "placing out" system. There was no legal regulation of this custodial system until the end of the nineteenth century, when reformers focused increased attention on child labor abuses.

White family records lend credence to Alden's cautionary note. Young Joseph's binding arrangement was terminated after one year when he was not sent to school as agreed. He was then "bound out" to a second farmer, who sent him to a district school but kept him in "most unfortunate" circumstances.[77] One family story relates how the boy was beaten for stopping to pick a berry when he was walking to church. His alleged offense was violating the Sabbath. Young Joseph White maintained contact with his biological family but remained in the binding arrangement for thirteen years, until he reached the age of twenty-one. Eventually he moved to Nebraska and later to Oklahoma.

The White family's declining fortunes, seen most starkly in the life of Flora's brother, occurred at a time of shifting attitudes toward poor people. Although Puritans associated economic prosperity with divine favor, other developments also shaped popular views on wealth and poverty. Michael Katz writes that before the twentieth century, it would have seemed "preposterous" to suppose that poverty could ever be eliminated. Biblical references supported the belief that most people would be poor throughout their lives, a condition that carried no disgrace. However, as early as 1821 Josiah Quincy, future mayor of Boston and president of Harvard University, made a distinction between "two classes of people"—the "impotent poor," who could not work due to old age, infancy, sickness, or "corporal debility," and the "able poor" who were capable of work. Over time, the concept of *pauperism* developed to describe the lot of the able poor. It was a label associated with indolence and vice, and eventually tarnished all poor people. Especially in the United States—where anyone with energy and talent could allegedly hope to prosper—being poor signaled personal failure. Katz notes that this new, moral view of poverty accompanied the growth of democracy and capitalism and produced public policy and private charity that remained "mean, punitive, and inadequate." Such attitudes provided a powerful incentive to work, thereby helping ensure a cheap labor supply in a market economy that was increasingly based on "unbound wage labor."[78] Katz notes that moral definitions of poverty found support in nineteenth-century Protestant theology, Charles Darwin's writings, hereditarianism, and—eventually—the eugenics movement of the twentieth century.[79]

Although both girls and boys could be "bound out," family lore suggests the Whites believed that a young boy needed a male role model in the home. It is also likely that Harriet White felt she could not prepare young Joseph for a trade, in this case farming. As her son filled out the remaining years of his binding commitment, Harriet White left Heath in 1872 and moved to Amherst, Massachusetts, with her two youngest daughters, Mary ("May") and Flora. Meanwhile, Hattie White (Harriet's second oldest daughter) entered Westfield Normal School to pursue a teaching career and graduated with honors. In 1874 the oldest White daughter, Emma, exercised another option available to young women in western Massachusetts. She married William Hillman from the nearby town of Hawley and moved west with him. The couple settled in Lincoln, Nebraska, where William was a ticket agent with the Rock Island Freight depot. The Hillmans became the parents of ten children.

As a young adult, Flora wrote a letter to her mother that reflected some of the insecurity and tension that appeared among the sisters as a result of the Whites' lost status and meager resources. Flora made a reference to one of her siblings, probably Emma, who was the only one of the sisters to marry. Flora wrote:

> "I've tried to raise my family to my own level" as a certain sister of mine remarked years & years ago when I was a little thing and "took in" what I heard. The aforementioned sister I am afraid is in the uncomfortable position of finding the family a little above *her* level. At any rate if there is further *lifting* to be done I think she is the one in most need of the hoisting.[80]

Flora's comments describe the hurt she felt at her sister's condescending characterization of the family's poverty and diminished status. As will be shown in chapter 3, Flora wrote her comments shortly after enjoying luxury travel on steamships bound for England and the Cape Colony in Africa. At that time, Emma and William Hillman were living in Nebraska, raising their large family on his modest salary. Despite Flora's lingering resentment, relations between the two sisters were sufficiently strong that in 1881 the Hillmans named their third daughter Flora. The first two Hillman daughters bore the names of Emma's other female siblings, Mary and Hattie. Around 1900, Flora Hillman died of tuberculosis, as did one of her younger sisters. Two years later, the Hillman family moved to Tacoma, Washington, for "health reasons" and remained there for the rest of Emma and William Hillman's lives.[81]

AN ACT OF KINDNESS

Harriet White's new home, Amherst, was located in the Connecticut River valley, one hundred miles west of Boston. It had a population of 4,035 in the 1870 U.S. Census, compared to Heath's population of 613. Amherst was home to two major institutions of higher learning: the private Amherst College, founded in 1821, and Massachusetts Agricultural College (later the University of Massachusetts), established in 1863 under the Morrill Land Grant to teach agriculture and science. In 1872, Amherst's largest employer was a factory, reportedly the largest producer of palm leaf hats in the United States.

At Amherst, Harriet White and daughters Mary and Flora lived in the home of the Reverend Isaac Esty, a widower and retired Congregational minister whose son, William Cole Esty, was a mathematics professor at Amherst College. Since Isaac Esty's wife died in 1872, it is likely that Harriet White ran his household in exchange for room and board. Esty, a graduate of Yale College and Andover Theological Seminary, had served congregations in Maine, Vermont, and New Hampshire, and he knew Joseph and Harriet White from being a supply minister at Heath. Late in life, Flora White wrote of Isaac Esty, "His ample library and his stimulating companionship were our constant joy. We called him grandpa & loved him as our very own."[82]

Like the Whites, Isaac Esty was descended from an old New England family that came to Salem, Massachusetts, during the seventeenth century. The Estys (also spelled Estey, Easty, or Estie) learned the importance of a good name through tragic family circumstances. Esty's direct ancestor, also called Isaac, was the husband of Mary Towne Esty who—along with her sister Rebecca Towne Nurse—was hanged as a witch in Salem in 1692. By most accounts the two women were among the most pious in the town. The aggrieved Mr. Esty lived twenty years following his wife's death. In 1702 he and twenty other colonists petitioned the Massachusetts General Court to publicly remove the infamy from the names associated with the Salem witch trials so relatives and progeny would not suffer reproach. Although the petitioners received no satisfaction, in 1710 Esty presented a memorial to the General Court, seeking remuneration for the harm his family had suffered. He cited the arrest and execution of his "beloved wife," noting his "sorrow and trouble of heart in such a manner, which this world can never make me any compensation for."[83] In 1711 Mary Esty's family received twenty pounds from the government for her wrongful execution.

Prior to moving to Amherst, Flora White may have attended a district school in Heath for a period of time; however, she recalled receiving most of her early education from her mother, including instruction in "Latin, Literature and Mathematics with thorough training in English Composition."[84] Flora attended public school in Amherst for two years and had a year of private instruction "with reading of World History and Literature."[85] In addition to her contacts through the Esty family, Flora benefited from the presence of her godmother, Laura Emerson, who "had a beautiful home in Amherst that was always open to us."[86] She was the daughter of Heath's physician, Dr. Joseph Emerson, and was distantly related to Ralph Waldo Emerson and the Whites. After the doctor's death in 1842, Sarah Cheney Emerson (Laura's mother), moved to Amherst with five children and purchased the historic home built in 1744 by Samuel Strong at 67 Amity Street. The gambrel-roof building is the "beautiful home" to which Flora White referred. One of Sarah Emerson's neighbors, nine-year-old Eugene Field (1850–1895)—later to find fame as a writer, poet, and essayist—parodied a popular hymn to express enthusiasm for the magnificent elms on her property. Field noted that if his dog had "wings like a dove" he would fly "away from this world of fleas" to "light on Miss Emerson's trees."[87] Laura Emerson bequeathed the home to the local historical society, and it has served as the Amherst History Museum since 1916.

When Isaac Esty died in 1875, he left the Whites some household belongings and money for Mary and Flora to enroll in a two-year teacher training program at Westfield Normal School, a coeducational institution in western Massachusetts that primarily served women of modest means. Late in life, Flora White recalled that Esty "made his home ours for many years," noting he was "a true saint" whose memory is "a deathless inheritance."[88] She understood that in providing her family with a home in Amherst—and giving her social capital and educational opportunity—Esty had bestowed a gift that would continue to provide benefits throughout her life.

CONCLUSION

Flora White spent her early life amid challenges and opportunities. The death of her father forced her family into poverty, which carried the stigma of personal failure. The rights of women were so limited that Flora's well-educated mother was not appointed *guardian* of her own minor children until nearly two years after his death. The destruction of the fragile ecosystem of the Berkshire hill towns and marginalization of Heath during to the First Industrial Revolution further limited the Whites' options for a secure life. The sale of the family farm—and binding out of eight-year-old Joseph—are perhaps the most poignant examples of the challenges the Whites faced during Flora's childhood. At the same time, Flora White enjoyed some advantages over other Massachusetts residents of the day. She was a white, native-born citizen in a society that privileged longtime Anglo-American residents. She had a proud family lineage with contacts that gave her access to educational opportunity and social capital. She could identify with a father who engaged in important social reform, and with a female forebear whose writing won acclaim in North America and Europe. As Flora White entered young adulthood and prepared for a career as a teacher, she pursued her desire for "more life, and fuller" by taking advantage of opportunities and working around challenges. It was a strategy she would continue to use for the remainder of her life.

NOTES

1. "Poetess, Educator Lives Quietly in Retirement," *Greenfield Gazette and Courier* (Greenfield, MA), July 14, 1947.

2. Ibid. In this case, "country" probably refers to New England and not to the United States.

3. Ibid.

4. Catherine White Moyer to Joseph White, 5 December 1941. Flora White Papers. Private collection. Moyer's statement reflected a widely held belief in western egalitarianism, later summarized by historian Ray Allen Billington: "Men were weighed on their present and future contribution to society, with total disregard for their background." See Ray Allen Billington, *America's Frontier Heritage* (New York: Holt, Rinehart and Winston, 1966), 151. Flora White, on the other hand, grew up in New England, in a society that had been established with the town, family, and school as the bases of social organization, as noted in Francis J. Bremer, *The Puritan Experiment* (New York: St. Martin's Press, 1976), 171–183. With industrialization, family influence remained important, as men from elite New England families shaped social and economic change to preserve their position with respect to others. See Betty G. Farrell, *Elite Families: Class and Power in Nineteenth-Century Boston* (Albany: State University of New York Press, 1993).

5. "Address at the Funeral of Mr. Joseph White, Heath, Oct. 18, 1861," Flora White Papers, private collection.

6. Florence Oetken Moyer in discussion with the author, July 19, 2005.

7. "Erving—Early Settlement," extracted from vol. II of Louis H. Everts, *History of the Connecticut Valley in Massachusetts*, 1879, http://www.franklincountyhistory.com/erving/everts/03html.

8. Bremer, *The Puritan Experiment*, 37.

9. Virginia De John Anderson, "Migrants and Motives: Religion and the Settlement of New England, 1630–1640," *New England Quarterly* 58 (1985): 339–383.

10. Bremer, *The Puritan Experiment*, 178.

11. Almira Larkin White, vol. 1 of *Genealogy of the Descendants of John White* (Haverhill, MA: The Chase Press, 1900), 10–11.

12. Bremer, *The Puritan Experiment*, 177–178.

13. Doctor Frederick Lewis Weis, "Lancaster's Part in the Founding of Heath," in *Sesquicentennial Anniversary of the Town of Heath*, Massachusetts, ed. Howard Chandler Robbins (Heath, MA: Heath Historical Society, 1935), 33.

14. Daniel R. Mandell, *King Philip's War: Colonial Expansion, Native Resistance, and the End of Indian Sovereignty* (Baltimore: Johns Hopkins University Press, 2010), 11.

15. Ibid.

16. Ibid., 12.

17. Ibid.

18. Ibid., 134.

19. Mary Rowlandson, *The Sovereignty and Goodness of God: Being a Narrative of the Captivity and Restoration of Mrs. Mary Rowlandson* (Cambridge: Samuel Green, 1682), in Almira Larkin White, vol. 1 of *Descendants of John White, 1638–1900* (Haverhill, MA: Chase Brothers Printers, 1900), 773.

20. Ibid.

21. Readers who wish to learn more about Captivity Narrative Studies—a field that has evolved since the 1990s—might begin with the work of Kathryn Zabelle Derounian-Stodola. In 2008 she wrote an essay review of three books that offer criticism on captivity narratives. One book (by Teresa A. Toulouse) links Mary Rowlandson's *The Sovereignty of Goodness* to the political instability that existed in Europe between 1660 and 1713. According to Toulouse, this period of upheaval created a cultural identity crisis among some elite New England clergy—for example, Increase Mather, who seized on the image of the passive female captive to reinforce his notion of social and religious authority. In that sense, Toulouse writes, Rowlandson's narrative reveals more about Anglo-American politics than about Metacom's War. See Kathryn Zabelle Derounian-Stodola, "Captivity, Liberty, and Early American Consciousness," *Early American Literature*, 43 (2008): 715–724; and Teresa A. Toulouse, *The Captain's Position: Female Narrative, Male Identity, and Royal Authority in Colonial New England* (Philadelphia: University of Pennsylvania Press, 2007).

22. Flora White, "Reply to Mr. Johnson," *Unity* 127 (1941), 119.

23. Mandell, *King Philip's War*, 144.

24. John H. Thompson, "Historical Address," in *Centennial History of Heath, Massachusetts*, ed. Edward P. Guild (Boston: Advertiser Publishing Company, 1885), 12.

25. John Keegan, *Fields of Battle: The Wars for North America* (New York: Vintage Books, 1995), 63.

26. The other wars for empire were the War of the League of Augsburg (1689–1697), or King William's War; the War of the Spanish Succession (1702–1713), or Queen Anne's War; and the War of the Austrian Succession, or King George's War (1743–1748).

27. John Bascom, "The Life of Joseph White, with Tributes of Friends," in *Lancaster, Mass., Heath, Mass., Joseph White* (W. J. Colton, 1884).

28. Pearle Tanner, "Heath and Its Families," in *Sesquicentennial Anniversary of the Town of Heath, Massachusetts*, ed. Howard Chandler Robbins (Heath, MA: Historical Society, 1935), 60.

29. Ibid., 61.

30. *History Proceedings of the Pocumtuck Valley Memorial Association*, vol. II (Deerfield, MA: Pocumtuck Valley Memorial Association, 1898), 376.

31. Tanner, "Heath and Its Families," 62.

32. "Heath—The Church of Christ in Heath," extracted from vol. II of Louis H. Everts, *History of the Connecticut Valley in Massachusetts*, 1879, http://www.franklincountyhistory.com/heath/everts/13.html.

33. Although there are multiple sources that document Harriet White's *preparation* for Troy Female Seminary, the existing archives at Emma Willard School in Troy do not show that she was a student there. Her attendance cannot be ruled out, however, because the current archival listing of students is substantially, but not entirely, complete. There is no listing of Harriet

White or Troy Female Seminary in the centennial history of Heath, which lists women of the town who received higher education.

34. Flora White's notation appears on p. 63 of the *Sesquicentennial Anniversary of the Town of Heath*. Flora White Papers, private collection.

35. David White to Joseph White II, 12 March 1851, Flora White Papers, private collection.

36. Kevin Sweeney, "Rum, Romanism, Representation, and Reform: Coalition Politics in Massachusetts, 1847–1853," *Civil War History* 22 (1976): 119.

37. William G. Bean, "Puritan versus Celt, 1850–1860," *The New England Quarterly* 7 (1934): 72.

38. Eric Foner, *Free Soil, Free Labor, Free Men: The Ideology of the Republican Party before the Civil War* (Oxford and New York: Oxford University Press, 1995), 21.

39. Bean, "Puritan versus Celt," 72.

40. Flora White wrote the following note in a copy of the *Sesquicentennial Anniversary of the Town of Heath, 1785–1935*: "Joseph White, son of David, represented the district (which included Heath) in the State Legislature in Boston & was a personal friend of Charles Sumner." Flora White Papers. private collection.

41. Ernest McKay, "Henry Wilson and the Coalition of 1851," *The New England Quarterly* 36 (1963): 338–357.

42. Ibid., 348.

43. Sumner mocked Butler's chivalrous behavior and charged him with "taking a mistress . . . who though ugly to others, is always lovely to him; though polluted in the sight of the world, is chaste in his sight . . . the harlot, Slavery." The statement recalled the abolitionists' repeated charge that slaveholders had sexual relations with their slaves. "May 22, 1856: The Caning of Senator Charles Sumner," http://www.senate.gov/artandhistory/history/minute/The_Caning_of_Senator_Charles_Sumner.htm.

44. Michael B. Katz, *The Irony of Early School Reform: Educational Innovation in Mid-Nineteenth Century Massachusetts* (New York: Teachers College, Columbia University, 2001), 6.

45. Ibid., 9.

46. Ibid., 11.

47. Thompson, "Historical Address," 11.

48. Flora White, "Heath Hills," in *Poems by Mary A. White and Flora White* (New York: Paebar, 1939), 16.

49. Edward Calver, *Heath, Massachusetts: A History and Guidebook* (Heath, MA: Heath Historical Society, 2009), 182.

50. Ibid.

51. Christopher Clark, *The Roots of Rural Capitalism: Western Massachusetts, 1780–1860* (Ithaca, NY: Cornell University Press, 1990), 287.

52. Spencer Miller Jr., "Address by Spencer Miller Jr.: An Interpretation of Its Founding in 1785 Upon the One Hundred and Fiftieth Anniversary, 1935," in *Sesquicentennial Anniversary of the Town of Heath Massachusetts,* ed. Howard Chandler Robbins (Heath, MA: Heath Historical Society, 1935), 19.

53. "Heath—The Church of Christ in Heath," extracted from vol. II of Louis H. Everts, *History of the Connecticut Valley in Massachusetts* (Philadelphia, PA: Louis H. Everts, 1879), http://franklincountyhistory.com/heath/everts/13.html.

54. Calver, *Heath, Massachusetts*, 182; *Centennial History of Heath*, 148.

55. Arthur Perry, "The Life of Joseph White, with Its Historic Antecedents," *in Lancaster, Mass., Heath, Mass., Joseph White*, n.d., private collection.

56. John Bascom, "The Life of Joseph White," in *Lancaster, Mass., Heath Mass., Joseph White*, n.d., private collection.

57. Perry, "The Life of Joseph White."

58. U.S. Census, Franklin County, Massachusetts, 1860.

59. Flora White, "Life Facts of Flora White and Family Recorded Mar. 18, 1939," Heath Historical Society, 1.

60. "Address at the Funeral of Mr. Joseph White, Heath, Oct. 18, 1861," Flora White Papers, private collection; Joseph White II's cause of death was inflammation of the stomach and bowels. *Massachusetts Vital Records, 1841–1910*, 147: 325.

61. Joseph D. White, "Reminiscent," n.d., Flora White Papers, private collection.

62. The Final Account of Harriet M. White, Administratix of the Estate of Joseph White, Late of Heath, Flora White Papers, private collection.

63. Calver, *Heath, Massachusetts*, 165.

64. "Address at the Funeral of Mr. Joseph White."

65. Ibid.

66. Ibid.

67. "Letter from Mrs. Sarah J. Hastings Nichols," in *Centennial History of Heath*, ed. Edward P. Guild (Boston: Advertiser Publishing Co., Aug. 19, 1885), 125.

68. Michael Grossberg, "Who Gets the Child? Custody, Guardianship and the Rise of Judicial Patriarchy in Nineteenth-Century America," *Feminist Studies*, 9 (1983): 244.

69. "J. D. White Life History," n.d., Flora White Papers, private collection.

70. Calver, *Heath, Massachusetts*, 164.

71. Golden Moyer Jr., "White, Joseph David," in vol. 1 of *Our Ellis County Heritage: 1885–1974* (Gage, OK: Ellis County Historical Society, 1974), 493; "J. D. White Life History."

72. Ruth Wallis Herndon and John E. Murray, eds., *Children Bound to Labor: The Pauper Apprentice System in Early America* (New York: Cornell University Press, 2009), 23.

73. Ibid.

74. Mary Ann Mason, *From the Father's Property to Children's Rights* (New York: Columbia University Press, 1994), 40–84.

75. Ibid., 79.

76. Lyman P. Alden, "The Shady Side of the 'Placing-Out System,'" *The Social Welfare Forum: Official Proceedings* (Boston: George H. Ellis, 1885), 201.

77. "J. D. White Life History."

78. Michael B. Katz, *The Undeserving Poor: America's Enduring Confrontation with Poverty* (Oxford: Oxford University Press, 2013), 5–7.

79. The eugenics movement promised to give human beings control over the process of natural selection by encouraging the reproduction of the fittest specimens of humanity.

80. Flora White to Harriet M. White, circa 1885–1886, Flora White Papers, private collection.

81. Grace Moyer Share, "Notes on the Lives of Mary Abby and Flora White" (unpublished manuscript). Flora White Papers, private collection, 1.

82. White, "Life Facts," 2.

83. "Tenth Generation," Ancestry of Ralph J. Turner, rockcreekexperiment.com.

84. White, "Life Facts," 3.

85. Ibid.

86. Ibid.

87. "Old Strong House (1744)," Historic Buildings of Massachusetts, http://mass.historicbuildingsct.com; "A Memory" in Eugene Field, *A Little Book of Western Verse* (New York: C. Scribner, 1892.

88. White, "Life Facts," 11.

Chapter Two

Nature Weeps

In 1896, Buffalo, New York, welcomed the annual meeting of the National Education Association (NEA) with a burst of civic pride. The meeting headquarters were located in Endicott Square, a ten-story Italian Renaissance structure named for the city's founder and billed as the world's largest office building. "[R]ich and elaborate" in its appointments, Endicott Square boasted "over a mile of marble corridor floor," and "the largest single skylight in the United States."[1]

In the hype that preceded the meeting, NEA members learned their host city had—in one century—grown from a "frontier trading post" to the "sixth largest commercial city." At the same time, Buffalo's public schools had evolved to become "an educational system of which . . . [the city] is justly proud."[2]

Amid such expressions of optimism, a thirty-six-year-old teacher introduced a note of incongruity into the meeting. Flora White of Boston read a paper to assembled NEA members that contained a bold statement: "It has long been a fancy of mine that nature covers her face and weeps whenever she beholds a schoolhouse."[3] Her words were remarkable in two respects. First, historian Kate Rousmaniere writes that there were significant gender restrictions at NEA meetings at the turn of the twentieth century, where the speakers were "all male, and almost all administrators."[4] While Rousmaniere may draw a distinction between speakers and presenters like White, she makes it clear that women's participation at the sessions was circumscribed at best. Although teachers were permitted to attend the NEA sessions, Rousmaniere reports that "they were prohibited from speaking. Their function was primarily to listen and learn from their superiors."[5] White's comment was also noteworthy because the people in her audience had spent their careers in educational institutions; moreover, *she too* had invested many years in schools, with successful results. Although White's paper largely criticized the overcrowding and lack of physical movement in schools (and proposed a program to develop fine- and gross-motor skills as well as cognitive skills in children), her criticisms constituted more than a passing complaint. They were a testimony to her revolt against the developing industrial model of public education, and her involvement in the formative period of the *new* education, later known as the progressive education movement.

White asked the group, "Now what do we want for our youth?" and then answered her question by quoting Tennyson: "'More life [,] and fuller.' I don't believe we can get beyond that."[6] As she argued for expanding and enriching students' lives, White also revealed her own desire for agency.

During Flora's infancy in Heath, an "old red schoolhouse" was one of her first visual images since the landmark building was adjacent to the White family farm.[7] Over the years, up to her 1896 presentation to the NEA, she gained considerable experience teaching in rural and urban schools. To explore ways in which White's career enhanced and frustrated her desire for agency—and shaped her thinking about effective pedagogy—it is important to first consider the state of schooling in Massachusetts during the nineteenth century.

COMMON—AND CLASSICAL—SCHOOL CURRICULA

By the time White presented her paper in Buffalo, reformers were already attacking rural education. They leveled criticism at one-room schools that, according to David Tyack, were subject to community control and characterized by "nongraded primary education, instruction of younger children by older [students], flexible scheduling, and a lack of bureaucratic buffers between teachers and patrons."[8] Herbert M. Kliebard notes that for much of the nineteenth century the teacher, though "often immature," was expected to personify community values and "mete out stern discipline to the unruly and dull-witted."[9] As industrialization and urbanization progressed, leading educators argued that such provincial places of learning no longer prepared students for the complexities of modern life. When White was born in 1860, Massachusetts was the most urban of the states, with three-fourths of its residents living in towns with populations over three thousand.[10] Nevertheless, rural schools continued to dot the countryside around Heath, then and throughout her adult life.

Some of Heath's schools dated back to the colonial period. Edward Calver's *Heath, Massachusetts: A History and Guidebook* references a 1772 deed for a brick school on Charlemont Hill where Colonel Jonathan White first cleared land for a farm. Early town meetings were held in the school, Heath's only public building when it incorporated in 1785. The brick school was later replaced by a frame structure known as the South Schoolhouse that remained standing until shortly before the publication of Calver's first edition in 1979.[11]

While the earliest Massachusetts schoolhouses had reflected the Puritans' desire to teach young people to read the Bible, the General Court passed a law separating church and state in 1827. (Battles over the appropriate amount and type of religious influence in public schools would continue, however, especially as the state's population became more pluralistic.)[12] In 1837, Horace Mann was appointed the first Secretary of the Massachusetts State Board of Education. Believing in "the perfectibility of human life and institutions," he poured his energy into achieving universal education through the establishment of a common school system.[13] The term "common school"—often used to describe U.S. public schools of the nineteenth century—reflects Mann's vision that school would be common to all people, and open to all children.[14] Drawing sufficient numbers of disparate groups of people together, Mann promoted some key ideas that shaped public education in Massachusetts and the United States. Among them were the beliefs that schools should be free, and not based on fees; they should be open to all; they should "foster morality and ethics" while avoiding "sectarian entanglements;" they should contribute to the public good and prepare students for success in life.[15] The staple of the common school curriculum was reading, with readers like those of William Holmes McGuffey infusing moral lessons into their content.

While public schools had existed prior to Mann's appointment, they functioned locally and autonomously, operating under the *district system* that divided a town into school districts, each of which managed its own school with funds from the town school committee and the state. The first four Secretaries of the Massachusetts State Board of Education (including Joseph White, first cousin of Flora's father) encouraged communities to abolish their district schools. They complained that the town school committees created rivalries through perceived inequities in the distribution of money; they also asserted that "prudential committeemen" (who oversaw individual district schools) gave teaching jobs to relatives and friends and built educational systems to meet their own material or personal requirements without considering the needs of children.[16]

Prior to the Civil War, the Massachusetts General Court enacted changes that would permit towns to abolish the district system, as well as additional reforms that expanded the state's role in public education. According to Michael Katz, these reforms, in aggregate, changed "the process of education."[17] For example, the legislature passed the first compulsory attendance law in 1852, withheld monies from the state school fund to force recalcitrant towns to open high schools, and provided support for local libraries. Still another reform enacted by the legislature—a cornerstone of Horace Mann's plan to establish a system of public education—was the founding of state normal schools.

The term *normal school* is derived from the French phrase *école normale,* denoting a school that would establish norms and serve as a model to others. In the United States, normal schools were teacher-training institutions. With Mann's support, the Massachusetts legislature established the country's first publicly funded normal school at Lexington in 1839 (which soon moved to Framingham); it was followed in the same year by a normal school at Barre (which closed in 1841 and reopened in Westfield in 1844) and by a third normal school that opened at Bridgewater in 1840.

In 1877 Flora White graduated from the two-year teacher training program at Westfield Normal School that prepared students to teach in the common schools of western Massachusetts. She may also have attended a common school for a portion of her youth. If so, White's writing indicates she did not place a high value on the experience. Under the heading "Flora White's Education & Schooling," she wrote in 1939 the following brief description of her academic preparation prior to moving to Isaac Esty's home in Amherst: "The most Educative instruction given by Mother—Harriet White (now a widow). Latin, Literature and Mathematics with thorough training in English Composition were given by her."[18] It would appear from this description that the provider of the *least Educative instruction* went without mention. When White was interviewed in 1941, she indicated that she had received a classical education (emphasizing Latin, Greek, literature, and history) that went well beyond the limits of a common school curriculum.[19]

In reflecting on her career, Flora White recalled that she and her sister Mary decided to "try . . . [their] hand" at teaching in a rural school in Hawley, Massachusetts (near Heath) before entering Westfield.[20] Although there are no records to characterize the experience, White later wrote a novel (published in 1942 but first drafted half a century earlier) that described a young female teacher in a rural school. White's narrative highlighted several pedagogical problems. The teacher was untrained and closely supervised by "Ephraim Pepperfield," a lay committeeman. He exerted an undue and counterproductive influence, opposed creative pedagogy, and valued the control of student behavior over intellectual development. Interestingly, the publisher's announcement on the jacket cover states that while White's novel is "pure fiction so far as the characters are concerned, we are assured that the experiences involved as well as the scenes depicted are absolutely factual."[21] As White gained teaching experience, her pedagogy contrasted greatly with the expectations of the fictional Pepperfield. Regardless of the situation at the rural school in Hawley, however, the experience did not dissuade the White sisters from entering normal school.

ALTERNATIVES TO PUBLIC EDUCATION

Equally important to Flora White's view of rural common schools was her understanding of alternatives to public education during her early years. Although Mann's vision was a common school open to all, many Massachusetts students were educated in private schools. Michael Katz writes that the expansion of public schools under Mann's leadership resulted in proportionately fewer of the state's children attending private institutions. He notes that during the course of the nineteenth century, the number of Massachusetts children at private, incorporated academies remained fairly stable. However, those attending "the more numerous, less prestigious, and often ephemeral unincorporated academies and other private schools dropped markedly." Katz reports that in 1840, 22 percent of Massachusetts schoolchildren were enrolled in private schools; by 1865 the number was cut in half. The spread of public high schools likewise "accompanied the decline in academy attendance."[22]

The *Sesquicentennial Anniversary of the Town of Heath* offers insight on early private school initiatives in the town. One essay notes that many young men studied under the Reverend Moses Miller, a Brown graduate and Heath's second minister from 1804–1840. Miller reportedly was the first person to take in male "scholars" at Heath. He apparently taught a classical curriculum, since some of the young men (day pupils as well as boarders in his home) were "preparing for college and others for the ministry."[23] Over time, Miller's instruction evolved into "select schools, with an imported master" [other than Miller].[24] Select schools were privately supported elementary or secondary schools whose students were *selectively chosen*, usually on sectarian, social, and/or economic bases.

Heath's select schools met on the second floor of a building in the town center called the Red House. It had a colorful history before being demolished in 1897, having served as an inn, a home for a family with sixteen children, and a temporary domicile for members of the Oneida tribe who gave exhibitions on their customs. On at least one occasion the Red House was an Election-Day bar where a "thirsty crowd" gathered to consume "intoxicating liquors." The beverage of choice, called "flip," was a mixture of homemade beer and rum.[25] It was the object of a drinking game described years later by the Reverend John C. Thompson, who, as an eleven-year-old boy, observed the 1815 Election-Day festivities in the Red House:

Those who wished to gain entrance could hardly find standing room, much less sittings; and so great was the demand for "flip" that, I well remember—it was difficult to keep a passage open from the bar to the fireplace . . . I . . . learned for the first time that there was a game in flip-drinking. . . . [A] ring of young men was being formed near the centre of the crowded room, for the purpose of social chat and flip-drinking. This ring was being continually enlarged. The method of enlargement was this: A young friend from without, was invited, or constrained to join them; and was given to understand the initiatory fee to their circle was a half mug of flip. . . . [I]t was not long before I felt an impressive hand upon my shoulder accompanied by an earnest invitation to come into the ring. My boyish pride, at being admitted into the circle of those so much older than myself, constrained me to order the initiating fee— the half mug of flip.[26]

Despite the lack of a proper educational facility in which to instruct advanced students, Moses Miller reportedly took a student-centered approach to his teaching. He is described in the town's sesquicentennial history as "the beloved pastor, who with untiring efforts, with his earnest, persistent, energetic labors aimed to educate and instruct his loved people, *most carefully studying their needs and necessities, and preparing his mental, moral and religious forces to meet their needs*" (emphasis added).[27]

Although Calver is unsure about whether girls were admitted to Miller's classes, Flora White repeatedly wrote that he tutored her mother in Latin, apparently in keeping with a practice Horace Mann described in 1853.[28] Mann noted that long after provisions for free public schools had been made in Massachusetts, "it was a common thing for boys only to attend them. In many towns, the first improvement in this respect consisted in smuggling in the girls, perhaps for an hour a day, after the boys had received their lessons and gone home."[29] Flora noted that Harriet White was well-educated, thereby voicing approval of the results of Miller's instruction and the informal setting in which it occurred. This is not surprising since student-centeredness would also become a hallmark of Flora White's own teaching.

Calver reports that "studious girls" in Heath, including Moses Miller's own daughters, were pupils of Mary Lyon while she was in the nearby town of Buckland, Massachusetts.[30] However, Lyon closed her Buckland Female School in 1830 and later spent three years (1833–1836) going from farm to farm, raising money for a higher education institution for women that became Mount Holyoke Female Seminary. Calver notes that Heath's citizens responded very favorably to Lyon's appeal (and to an appeal from the all-male Amherst College), indicating they placed a high value on education. He offers additional evidence that "Heath people took to education" by stating that the town produced, in one year, a sufficient number of teachers to meet its own needs while supplying forty teachers to neighboring towns.[31] Sarah D. Locke Stow provides more detail on the extraordinary support Heath residents gave Mary Lyon, considering the size of the town. Over a three-year period, Lyon received pledges from over eighteen hundred people in ninety different New England towns for a total of $27,000. Only three towns (Boston, Easthampton, and Conway) pledged more than Heath. For purposes of comparison, Boston pledges amounted to $6,720; Easthampton $1,850; Conway $1,405; and Heath $1,200. Only fourteen towns (including the four mentioned above) gave Lyon pledges of more than $500.[32] The generous donations allowed Lyon to advance her five major objectives at Mount Holyoke: inculcating a "social and domestic character" in her students; encouraging physical culture; encouraging the ethos of "disinterested benevolence" within the school community; converting each member of the school family to Christianity; and providing students with as thorough an academic preparation as possible.[33]

It may be that in tutoring girls like Harriet White (born in 1825), Moses Miller was trying to meet the needs of young women who were either preparing for a seminary education or were unable to avail themselves of one after Lyon closed her Buckland school. It is clear, however, that many of the teachers Heath produced were women. Throughout the nineteenth century in Massachusetts, teaching was becoming a female occupation. In 1840, 61 percent of the state's teachers were men; by 1865, the percentage was only 14 percent.[34] This trend would continue until—by 1906—males constituted just 10 percent of the state's teachers, with most men still in the profession having moved into administration.[35]

A PUBLIC, PRIVATE, AND NORMAL SCHOOL EDUCATION

In 1939, Flora White acknowledged spending two years in public school in Amherst but provided no details about the experience. Amherst had a coeducational high school, but there is no indication that White was one of its graduates. (A high school diploma was not required for entering Westfield; as late as 1890, only 22 percent of its students were high school graduates, due to the small number of high schools in the counties Westfield served.)[36] It is likely that, in acknowledging her Amherst public school attendance but saving the detail (and praise) for the informal, individualized instruction she received from her mother and Isaac Esty, White revealed an attitude that the Amherst public school was better than a rural common school, but less helpful than the "stimulating" educational experience she had at Esty's home.[37] In her reminiscence, White provides specifics about the year between public school and normal school in which she followed a classical curriculum, studying world history and literature under "private" instruction. White cites four authors whose books she read—"Gibbon, Hume, Motley, MacCauley."[38] Here White is likely referring to historians Edward Gibbon, John Lothrop Motley, and Thomas Babington MacCaulay, as well as philosopher David Hume—all challenging writers for a young woman of fourteen or fifteen. Existing sources on Westfield Normal School (the institution's records as well as White's) provide a fuller picture of her educational experiences after she left Esty's home to study for a teaching career.

Westfield was established as the first publicly supported, coeducational normal school in the United States. Given the feminization of teaching, an overwhelming proportion of Westfield students (nearly 89 percent) were women when Flora and Mary White enrolled there in 1875.[39] Although tuition was free, each Westfield student could expect to spend about five hundred dollars to complete the two-year program due to the cost of room, board, books, supplies, and transportation. The White sisters were able to use Isaac Esty's bequest to meet expenses; however, five hundred dollars was a considerable sum since a normal school graduate earned only fifteen to twenty dollars per month during a six-month school year.[40]

Flora White highlighted the name of one normal school faculty member in her 1939 writing of "Life Facts": Joseph Gould Scott, head teacher at Westfield during the White sisters' attendance. Scott taught classes in physics, physiology, botany, and zoology; as such, he provided White with an education in the sciences to complement the classical curriculum she received from her mother and Isaac Esty. White recalled that her sister Hattie (a Westfield graduate) said "much about this remarkable teacher who had been a pupil of [Harvard scientist] Louis Agassiz." Flora added, "We formed an ardent and life long friendship and this devotion never wavered."[41] Scott went on to serve as Westfield's principal from 1877–1887 and died in 1889 at age fifty-three.

Scott followed John W. Dickinson (1825–1901), who served as principal during Flora and Mary White's attendance at the normal school. (White also cites Dickinson in her 1939 memoir, referring to him not by name but as "Sec. of Board of Education.")[42] Dickinson succeeded Joseph White (the first cousin of Flora's father) in 1877 and remained in that office until 1893. While he was Westfield's principal, Dickinson taught classes in rhetoric, psychology, didactics, and moral philosophy. He set the tone at the normal school by subscribing to the philosophy of Johann Heinrich Pestalozzi, the famous Swiss educator. Pestalozzi believed a teacher should approach instruction by first taking the interests of the child into account rather than the demands of the subject matter. Once engaged, Pestalozzi contended, the child could be led by the teacher to the desired place. Pestalozzi's pedagogical approach was popularly known as *object teaching*, which occurred when the teacher began instruction with a concrete object to gain the child's attention. (The object was supposed to relate to the child's world and also serve as a medium for bringing the child into the world of the teacher.) In addition to his support of object teaching, Dickinson believed learning occurred in stages associated with the age of the child, and he advocated a holistic approach to child study that incorporated new behavioral sciences. When the White sisters graduated from Westfield, Dickinson was working on a book titled *Psychology for Normal Schools*. He was a frequent speaker at NEA meetings on such topics as "Knowledge," "Methods of Professional Training," and "Methods in Teaching."[43]

John W. Dickinson's student-centered approach to teaching foreshadowed the pedagogical style Flora White developed during her career. In particular, she concurred with his view that teachers should value the individual characteristics of students, and refrain from "annihilating" them.[44] Dickinson's close association of object teaching with science and nature was also consistent with outdoor education experiences that became part of White's school program. Dickinson emphasized daily exercise and healthy habits, as did White. He continued to be a force in her life when, in 1892—as Secretary of the Massachusetts State Board of Education—he urged her to return to Westfield as a faculty member. She accepted, citing the "acute" need to introduce teachers to new methods.[45]

Despite all the benefits White derived from Westfield, some practices at the school revealed a deep gender bias, reflecting attitudes widely held in U.S. society and propagated by medical and scientific authorities throughout the nineteenth century. For example, members of the Massachusetts State Board of Education visited Westfield in 1867 (during the approximate period when Flora White's older sister Hattie attended there) and discovered at this largely female institution "many cases of failing health, headaches, sleeplessness, arising evidently from too much brain work." They concluded that "since the brain of an adult is not capable of more than four hours hard work a day, a young person cannot work to advantage more than three." Thereafter, Westfield prohibited "unreasonable rising and study" on the part of its students.[46] This view reflected a cult of invalidism during the mid-nineteenth century in which physicians warned that too much activity unnerved women, creating a host of maladies from hysteria to dyspepsia. People believed the uterus was connected to the nervous system, so overexertion might lead to weak and degenerate offspring.[47] As late as 1873, Dr. Edward H. Clarke of Harvard Medical School blamed college education for a range of female disorders, including neuralgia, uterine disease, and hysteria.[48] Women were taught to conserve what little energy they had, since expending it in one area such as intellectual work removed it from another area considered more gender appropriate such as childbearing.[49] This did not apply to black and lower-class women, who were expected to engage in hard physical labor.

A FEMINIZED OCCUPATION IN AN INDUSTRIAL ERA

Gender bias continued to affect Flora White's work life when, following graduation, she began teaching in a city school system. David Tyack documents the disparity in pay that existed between male and female teachers in city schools in the United States. He reports that in 1870 men teachers earned an average of thirty-five dollars per week while women teachers earned twelve dollars; in 1880 men teachers earned an average of thirty-one dollars a week while women teachers earned twelve dollars; in 1890 men teachers earned an average of thirty-three dollars a week while women teachers earned thirteen dollars. In discussing the wage disparity, Tyack explains that teaching was one of the few "large and respectable occupations" open to women, and—since they were willing to work for less than men—school boards kept costs down by readily employing them.[50] Women faced a more difficult job market in school administration, as evidenced by U.S. Commissioner of Education reports that some superintendents preferred men as elementary principals due to their perceived executive ability and skill as firm disciplinarians.[51] Tyack and Elisabeth Hansot note that as schools became larger and more bureaucratic, women lost "even their tenuous toehold on good jobs,"[52] as evidenced by the decline in the number of women in elementary principalships. Kathleen M. Brown writes that "powerful elites subscribed to the belief that men should supervise men while women should teach children. This belief translated into the practice of hiring male superintendents to supervise male principals, who, in turn, managed a largely female faculty."[53] Tyack and Hansot also report that boards sought men for leadership roles in the belief that "maleness gave the schools a higher social credit rating because of the higher general standing of men in society."[54]

Flora White pursued her teaching career during the period known to historians as the Second Industrial Revolution (1870–1914). The era began with the introduction of the Bessamer process in the U.S. steel industry and culminated in mass production through a progressive assembly procedure that came into use by the First World War. During this period the corporation became the dominant form of business organization. In 1911 Frederick W. Taylor (who drew from his experience in the steel industry) published his widely read *Principles of Scientific Management*, emphasizing the importance of efficiency in organizations.[55] Evidence of an early application of the industrial model to schools (with an accompanying gender bias) can be seen in an 1874 commentary on the feminization of teaching. The commentary was part of a larger document titled "Statement of the Theory of Education in the United States of America." It was signed by Joseph White, Secretary of the Massachusetts State Board of Education (and first cousin of Flora's father), along with chief school officials of several other states, college and university presidents, and superintendents of city school systems. The following is an excerpt of the "Statement," printed by the U.S. government:

> The pupil, coming directly from home influence, finds a less abrupt change upon entering the school under the charge of a female teacher. The female character, being trained by experience in family-supervision to the administration of special details wherein division of labor cannot prevail to any great

extent, is eminently fitted to control and manage the education of the child while it is in a state of transition from caprice to rationally-regulated exercises of the will; and the development of individuality is generally more harmonious up to a certain age if the pupil is placed under female teachers. The comparatively small cost of female-labor, also, largely determines its employment in all public schools.[56]

Apart from acknowledging wage discrimination in schools, the "Statement" reinforced a widely held view that female teachers were appropriate nurturers of younger pupils but less suitable for older students. It also suggested a pigeonholing of women that Flora White would reject by her own actions. (For example, at age twenty-five she accepted a position teaching English History and Literature at a boys' preparatory school in the Cape Colony in southern Africa, with students aged ten to fifteen.) Whereas the "Statement" implied a business/industrial model of schooling with terms like *supervision, division of labor, control,* and *manage,* White took a different approach, as seen in her 1896 paper presentation to the NEA in which she criticized efforts to standardize education:

Get percentages on joy and exuberance of spirits [i]f you would make safe, sane and righteous standards for your schools. If the pulses do not beat faster, longings grow stronger, doubts further deepen, and the joy of life tingle along the nerves, of what avail think you will the school and all its bookishness be toward producing a stronger, nobler race.[57]

Despite her sentiments, however, the industrial model gained wide usage among leaders of organizations during the late nineteenth and early twentieth centuries. It was increasingly applied to schools, as seen in the broad support the previously discussed "Statement" received from the country's educational leaders. Paralleling discussions about *how* to teach U.S. students during this period were debates on *what* to teach them, as seen in deliberations on vocational education and the role of humanist values in the curriculum.

Drawing on their experiences in Hawley and Westfield, Flora and Mary White graduated from their two-year teacher training program and sought positions in the common schools. They found jobs in the general vicinity of Springfield, Massachusetts. It was a city with a population of 31,043 in 1875, located on the Connecticut River—some ten miles from Westfield and sixty miles from Heath.[58]

TEACHING IN URBAN PUBLIC SCHOOLS

Springfield's economic boom began during the Civil War when the Confederate capture of Harper's Ferry left the Springfield Armory as the only government-owned gun manufacturing facility under Union control. During the war, the city's private arms producers such as Smith and Wesson also received government contracts. At the war's end, Springfield's skilled workforce found employment in new industries that located in the city. Immigration increased, and Springfield's population doubled between 1880 and 1900.[59]

Flora White's "Life Facts" show that, following graduation in 1877, she first taught in public schools in West Springfield and then in Springfield. Census records, school reports, and city directories indicate that during this period Flora and Mary White were boarders in the towns of West Springfield and nearby Chicopee. Their mother lived with them as did (for a brief period) their sister Hattie. When Flora began teaching at Springfield in the fall of 1881, she was assigned to teach grade seven at Worthington Street School. In 1882–1884, she taught grades 1 to 3 at School Street School and then resigned, accepting a teaching position in the Cape Colony in southern Africa where she lived from 1885 to 1887. Meanwhile, Mary White continued to teach in the primary grades at two different Springfield schools (Worthington Street and School Street) until after Flora returned.[60]

Flora White's correspondence shows that even before leaving the Cape Colony to return home in 1887, she had decided to open a private school in Springfield. In letters home she expressed dissatisfaction with the experience Mary was having in the Springfield Public Schools and urged her to resign. Flora wrote, " You have had enough of the Public School and it wears on you too much."[61] Leaving public education proved to be an important exercise of agency on Flora White's part; therefore, the reasons for her departure need to be explored.

Local histories indicate that circumstances in the Springfield Public Schools were difficult when the White sisters taught there, due to financial shortfalls. In 1865, the system hired its first superintendent when the growth of the city convinced officials that the size and complexity of the schools required expert leadership. Admiral P. Stone, the second superintendent from 1873 to 1888 (during Flora White's employment), is remembered for having served during a nationwide financial depression that reduced appropriations in Springfield. One local history noted, "Mr. Stone by his ability in organization did much to bring the schools uninjured through the trying experience."[62] While such difficulties may have contributed to White's feelings about teaching in public schools, there were other factors at play as she pondered her next teaching assignment.

Like many other communities in nineteenth-century America, Springfield evolved from providing education in a village school to delivering it through a bureaucracy, a process Tyack details in *The One Best System: A History of American Urban Education.* He documents how school boards in growing communities built structures since dubbed "egg-crate school[s]" with crowded classrooms.[63] Teachers addressed the problem of maintaining order among "many different social classes" by keeping the students continually busy, forcing them to compete for the limited praise, and terrorizing them with the prospect of being degraded.[64] Flora White concurred with Tyack's assessment of public education, writing, "The crowding of our schoolrooms is our greatest sin against childhood."[65]

Despite White's decision to leave the Springfield Public Schools, there were no lasting ill feelings with her employer. In fact, the third Springfield superintendent, Thomas Balliet, permitted White to prominently feature his name as a reference for the private school she founded in 1897 in Concord, Massachusetts. Balliet was widely acclaimed as an educational leader and credited with making the Springfield Public Schools into "one of the most *efficient* [emphasis added] and progressive systems in the country."[66] Following his service in public education he became dean of the School of Pedagogy at New York University, retiring as dean emeritus in 1919. (The valuing of efficiency in a school superintendent, and the influence of U.S. business leaders and business values on public schools, is fully explored in *The Cult of Efficiency* by Raymond E. Callahan,[67] whose thesis is revisited in an edited book, *Shaping the Superintendency*, by William Edward Eaton.)[68]

LIFE CHANGES

In spite of her dissatisfaction with the growing industrial model in public education (as seen in her criticism of standardization and overcrowding and her belief that her sister should resign her teaching position), the most compelling reason for Flora White to leave Massachusetts and travel to the Cape Colony in 1885 was the health of her sister, Hattie, who was teaching in the Huguenot Seminary at Wellington. Hattie had suffered a "breakdown," and Flora went to the Cape Colony to lend assistance.[69]

The Huguenot Seminary had been founded eleven years earlier by Abbie Park Ferguson and Anna E. Bliss—both daughters of Congregational ministers and graduates of Mount Holyoke Seminary in Massachusetts. They went to Wellington (about seventeen miles from Cape Town) at the invitation of the Reverend Andrew Murray, moderator of the Dutch Reformed Church. Murray was troubled by what he perceived as a dearth of rigorous academic instruction for middle-class white girls in the Cape Colony. Inspired by Fidelia Fiske's 1866 book, *Recollections of Mary Lyon, with Selections from Her Instruction to the Pupils at Mt. Holyoke Female Seminary*, Murray contacted the Massachusetts school. Ferguson and Bliss responded, bringing the curriculum, rules, traditions, and architectural plans of Mount Holyoke to the colony. Their purpose was to provide a secondary education and teacher training to white women between fifteen and twenty years of age.[70]

Although Hattie White had graduated from Westfield and not Mount Holyoke, she was fully engaged in the missionary effort at Huguenot Seminary. In deciding to travel to the Cape Colony, Flora was undoubtedly aware that Hattie's view of religion differed from her own. Flora White had become an Episcopalian when she was working in Springfield, and her conversion was not a solitary endeavor. Flora, her mother, and sister Mary regularly attended Springfield's Christ Church, the largest Episcopal Church in western Massachusetts, where the Reverend John Cotton Brooks (1848–1907) was rector. The Whites became friends of Brooks, who, like Isaac Esty, gave them additional social capital. Brooks was a member of a prominent Massachusetts family whose ancestors, like the Whites, arrived at Salem during the Puritan migration of the 1630s. (His brother, Phillips Brooks—rector of Boston's Trinity Church and briefly Bishop of Massachusetts—was best remembered as the lyricist for "O Little Town of Bethlehem.") John Cotton Brooks was a Phi Beta Kappa graduate of Harvard who, in considering the ministry, thought about attending Andover Theological Seminary where his grandfather was among the founders. Brooks's biographer notes, "Although it [Andover] was a Congregational school, it was thought that a year spent there would be a good foundation for the work to be continued elsewhere. The excellence of the course in Hebrew especially appealed to him."[71] Brooks decided to spend a year at Andover and the following two years at Philadelphia Divinity School, from which he graduated in 1876.

John Cotton Brooks's grounding in the Congregational and Episcopal traditions was likely helpful in his relationship with Flora White, who continued to identify as an Episcopalian for the remainder of her life. In 1939 she acknowledged Brooks's great influence on her family. White wrote:

> This relationship [with John Cotton Brooks] was a strong force in our lives though cut short by our leaving Springfield and the death of our loved Rector & long illness of his wife. We were often there in the earlier days of his ministry to celebrate the birthdays, to meet his brother Phillips Brooks as well as Mrs. Brooks their mother & other members of the family.[72]

Even given Brooks's familiarity with the Congregational and Episcopal traditions, White's conversion is somewhat surprising, in light of her Congregational roots and formative experience with Isaac Esty. Her actions may be explained in part by Mary Sudman Donovan, who reports that an unusually large number of U.S. women writers and educators converted to the Episcopal Church in the mid-nineteenth century. Included in this group were Catharine Beecher, Harriet Beecher Stowe, Emma Willard, and Sarah Josepha Hale.[73] Donovan explores reasons for the Episcopal Church's appeal to prospective members, citing its "high social status" and traditional ritual during a time when "all things English" were in vogue in Victorian America.[74] (At the mid-nineteenth century, Donovan notes, the Episcopal Church ranked sixth in membership and third in property value among U.S. churches, an indicator of its members' socioeconomic status.) She adds that some people joined the Episcopal Church in reaction to the emotional excesses of the Great Awakening, preferring "the order and dignity" of Episcopal worship and "the conservative tradition of its intellectual life" that made the Church less vulnerable to being overwhelmed by popular trends.[75] However, both Donovan and Kathryn Kish Sklar, biographer of Catharine Beecher, suggest there was a theological reason for a woman writer and/or educator to convert to the Episcopal Church. It related to a view of children as regards original sin. Since Flora White spent a career promoting the education of children, this viewpoint merits consideration.

When Beecher was writing *Religious Training of Children*, she concluded that only the Episcopal Church treated children appropriately. Beecher explained, "For they [Episcopalians], by baptism, *do* [erase] the evil done by Adam's sin, so that the child can be successfully *trained* by a *religious growth.*"[76] Traditional Calvinism viewed children as corrupt, their "inherent evil" being redeemed later in life by a "conversion of spiritual rebirth."[77] Other Protestant churches (besides the Episcopalians) preferred a "testimony of rebirth" over training in childhood.[78] Since rebirth generally occurred in early adulthood, there was, for these churches, a congruence between a person's physical growth and the culture's view of her/his spiritual growth. In this manner, children proceeded from a state of corruption to a state of purity, with knowledge fostering and accompanying that progression. Sklar notes, however, that popular thought during the nineteenth century "turned this progression on its head," so that when Beecher wrote *Religious Training of Children* in 1864, children were seen as innocent at birth but gradually corrupted by the world around them.[79] Education therefore became focused on preserving children's innocence rather than eradicating their sin. However, as Beecher pointed out in *Letters to the People on Health and Happiness,* "innocence could not be preserved without ignorance."[80] Since one had to know evil in order to deal with it successfully, Victorian parents set about the "impossible task" of preserving natural innocence while acknowledging that exposure to evil was inevitable and even necessary.[81] Sklar states that Beecher foresaw the development of a moral dilemma around this issue, "long before the culture completely boxed itself into the predicament."[82] In the end, however, Catharine Beecher rejected the doctrine of natural depravity but continued to see the world as sharply divided between good and evil, thereby demonstrating an inability to entirely abandon Calvinism.

Daniel T. Rodgers provides additional insight into nineteenth-century attitudes toward children and education. He writes that after 1830, northern, middle-class children in the United States received conflicting messages as they moved from infancy toward adulthood. By the end of the nineteenth century, agencies that shaped children (including most schools) were unsure about whether to integrate children into society or to preserve them from it. Amid a widespread uncertainty about the transformation of the United States from an agricultural society to an industrial and urban order, these agencies were torn between an impulse to educate children into adult roles, and a desire to seize on children as a corrective for adult shortcomings. [83]

In joining a church that rejected a belief in the depravity of children while emphasizing their religious instruction, Flora White made a spiritual choice that was consistent with her pedagogical philosophy. In addition to theological reasons for her conversion, it is likely that she was sensitive to social class and valued worship services that eschewed strong emotional expression. These points will be amplified in the next chapter. Over time, Flora White would lend her support for a summer educational program that the Episcopal Church established in her home town of Heath. Calver notes that in 1910 Flora White and her sister Mary gave Archdeacon Charles Sniffen of the Diocese of Western Massachusetts "the house just south of the common as a summer location for St. Faith's Training School for Deaconesses . . . [where] girls from isolated communities were to be prepared for confirmation." [84] The building, called Mission House, was overseen by Deaconess Susan Knapp, director of St. Faith's School, which was located on the grounds of the Cathedral of St. John the Divine in New York City.

Hattie White, on the other hand, continued to be strongly influenced by the Calvinism of her Congregational background until her death in 1904. After arriving in the Cape Colony, Flora sent letters home indicating that Hattie practiced a type of evangelical faith that her younger sister sometimes found off-putting. (Flora wrote of Hattie's colleagues at the Huguenot Seminary, "I think they have begun to try & convert me and I don't just fancy it.") [85] As will be discussed in the next chapter, when Flora made plans for founding a school in Springfield, she decided to include her sister Mary but not her sister Hattie, in part because of Hattie's strong evangelical bent.

Calver explains Flora's eventual reconciliation of the two traditions by noting that most people who participated with her in her summer intellectual colony at Heath (from 1896 through her death in 1948) were Episcopalians; however, they claimed to become "Congregationalists during the summer." [86] Heath never had an Episcopal church, but Calver notes that for the "purists," an Episcopal priest celebrated an early morning communion service, using the facilities of St. Faith's School. [87]

Meanwhile, religious affiliations in Heath fluctuated. During the first half of the nineteenth century other religious groups, in addition to Congregationalists, had established churches in the town (Baptists in 1801, Unitarians in 1825, Methodists in 1859). However, by 1891 the town's population (and church attendance) had so declined that the churches were having difficulty paying ministers' salaries. Representatives met and in 1892 drafted a constitution and bylaws for a new church known as the Union Evangelical Church of Heath. It would replace the existing churches, which agreed to dissolve. The Union Church, as it was called, was located in the building that the former Congregational Church constructed in 1833 when Heath's population was at its peak.

Although histories of Heath document the "Great Revival" in the sixteenth year of Moses Miller's ministry (1822 to 1823) when 121 people joined its Congregational Church by profession of faith,[88] by 1861 even "godly" Joseph White II had difficulty reconciling his beliefs to the requirements of the "visible Church" of his day.[89] However, churches—like schools—had to adjust to changing times. Unbeknownst to the new members of the Union Church, returning Heath natives, "summer Congregationalists," Calvinists—and even an agnostic Jew would soon establish vacation residences in the town, availing themselves of its beautiful scenery. As a result, the pulpit of the Union Church would regularly feature some of the most famous clergy in the United States whose sermons would provide theological perspective on the dilemmas of modern life. In 1943, one member of the group—Reinhold Niebuhr—would offer from the Union Church pulpit a simple prayer for grace, courage, and wisdom that would find credence throughout the world. Known as the "Serenity Prayer," it crossed religious boundaries in the midst of global conflict.

CONCLUSION

In summary, Flora White's experiences as a student and teacher explain the ambivalence she felt about schools. Her perspective was a result of firsthand experience with a variety of curricula and pedagogies in a range of settings. Sometimes White's classroom was her home, where she explored classical texts under the tutelage of a loved one. At other times *she* was in charge of a classroom with many students, in a mass education model reflecting a society undergoing rapid industrialization. As a normal school student, White was influenced by educators who took a Pestalozzian, child-centered approach that would become a hallmark of her teaching. Their views did not represent a consensus in the society at large. As Rodgers notes, the late nineteenth century was a time of widespread societal uncertainty about how to educate children—whether to ignore their unique characteristics and prepare them for adult roles, or utilize them as a corrective for adult society. For some women educators, the dilemma was spiritual as well as professional and, in this context, White's conversion to the Episcopal Church appears to have reconciled her view of children with her own pedagogical beliefs. Regardless of how she came to terms with this issue, it was clear that Flora White was working in an environment of widespread gender discrimination in which

women teachers were paid less—and afforded many fewer leadership opportunities—than men. As she grew into a progressive educator who would seek
ways to enhancing the development of children, she would also look for
opportunities to promote the development of young women beyond the limitations imposed by those around her.

NOTES

1. Arthur Stocks, "Buffalo and Its Attractions," *The School Review*, 6 (1896), 496.

2. Ibid., 494.

3. Flora J. White, "Physical Effects of Sloyd" (paper presented at the annual meeting of the National Education Association, Buffalo, NY, July 1896).

4. Kate Rousmaniere, *Citizen Teacher: The Life and Leadership of Margaret Haley* (Albany, NY: State University of New York Press, 2005), 106.

5. Ibid.

6. White, "Physical Effects of Sloyd," NEA paper, 1.

7. Joseph D. White, "Reminiscent," n.d. Flora White Papers. Private collection; Edward Calver, *Heath, Massachusetts: A History and Guidebook* (Heath, MA: Heath Historical Society, 2009), 33.

8. David B. Tyack, *The One Best System: A History of American Urban Education* (Cambridge, MA: Harvard University Press, 1974), 14.

9. Herbert M. Kliebard, *The Struggle for the American Curriculum, 1893–1958* (New York: Routledge, 1989), 1.

10. Robert T. Brown, *The Rise and Fall of the People's Colleges: The Westfield Normal School, 1839–1914* (Westfield, MA: Institute for Massachusetts Studies, Westfield State College, 1988), 9.

11. Calver, *Heath, Massachusetts*, 33.

12. See Tyack, *The One Best System*, 104–109, for a discussion on Protestant-Catholic conflicts over religion in public schools.

13. Lawrence A. Cremin, *The Transformation of the School: Progressivism in American Education, 1876–1957* (New York: Alfred A. Knopf, 1969), 8.

14. Ibid., 10.

15. Wayne Urban and Jennings L. Waggoner Jr., *American Education: A History* (New York: Routledge, 2004), 135.

16. Michael B. Katz. *The Irony of Early School Reform: Educational Innovation in Mid-Nineteenth Century Massachusetts* (New York: Teachers College, 2001), 54.

17. Ibid., 13.

18. Flora White, "Life Facts of Flora White and Family Recorded Mar. 18, 1939," Heath Historical Society, 2.

19. Miss Pickwick, "Girl about Town," *The Daily Oklahoman*, February 9, 1941, C5.

20. Flora White, "Life Facts," 3.

21. Flora White. *Bloodroots in the Wake of Circumstance* (Kansas City, MO: Burton, 1942), 84–91.

22. Katz, *The Irony of Early School Reform*, 12.

23. Pearle Tanner, "Heath and Its Families," in *Sesquicentennial Anniversary of the Town of Heath, Massachusetts, 1785–1935*, ed. Howard Chandler Robbins (Heath, MA: Heath Historical Society, 1935), 116.

24. Calver, *Heath, Massachusetts*, 185.

25. Ibid., 161–162.

26. Ibid.

27. Tanner, "Heath and Its Families," 116.

28. Flora White penned a notation on the cover page of Spencer Miller, *Joseph Miller of Newton, Massachusetts: His Descendants in America and His Ancestry in England* (New York:

Privately Printed, 1942). She wrote, "The grandfather of Spencer Miller, Rev. Moses Miller, coached Harriet White, mother of Flora, in Latin to prepare her for the Seminary of Troy, NY now a college." Flora White also wrote on page 116 her copy of the *Sesquicentennial Anniversary of the Town of Heath*, "Rev. Moses Miller tutored Harriet Mayhew White in Latin[,] Higher Mathematics, Literature [,] etc. in preparation for the Seminary."

29. David Tyack and Elisabeth Hansot, *Learning Together: A History of Coeducation in American Public Schools* (New York: Russell Sage Foundation, 1992), 13.

30. Calver, *Heath, Massachusetts*, 175.

31. Ibid., 185.

32. Sarah D. Locke Stow, *History of Mount Holyoke Seminary, South Hadley, Mass: During Its First Half Century, 1837–1887* (North Hadley, MA: Mount Holyoke Seminary, 1887), 59.

33. Dana L. Robert, *American Women in Mission: A Social History of Their Thought and Practice* (Macon, GA: Mercer University Press, 1996), 96.

34. Katz, *The Irony of Early School Reform*, 12.

35. Brown, *The Rise and Fall of the People's Colleges*, 9.

36. Ibid., 94.

37. White, "Life Facts," 3.

38. Ibid.

39. Brown, *The Rise and Fall of the People's Colleges*, 128.

40. Ibid., 54.

41. White, "Life Facts," 12.

42. Ibid., 5.

43. Brown, *The Rise and Fall of the People's Colleges*, 51.

44. Ibid., 49.

45. White, "Life Facts," 5.

46. Brown, *The Rise and Fall of the People's Colleges*, 52.

47. Stephanie L. Twin, "Women and Sport," in *Sport in America: New Historical Perspectives*, ed. Donald Spivey (Westport, CT: Greenwood Press, 1985), 196.

48. Ibid., 201.

49. Carroll Smith-Rosenberg and Charles Rosenberg, "The Female Animal: Medical and Biological Views on Woman and Her Role in Nineteenth Century America," *Journal of American History* 60 (1973): 340.

50. Tyack, *The One Best System*, 62.

51. Ibid., 63.

52. David Tyack and Elisabeth Hansot, *Managers of Virtue: Public School Leadership in America, 1820–1980* (New York: Basic Books, 1982), 181.

53. Kathleen M. Brown, "Pivotal Points: History, Development, and Promise of the Principalship," in *The SAGE Handbook of Educational Leadership*, ed. Fenwick W. English (Los Angeles: SAGE Publications, 2011), 90.

54. Elisabeth Hansot and David Tyack, *The Dream Deferred: A Golden Age for Women School Administrators* (Stanford, CA: Institute for Research on Educational Finance and Governance, School of Education, Stanford University, 1981), 13.

55. Frederick W. Taylor, *The Principles of Scientific Management* (New York: Harper and Row, 1911).

56. U.S. Bureau of Education, "A Statement of the Theory of Education in the United States of America as Approved by Many Leading Educators" (U.S. Government Printing Office, 1874), 19.

57. Flora J. White, "Physical Effects of Sloyd" (paper presented at the annual meeting of the National Education Association, Buffalo, New York, July 1896).

58. Laurel O'Donnell, 1999–2005. "Christ Church Parish—Springfield, Mass.—Rev. John Cotton Brooks, http://www.hampdencountyhistory.com/springfield/christchurch/cc069.html.

59. "Springfield History," http://www.quadrangle.org/springfield-history.htm.

60. Michele Plourde-Barker to author, 24 August, 2004, private collection.

61. Flora White to Harriet M. White and Mary A. White, 6 March, 1887, Flora White Papers, private collection.

62. Eugene Clarence Gardner, *Springfield Present and Prospectives: The City of Homes* (Springfield, MA: Pond and Campbell, 1905), 34.

63. Tyack, *The One Best System*, 44.

64. Ibid., 54.

65. White, "Physical Effects of Sloyd," NEA paper, 3.

66. "Balliet, Thomas Minard," vol. 1 of *Biographical Dictionary of American Educators* (Westport, CT: Greenwood Press, 1978), 81–82.

67. Raymond E. Callahan, *Education and the Cult of Efficiency: A Study of Social Forces That Have Shaped the Administration of Public Schools* (Chicago: University of Chicago Press, 1962).

68. William Edward Eaton, ed., *Shaping the Superintendency: A Reexamination of Callahan and the Cult of Efficiency* (New York: Teachers College Press, 1990).

69. Flora White to Harriet M. White and Mary A. White, 6 June 1887, Flora White Papers, private collection.

70. Sarah Emily Duff, "Head, Heart, and Hand: The Huguenot Seminary and the Construction of Middle Class Afrikaner Femininity" (Master's thesis, University of Stellenbosch, 2006).

71. James Clement Sharp, *John Cotton Brooks* (Cambridge: Harvard University, 1909), 40.

72. White, "Life Facts," 15.

73. Mary S. Donovan, *A Different Call: Women's Ministries in the Episcopal Church, 1850–1920* (Wilton, CT: Morehouse-Barlow,1986), 20. See also Kathryn Kish Sklar, *Catharine Beecher: A Study in American Domesticity* (New York: Norton, 1976), 79–88.

74. Donovan, *A Different Call*, 18–21.

75. Ibid., 19–23.

76. Sklar, *Catharine Beecher*, 260.

77. Ibid., 261.

78. Ibid.

79. Ibid.

80. Ibid.

81. Ibid.

82. Ibid.

83. Daniel T. Rodgers. "Socializing Middle-Class Children: Institutions, Fables, and Work Values in Nineteenth-Century America," *Journal of Social History* 13 (1980): 354–367.

84. Calver, *Heath, Massachusetts*, 190.

85. Flora White to Harriet White and Mary White, 4 October 1885, Flora White Papers, private collection.

86. Calver, *Heath, Massachusetts*, 192.

87. Ibid.

88. Howard Chandler Robbins, "The Church of Christ in Heath," in *Sesquicentennial Anniversary of the Town of Heath, Massachusetts*, ed. Howard Chandler Robbins (Heath, MA: Heath Historical Society, 1935), 139.

89. "Address at the Funeral of Mr. Joseph White, Heath, Oct. 18, 1861," Flora White Papers, private collection.

Chapter Three

Finding Her Voice

Flora White gazed out on the Atlantic Ocean as she penned a letter to her mother and sister Mary in Springfield. It was August of 1885, and White was en route to Cape Town by way of Madeira on the passenger ship *Spartan*. She wrote:

> [T]he Spartan has been rolling so outrageously since we came on board that you could not write with any peace. I was sick one day as we came thro' the bay of Biscay—a little sick only I paid two tributes to Neptune but it was not in the least bad, not half as bad as the little stomach trouble we have at home. The ship rolled like anything & gave one's insides a regular shaking up. [1]

Shortly before her arrival at Cape Town she wrote, "I really am a fine sailor and stand the rolling beautifully—in fact I rather like it today. I have been exalting myself generally but I await your reprimands. You are both home now and I do hope well & happy as I am."[2]

White's travel was made possible by important economic and technological developments during the nineteenth century that allowed growing numbers of U.S. women to cross the Atlantic. Although their culture had long accepted and even encouraged men's travel (as, for example, in exploration, commerce, and the military), few U.S. women had journeyed beyond their national borders by the early nineteenth century. Those who did were "accidental" tourists accompanying their fathers or husbands, largely for commercial or political reasons.[3] However, with the advent of steam-powered ships of the 1820s—and the subsequent introduction of "luxurious 'steam palaces'" that traversed the Atlantic beginning in the 1860s—women began to go abroad in larger numbers, and for their own reasons.[4]

Scholars suggest that foreign travel provided women with many benefits. Casey Blanton wrote that the increased democratization of travel and the gradual democratization of women's roles in the nineteenth century allowed well-educated, upper-class, single, white women to escape the rigidity of Victorian society and journey to remote places.[5] Beatrice Bijon and Gérard Gacon[6] as well as Alison Blunt[7] noted that the women who wrote about their travels experienced an increase in individual freedom. According to Blunt, this was because travel presented the opportunity to transgress or question ideas that were accepted at home.

Some scholars contend that, in addition to the benefits foreign travel afforded women, it was especially advantageous to Americans. Mary Suzanne Schriber writes that foreign travel played an important role in constructing a national identity by giving U.S. citizens an opportunity to interact with "the other."[8] (That is, in recognizing what they *weren't,* Americans also identified what they *were* as a group.) In addition, foreign travel gave Americans a sense of cultural and intellectual superiority over their fellow citizens—especially after the Civil War when travel became "an instrument of social leverage" in a "ferociously competitive economy" in which class-conscious people improved their status by "the performance of leisure."[9] By the last quarter of the nineteenth century both old and new-monied Americans were escaping the "massive influx of immigrants" by traveling to Europe on the decks of the same steamships that carried U.S.-bound Europeans in steerage.[10] Schriber noted that the "vulgarity and disorder" that many established Americans associated with immigrants caused the "traveling classes" to envision the high culture of Europe as "yet more desirable and genteel."[11]

White's travel was part of what Drew Keeling described as the "greatest intercontinental migration in human history" when—after the Civil War until the beginning of World War I—unprecedented numbers of people crossed the Atlantic between Europe and the United States. The steamship traveler's experience was largely determined by social class. Those in the "traveling class" (usually tourists, businessmen, and diplomats) had accommodations in cabins, on or above the main deck, where they could escape the noise below, and enjoy fresh air and pleasant views. On the other hand, "migrants"—the group constituting three-fourths of the travelers on board—stayed below the deck in "steerage" (so-named because the mechanism for steering the ship had once been located there). Although migrant fares were one-third that of the traveling class, the reduced price also meant having to contend with poor ventilation, noise, and the close proximity of mail and cargo storage.[12]

Flora White had a cabin and enjoyed the privileges of the traveling class; this was possible because transportation was provided under her employment agreement. In fact, although teachers were less advantaged than many U.S. traveling women, some journeyed great distances to perform their professional duties during the late nineteenth century. In *Mary Lyon and the Mount Holyoke Missionaries,* Amanda Porterfield highlighted the large number of white women from New England who (like Flora's sister Hattie) traveled to Persia, India, Ceylon, Hawaii, and Africa as teaching missionaries from Mount Holyoke Female Seminary.[13] The school prepared teachers to assist in the work of the American Board of Commissioners for Foreign Missions. Some scholars, such as Lamin Senneh, have discussed the ambivalent and even negative feelings of many Westerners toward Western missionary activity in the rest of the world.[14] Porterfield, however, noted that while the Mount Holyoke missionaries' goal was to convert large numbers of women to Protestant Christianity, they also promoted female literacy, monogamy, and a concern for the well-being of women and children. She contended that the missionary women contributed to cultural change in many parts of the world as traditional cultural views combined with missionary ideals to form a new synthesis. Although Flora White was only tangentially connected to Mount Holyoke's overseas efforts through her sister Hattie's work at the Huguenot Seminary in Wellington (designated a Daughter School of Mount Holyoke in 1874), the connection is an important one. The extant correspondence from White's two-year residence in the Cape Colony documents a critical period in the evolution of her thought. As she encountered *the other* and faced obstacles to her quest for agency, she further developed her identity in gender, class, racial, and national terms. In time, White would come to view the Cape Colony as a secluded place of retreat where she could reflect, focus on her students, and make some important decisions about her personal and professional future.

FIRST ENCOUNTERS WITH THE OTHER

Prior to boarding the *Spartan* to journey to the Cape Colony, White had traveled by steamer to Liverpool and then by train to London, where she spent several days. She was accompanied by Abbie Ferguson, co-founder of the Huguenot Seminary, who became ill in London. White dutifully stayed inside with Ferguson for two days, but when she showed signs of improvement White took that opportunity to tour the city. She consulted a guide book and later wrote to her mother, "I started off by myself. Imagine me prowling about the big city alone—It is very easy & does not seem bigger than any city when you are in it."[15] White enthusiastically toured architectural and historical sites and reported, "It is great fun to shop here. . . . Everybody was *very* attentive & they all took care to let me know that they knew I was an American. Nobody takes *me* for an Englishwoman you may be sure. And I am *very* glad of it."[16] This comment illustrates Schriber's point that foreign travel helped Americans construct a national identity by interacting with *the other*. It also represents a change in attitude because, in White's correspondence prior to arriving in London, she appeared to identify more closely with

New England than with the United States. For example, just after arriving in England—as she looked out the window of the train that went from Liverpool to London—White wrote a letter to her mother and sister in which she compared the English scenery to that of her home. After complimenting the "solidarity" of the English buildings as well as the beautiful, well-manicured (even "perfect") countryside, White made it clear that *home* was New England rather than the United States:

> Nature has done twenty times more for *New* England than *Old*. This lovely English scenery gives you the sweetest sense of comfort but no inspiration. I could not help after a little thinking of our wild streams & tall heaven-reaching trees. The great boulders-cliffs, mountains-rivers-Oh! there is such a difference!
>
> However, I do think that a wholesale introduction of this splendid masonry that upholds Old English roads would be in no wise injurious to our N. Eng. Highways or its scenery.[17]

As she interacted with *the other* in London, White encountered gender roles that surprised her. In a letter mailed from Madeira she wrote her sister Mary about the daring behavior of a female acquaintance in the English capital city: "Did I tell you that . . . [the acquaintance] took a cab & went to the theatre stark alone, on her way out! In London—think of it—and home alone at 11 o'clock. Who would do such a thing even in Springfield."[18] White also demonstrated an awareness of social class in criticizing women on "one of the worst streets in London—A thieves' resort—where murders are common & dark & dirty & literally *heaped* with babies—real pretty babies some of them if they had been washed & oh—*such looking* women."[19] White's class consciousness was evident when, before boarding the *Spartan* for the Cape Colony, she attended a worship service conducted at the Metropolitan Tabernacle by Charles Haddon Spurgeon. The most popular preacher in London, Spurgeon was a Particular Baptist with no formal theological training.[20] White's letters indicate she was not impressed by Spurgeon's strong emotional appeal to his congregation, composed largely of people from the working and lower classes of British society. She reported that Spurgeon, "a decidedly common looking . . . plain, unpretentious man" (who she said could be easily mistaken for a "Yankee Methodist") encouraged members of the large audience to "break down," and nearly brought them to tears as he preached. White contended that he "perverted the text . . . in every conceivable way to suit his idea and illustrations."[21] She concluded that the service left her cold, writing, "I might as well have gone into the woodshed for all the religious emotions it awakened."[22] Contrasting Spurgeon's "vulgarisms" with the sermons of her Episcopal rector in Springfield,

John Cotton Brooks, White noted that the rector "speaks to humanity at its highest," while Spurgeon "speaks to humanity at its lowest."[23]

Despite her criticism, White admitted she could not help but admire Spurgeon, who "was so earnest—so simple & simply sincere & reverent—really reverent." She added, "His whole life is so infused with the desire of instilling some religion, feeling & emotion into the masses of the indifferent & low that he does not get beyond it."[24] In the letter, White demonstrates an ability to rethink ideas she accepted at home, thereby supporting Blunt's finding. White acknowledges that while John Cotton Brooks's sermons moved her, some congregants found his intellectual messages difficult to understand. Such people, according to White, listen to the rector's complex ideas and say "what does he mean."[25] White's letters also support Mary Sudman Donovan's analysis of factors that motivated some nineteenth-century women to join the Episcopal Church. Among the factors she discussed were the high socioeconomic status of Episcopalians and the perceived emotional excesses of evangelical churches. White's reaction to the service at the Metropolitan Tabernacle demonstrates her strong awareness of social class as well as a desire for dignity in a worship service. A preference for dignified worship is also apparent when White subsequently writes from the Cape Colony, describing a service in the Dutch Reformed Church. She notes approvingly that the clergyman is "not a fanatic," but a "staid, orthodox minister."[26] She indicates, however, that staidness can be overdone. "The service was wooden," White observes, "and the seats excruciatingly so."[27]

GROWING INDEPENDENCE

Flora White's travel letters during the summer of 1885 also demonstrate her growing self-confidence and—in keeping with the findings of Bijon and Gacon and Blunt—greater sense of individual freedom as her trans-Atlantic voyage progressed. Upon leaving the United States for Liverpool, White told herself, "there is nobody I want to know except those lovely looking people [Mrs. Babcock and her daughter Mrs. Martin, both of Chicago] who kept by themselves & noticed no one. . . . I did not expect in the least to become acquaintances with them."[28] By the time she arrived in England White wrote, "I formed such a *pleasant* friendship on board the steamer with those Chicago people. . . . Mrs. Martin & I are going to write one another."[29] After leaving London she assured her mother and sister, "I am so glad I came. I've not had a second of regret & won't."[30] Later, as White traveled toward Cape Town on the *Spartan,* she viewed her trip with optimism—even exhilaration—writing, "I do not have a single feeling of dread about anything and mean to enjoy everything and everybody."[31]

White's optimism and high self-esteem were reflected in her dealings with fellow passengers. She easily interacted with women and men, most of whom were not Americans. On August 30 she wrote, "Everybody is so very nice to me that I am afraid my head will be quite turned with attention. I have had so many toasts & speeches & compliments & things made to me I feel like locking my cabin door & not coming out at all."[32] White reported that her fellow travelers looked to her for entertainment. To their delight, the spirited young woman staged *tableaux* (depictions of scenes) and arranged other group activities.[33] For example, White convinced passengers to dress up in a "sheet and pillow masquerade" explaining, "You could not tell the gentlemen from the ladies."[34] She also organized singing, persuaded an English traveler to give a talk on London, and narrated a "comic pantomime" of the Eve of Waterloo, with six passengers acting the parts. White reported, "It was simply killing."[35] As the *Spartan* approached Cape Town and White's "*splendid* time" was drawing to a close, she related that the passengers presented her with "a lovely bow & arrow [from a Hiawatha *tableau*] for a reminiscence of our voyage."[36] White's letter suggests the group enacted Henry Wadsworth Longfellow's epic poem, "The Song of Hiawatha," which had a large circulation in the United States and Europe. Written in 1855, the poem is an example of American Romanticism rather than an accurate representation of Native American oral tradition.[37]

Shortly before her arrival in the Cape Colony, White received a veiled warning from the ship captain, suggesting her future encounters with a different type of *other* that might thwart her freedom and growing independence. White wrote, "The Capt. made me promise to *write* him if I got blue and wanted my address. He told me over and over again not to change or allow myself to *rust*."[38] In fact, White would struggle during the next two years to live a full life in a time and location where women's roles were circumscribed. As the captain anticipated, she would confess to being "a little blue" on more than one occasion.[39]

AN OUTSIDER IN THE CAPE COLONY

When Flora White got her first glimpse of Cape Town—with flat-topped Table Mountain providing a magnificent backdrop to the harbor—she entered a world in which she was an outsider. As an American in a British colony, an Episcopalian in a Dutch Reformed (Calvinist) household, and a woman teacher in a boys' school, White encountered *the other* constantly—but at the steady, slower pace of those who now surrounded her. The spontaneous young woman who explored London on her own and directed the entertainment of travelers on the *Spartan* would come to view her Cape Colony experience as a "hermitage."[40] Nevertheless, the two years in the colony provided White with new exposure and a secluded place of retreat that she would put to productive use.

White's letters reveal that the social capital she acquired in Amherst assisted her in making contacts among upper-middle-class residents of the Cape Colony. One letter reported on a visit with the Ferguson family at the Huguenot Seminary, including Maggie Ferguson, niece of the school's co-founder. White wrote that Maggie's mother "knows lots of people that we do—Amherst people & the Foster girls—Mrs. Hopkins & Mrs. Kelsy." White said the Ferguson residence seemed "natural and home-like and American," adding that she and Maggie were awakened by a servant who brought them each "an elegant cup of chocolate."[41] Other letters indicated White found it comforting to encounter Americans in the Cape Colony, whether they came from New England or not. For example, she wrote her mother and sister, "A Mrs. Riddell from New Orleans is here with her children—a dear little boy & girl. I think they will make it their home here. They have rooms near the Sem—it seems so nice to see some real American children."[42]

Prior to White's arrival, the Cape Colony had developed "a complex, racially stratified society" with simmering social tensions that culminated twelve years after her departure in the South African War of 1899–1902, also called the Second Boer War.[43] (The First Boer War ended in 1881, well before White's journey to the Cape Colony.) The colony's conflicts were a result of an interesting political and social history in which rival European powers sought to exploit the indigenous people and their land.

The Cape Colony was the creation of the Dutch East India Company, or the *Verenigde Oostindische Compagnie* (VOC). During the seventeenth century, the VOC was the most powerful trading corporation in the world. Founded in 1602, and existing under a charter from the Dutch government, the VOC operated as "as state outside a state" with sovereign rights in and east of the Cape of Good Hope.[44] In creating the Cape Colony, the VOC directors' initial objective was to establish a small, fortified base at the southern tip of Africa that would function as a halfway station for ships sailing between Europe and the East Indies. The directors hoped they could maintain a viable station that would serve the company's commercial interests without encouraging large-scale European settlement. Nevertheless, the colony's population grew. Over time it became integrated into the structure of the VOC's "mercantilist empire," with a level of "capitalist farming that responded closely to market forces."[45] Soon Cape Town served as a major port and trading center, and the colony's major occupations—arable agriculture, pastoral farming, and wine production—required a labor force.

Within a decade of its founding, the colony was well on its way to becoming the diverse society Flora White encountered in 1885. That society was comprised of the descendants of indigenous, pastoral people known as the

Khoikhoi (whom whites called *Hottentots*, a pejorative term today). There were also descendants of mostly Dutch but some German "free burghers" who established farms when the VOC released them from their employment contracts.[46] There were the progeny of French Protestants (Huguenots) who escaped their homeland for the Netherlands, and settled in the Cape Colony in the 1680s. The Huguenots were speaking Dutch rather than French within a generation of their arrival. Finally, there were the descendants of slaves who came to the Cape Colony through VOC's participation in the notorious slave trade.

As early as 1658, the VOC arranged for the first group of enslaved persons to be brought on credit to the Cape Colony's burghers. The one hundred seventy slaves—many of whom were children—arrived on the *Amersfoort*, a VOC merchant ship that intercepted a Portuguese slaver bound for Brazil. The slaves aboard had originally been captured by the Portuguese in present-day Angola. Since the VOC controlled the slave trade in the Cape Colony, free burghers were not permitted to trade slaves there. Over time, the VOC brought a total of 4,300 slaves to the Cape Colony on company-sponsored voyages.[47] Slaves were also procured in a somewhat "haphazard fashion" from Dutch and French ships returning from the East Indies, from Portuguese traders returning from Mozambique and Madagascar, and from some "English interlopers" in the slave trade.[48] As a result, most Cape Colony slaves did not originate in Africa, but instead represented highly diverse linguistic, religious, and social backgrounds. While some came from Mozambique, most slaves were brought to the Cape from Madagascar, Indonesia, India, and Ceylon.[49]

In the first few years following Dutch settlement of the Cape Colony, Europeans enjoyed fairly cordial relations with the Khoikhoi; however, by 1713 the pastoral society of these indigenous people was disintegrating, and they became a major source of labor for the colony's white settlers. Leonard Thompson writes that the southwestern Khoikhoi became a "subordinate caste in the colonial society, set apart" from the whites and the slaves; "technically free, but treated no better than the slaves."[50]

In 1795 the British captured the Cape Colony from the Dutch, only to have the Dutch regain it by treaty in 1803. Britain then reconquered the colony in 1806 and, in 1820, transformed it by transplanting lower-middle-class settlers from the British Isles and setting them up on lots of approximately one hundred acres. The newly arrived British called the earlier European group *Boers,* the Dutch word for farmer. (Over time the word took on a derogatory meaning, and the preferred term today is *Afrikaner*.) Although Cape Colony slaves were technically emancipated in 1834–1838, both the British settlers and the Afrikaners had an interest in controlling non-European labor. Tensions mounted between the British and Afrikaners, and in 1836 to 1845 between five thousand and fourteen thousand frontier Afrikaners and their servants migrated out of the Cape Colony in what became known as the Great Trek. They founded the Orange Free State and the South African Republic (Transvaal)[51] which, along with the Cape Colony and Natal, would join in 1910 to form the Union of South Africa.[52]

Following emancipation, the Khoikhoi and the former slaves had the same legal status, and—despite their varying cultural backgrounds—were referred to comprehensively as "the Cape Coloured People."[53] The term stuck and would become one of four main racial categories recognized by the South African government in the twentieth century. In addition to colored, the other categories were whites (the ruling class); Bantu-speaking Africans who constituted the majority of the population; and Asians, who were brought from India as indentured laborers beginning in the 1860s. Thompson wrote that after emancipation—as in the United States—the rhetoric of freedom in the Cape Colony did not stop the exploitation that occurred there. The colony's deep societal divisions were not lost on Flora White, who reported, "it seems no one but the lower classes are expected to ever sit on any public sitting place. However we *stood* and had such a lovely sea view."[54]

Readers may wonder how Flora White could have characterized living amid such simmering social tensions as a hermitage. The answer is found in a 1900 paper she presented in Washington, D.C., to the American Social Science Association titled "The Boers of South Africa, in Their Social Relations."[55] Published in 1901 in the *Journal of Social Science*, White wrote and read the paper during the period when Britain was conquering the Afrikaner republics. The paper reveals White's strong bias in favor of her own cultural heritage as she compares the society created by Afrikaners with that of the United States. Noting that both societies were founded by "determined, virile" people who sought "new life on a new continent from a love of independence and strong convictions," White attributes the difference in their progeny largely to "physical and geographical" factors.[56] Whereas the American colonists encountered "a long line of seaboard," "vast woodlands," plentiful watercourses, and relative proximity to the "fermenting" life of Europe, White contended that Afrikaners were greeted by a "barren shore, skirted with still more barren mountains." While the American environment resulted in an energetic society characterized by manufacturing and commercial success, Afrikaners live in a place of "slow, retarded growth" where "There was only a dull stretch of level land, and a changeless, unveiled sun, upon which they could rely."[57]

According to White, there were particular challenges for women of European background who married Afrikaner men:

> [M]any times I have seen Boer youths return from their college life, with charming brides taken from the midst of Edinburgh society. These girls knew their fate, the lonely farm life, the foreign speech, the patriotism of their

husbands, yet they accepted it. And the children of these women, are they any less Dutch than their fathers? Indeed, they are not. It is Dutch blood, Boer blood, if you please, which dominates South Africa. And it is my belief that it will not be permanently conquered.[58]

However, White went on to assert that the Afrikaners are not without merit:

They are sober, thoughtful, and slumberously passionate, strong-limbed, clear-eyed, and with a wide kindliness of nature that suggests the breadth of the veldt [or *veld*, meaning "open country"]. . . . They still believe in God, and have respect unto their fathers. They love heroism and all heroes, both of the past and present, and their faith in the genius of their own race is so unbounded that they stubbornly refuse to be stuccoed with the ideas, ways, and opinions of other men, but insist that they must develop along their own line and no other.[59]

LIVING AND TEACHING AT THE PAARL

Flora White did not arrange to live at the Huguenot Seminary with American women who were focused on improving the intellectual and moral development of the Cape Colony's white female population. Instead, she boarded in a rural environment at the home of her principal Mr. le Roux, his wife, and children. The le Roux home was located in the Paarl (Dutch for "pearl"), some ten miles from Wellington. It was a fruit-growing region known by its easily recognizable landmark, the large granite Paarl Rock, or Pearl Mountain. The region's European settlement dated back to the seventeenth century with the arrival of free burghers and Huguenots, whose concept of private property conflicted with the Khoikhoi people's communal land use. The Khoikhoi were defeated in a local war and further decimated by European diseases. Some moved inland or worked as laborers on local farms.

While she lived in the area, White taught in English in what was then called the Paarl First Class Public School, the forerunner of today's Paarl Boys' High. Her description of the institution as a preparatory school suggests it offered a classical education reminiscent of an English public school more than a U.S. public high school of the period. In White's early letters home, she praised Mr. le Roux for keeping his school "in excellent working order."[60] However, while White initially described Mrs. le Roux as a "home-spun little woman" who lived "plainly but well,"[61] over time the letters communicated a dislike for the woman, whom White described as selfish, jealous, unchristian, and having few friends. (White would later remind the American Social Science Association that, as with other groups of people, there were good and bad Boers.) When Mr. le Roux left his post several months before White's return to Massachusetts, White moved to the Huguenot Seminary and indicated that her boarding situation had improved. Her correspondence also shows she assumed some of Mr. le Roux's duties after his departure and before the arrival of the new principal.

In her letters home, Flora White reported that Hattie's health was improving, and she acknowledged that her sister had previously been "dyspeptic."[62] During the nineteenth century dyspepsia was widely thought to be a result of a woman's overengagement in physical or mental activities. In her correspondence, Flora reported that Hattie's fellow teachers expressed fear that she would have another breakdown if her younger sister left the colony.

As for Flora White's classes, her early letters home suggest she was getting on well with her students and feeling "quite enthusiastic" about her job.[63] Within three months of her arrival, she considered accepting an administrative assignment, an opportunity she would not have had in the Springfield public schools. White wrote:

> There is a girls school here at the Paarl & I have been asked to take charge of it. I would like to. It has been badly managed & a great need is felt of having a change created. I think perhaps I shall take charge of the Primary Department another quarter. I am not sure. There is certainly more need of good teaching there than Mr. le Roux's school. . . . There is nothing to influence my taking it except my own personal choice in the matter. Mr. le Roux would be very sorry to have me go from his school but he would get the benefit of it if I did as the boys from the Primary school go into his so he is willing I should do it just as I like in the matter.[64]

Subsequent letters suggest White decided to remain at the boys' school with Mr. le Roux and was pleased with the result. On August 9, 1886, she wrote her mother about fifteen "nice little boys" aged ten to twelve who comprised her Grammar class. White explained, "They are not very bright scholars, but I mean to make them as I never enjoyed teaching any pupils more than the boys of this school."[65] In another letter she reported that her students were away from school for two days, taking standardized tests. White expressed the hope that they would do well, adding, "I have worked ever so hard for them and I think the boys appreciate it. I am not tired now though."[66] On another occasion White wrote:

> I am as well as can be and very much interested in my boys and work. They are such nice boys—one of them, a handsome Jew, who is gentlemanly and a beautiful scholar is going to leave in a few days—His people are going up to the Diamond Fields to live—He feels very badly about leaving school but thinks his father will be able to send him back as a boarder after a few months—They have not been in the Colony but a few years and came from London.[67]

White's letter refers to the fact that she was in the Cape Colony during the period Thompson calls "the peak of British imperialism" in southern Africa.

He noted that it coincided with the exploitation of the world's largest diamond deposits and substantial gold deposits there. By the end of the nineteenth century southern Africa had become—for the first time—"a significant contributor to the world economy."[68] For the family of White's student, the prospect of immediate financial gain overshadowed the need for regular school attendance, at least in the short term. The materialism in the diamond and gold fields, and the war, likely motivated White to state, years later, to the American Social Science Association:

> "Civilization," that word is now the war-cry of the Anglo-Saxon race. It should stand only for what is wise and excellent and righteous; but are we now fast making it stand for those things we have most reason to deplore, for dependence on luxury, for greed of gain, for unscrupulous acts, cheap opinions, and cheaper faiths?[69]

Flora White's remarks foreshadowed her later criticism of global developments in which Western nations exploited people of color and their land. For example, in 1941 White published a response in *Unity* magazine denouncing British imperialism in India and Africa, as well as "dishonorable" U.S. actions that included lynchings and discriminatory laws for African Americans, poor treatment of Native Americans, and the "massacre" of Filipinos.[70]

While she was in the Cape Colony, one of White's pupils perceived a need to defend *her* in print. After she encountered some resistance to the idea of a female teacher in a boys' school, one student wrote "a piece in the paper . . . stating that he would defy the Paarl to produce a more competent or capable teacher than Miss White." Flora confided in a letter to her mother that this was "too silly & boyish a thing to do. . . . But I liked the boy's spirit in standing up for his teacher."[71]

White's letters home reveal her preference for the pedagogy of active learning, a predilection that would characterize her teaching in progressive schools after she returned to the United States. For example, she responded to a letter from her sister Mary by writing, "[Y]ou don't seem to think much of my dear little school. You make me laugh calling them brats & bedlam."[72] The following year, when Flora and her sister Hattie prepared for a student concert in Wellington, Flora referred to "about 20 children in all, such splendid bright-rollicking boys, just as affectionate and sweet as they can be."[73] When she and Hattie took the children into the laundry room to practice, she described the scene as follows: "You should have seen the little fellows there, singing with might—and . . . me tapping out the time with a broom stick as demurely as possible. They just graded in size, each one a tiny bit higher than the next younger—Such dear little fellows I never saw—they went right for my heartstrings with a tug."[74]

Another letter describes a pageant given by the older boys that recalled White's *tableaux* on the *Spartan*:

> They have a few scenes from King John and a little modern drama besides. Maggie [Ferguson] and I made a complete set of armor for King John out of paste board covered with tin foil—The shield was of dark glazed paper bordered with silver and a huge lion in the center—the result of my artistic genius?—we got a real helmet and covered it properly and managed the whole thing very nicely. [75]

Flora White's correspondence also suggests she was responsive to individual student needs. For example, one night while reading in the le Roux home White was approached by a representative of five boys who boarded in the dormitory outside. They wanted to join her and asked if they could come inside for a prayer. She did not want to refuse them and requested that they return at nine o'clock. White stopped what she was doing and used the available time to write a prayer that would be appropriate for them. [76]

White's responsiveness to students is also apparent in her letters home about one particular pupil, Eugene Marais. She wrote her mother and sister Mary:

> I am sure the boy has genius and I am so anxious to have it developed—He is such a sweet demure boy that cares only for reading and being in the fields by him self—He has read Dante & Petrarch, Milton, Shakespeare—in fact nearly all the classics but of course knows nothing of Modern Literature—I mean that which is first afloat now. [77]

White went on to say that Marais, who "comes from the Transvaal and is of French Huguenot descent," has written verse "full of patriotic resentment against English rule for the Colony." [78] White promised to send some of his poems to her mother and sister so they could show them to John Cotton Brooks and others in Springfield "and see what they say of my little boy poet." [79] She opined that young Marais had the scholastic ability to "be about in the Sophomore class at Amherst or any ordinary college—and he is about 15 now I think." She further stated, "I don't know as you will be interested in all this about my boys but they are the only thing I have to interest me." [80] In the letter, White shared a long talk she had with Eugene Marais in which he described becoming agitated at school when he observes or hears something of interest and is unable to write it down for an hour or two. He explained that, with the passage of time, the feeling goes away and he no longer thinks about it.

White's assessment of Eugene Marais's (1871–1936) brilliance was well-founded. Before he finished school, some of his verses were published in *The Paarl District Advertiser*. [81] At age twenty-one, he became the publisher of a newspaper, *Land en Volk* (Land and People). However, Marais's work as an aggressive investigative journalist created enemies in the government of Transvaal president and Afrikaner folk hero Paul Kruger. In 1896 Marais went to London where he studied law, medicine, and psychiatry. When war broke out between the British and the Afrikaners in 1899, he was paroled as an enemy alien. Today Eugene Marais is considered to be one of the greatest Afrikaner poets. He is also acknowledged as the father of ethology, the scientific study of animal behavior. Marais began taking opiates at an early age when they were thought to be nonhabit forming and safe, and became addicted as a result. He took his own life at age sixty-five.

During her stay in the Cape Colony, Flora White kept homesickness at bay by seeking solace in the le Roux garden, visiting her sister Hattie, riding horses or playing an occasional game of tennis with Seminary acquaintances, and visiting picturesque sites in the countryside. She drew sketches of her surroundings and sewed her own clothes (mailing drawings of her creations to her mother and sister). However, White's feelings about the environment she encountered as a woman living in the Paarl are best summed up in a letter she wrote several months before returning home:

> It will seem so sweet to have real companionship again after these two years of hermitage. I hope I have not grown crusty [an apparent reference to the captain's earlier warning]. I am firmly convinced though that prolonged stay would transform me outwardly and as far as all practical purposes are concerned entirely into a wide, stolid, prolific Dutch "Vrau." You will have to pinch me to keep me in trim. I never think to smile now. I incline my head slowly and very slightly to show recognition, and impassively shake hands on all possible occasions. However I am not seriously alarmed but when the presence is removed I shall rebound fast enough. I find that I am of a very cock-like and rubbery temperament. I can sustain a good pressure without being ultimately affected by it. [82]

As Flora White moved into her second year of teaching, her letters contain ongoing deliberations between the sisters on where they would teach the following year. Flora had enough money to come home, but Hattie's savings were more meager. Flora wanted Mary to have the opportunity for overseas travel and offered to take her place in Springfield if she preferred. In one letter, Flora tried to make a humorous point about her willingness to keep Mary happy. She did so by exhibiting cultural narrowness and racial insensitivity as she poked fun at traditional African dress. White wrote, "You know quite well I would joyfully sit wrapped in a pocket handkerchief the entire year or even go with nothing on but a collar & pair of boots . . . and robe you in ermine both summer and winter if I thought that by doing so I could increase the sum of your happiness." [83]

Although unstated, one of the sisters needed to live with their mother. After weighing all factors, they reached a decision, and on June 29, 1887, Flora White left the Cape Colony for the United States. A letter to Mary four months earlier indicates Flora was already anxiously awaiting her departure:

> May [Mary] I leaned out of the window in my room just now and let myself imagine as the breeze came rushing in that I was on my way home crossing the sea. Ah—I will tell you it is a strange feeling. I hardly dare indulge it. What will the reality not be! I am afraid that I will be almost beside myself when that comes. I have been reading the hymn "Thou art coming, Oh my Savior" and I thought of you as saying the first part of the second verse for my coming. [84]

White's letters show that, in the months before she returned to Massachusetts, she was already exercising her agency by envisioning a new place where she and Mary might live and teach. At the time, Mary White was a teacher in the Springfield public schools. Flora's letters deplored Mary's work load and urged her to resign so the two sisters could open a private school that would also serve as their residence. (White suggested that Hattie not be included in the venture, for two reasons. Her evangelical Christianity would be a problem, and she might assert her prerogatives as older sister). In letters to Mary, White rejected the U.S. public school practice of seating students in rows of desks (another instance of a traveling woman criticizing practices at home). She envisioned furniture that would, in later years, characterize progressive schools:

> I do dread your going on in the Public School and I think if you have a comfortable house and a nice little school in it you will be much better off than now. Don't you think you could send a doz. or so chairs and 1 or two low tables, like the kindergarten table, for them to sit around in place of desks. Would not Mr. Bradley let you have them? [85]

White described the imagined place further:

> I care more about a plot of ground than the house & we would only be cozy in small quarters—I can't explain to you now the tremendous importance in my mind of the plot of ground if our school becomes what I want it to become. It would be nice if we could have a house quite to ourselves. . . . I want the school rooms a part of the house or at least joined to it in some way when we have our own. [86]

In addition to documenting Flora's growing independence and development as an educator, the Cape Colony letters reveal her relationship to her sister Mary. The two women were very close throughout their lives. After Flora's 1887 return to Massachusetts, they spent most of their remaining years living together, pursuing complementary personal and career goals.

However, the letters show Flora to be the dominant sister in the relationship, as seen in her willingness to risk foreign travel, envision their professional futures, work through the logistical details, and implement their plans. This view is supported by a 2003 interview of Grace Moyer Share, the sisters' great niece, who reported that, of the two women, Flora was "definitely the leader."[87]

Shortly before Flora's departure, she wrote her mother that "letters have made it 'plain' to Hattie that she will not come back here again at least for a number of years." Flora added that she was glad about this development, noting that Hattie had greatly improved and would be "jolly & kind & sweet" and enjoyable to be around when she returned home.[88]

White family correspondence indicates that Hattie continued to live overseas. In 1888 she wrote her sister Emma and brother Joseph from Hauptwil Castle in Switzerland, a physical and spiritual sanitorium for believers in divine healing. Hattie went there on the recommendation of the Reverend Andrew Murray, whose letter to Mount Holyoke resulted in the creation of the Huguenot Seminary.

An undated letter from Hattie to Joseph and Jennie White indicates that Hattie traveled to Bonn and Cologne in Germany, and to the Isle of Wight. According to the sesquicentennial history of Heath, after teaching seven years at the Huguenot Seminary—and prior to her death in 1904—Hattie White was a missionary in the Barbados and "was connected to a mission in New York City." The history also described Hattie White as "a woman of brilliant attainments, and because she was so capable, overestimated her strength and her health failed."[89] A 1929 article in a local Massachusetts newspaper repeated the same information verbatim, and it is likely in both cases to have been furnished by Hattie's sister Flora.[90] In 1939, when Flora White was the last person living in Massachusetts in her immediate family, and writing to a limited audience, she was more direct: Hattie was in the hospital at Northampton, Massachusetts and "died of a cancer that for religious reasons she refused to have removed."[91]

During her stay in the Cape Colony, Flora White gained a sister-in-law. In 1881 her brother Joseph had moved to Lincoln, Nebraska, where their sister, Emma Hillman, lived with her large family. While at Lincoln, Joseph worked on a farm for one year and spent the following year driving a horse and buggy in northern Iowa and Minnesota "buying soldiers additional homesteads."[92] When the railroad was built from Lincoln to Beatrice, Nebraska, he worked in the nearby town of Pickrell for a Lincoln grain and coal dealer. He also served as county supervisor. In 1887, Joseph White married Mrs. Jennie Knight, mother of a four-year-old girl, Grace. Born in 1863 at Fort Hunter, New York, Jennie Johnson Knight had moved with her parents to Denison, Iowa, and in 1879 married a man somewhat older than she who, according to family lore, was abusive when he drank. She divorced him and, with her daughter in tow, moved to Pickrell to the home of her ex-husband's relatives, one of whom worked for Joseph White. (At the time, the U.S. divorce rate was low—2 percent in 1865 and 4 percent at the end of the nineteenth century.)[93] Upon arriving in Pickrell, Jennie Knight gave piano lessons, and Joseph became her student so they might become better acquainted. Following their marriage, Joseph and Jennie White had three children of their own, two of whom lived to adulthood. Around 1897 the family moved to Beatrice, Nebraska where Joseph served as county clerk.

Although the marriage of Joseph and Jennie White was by all counts a happy one, the union of her parents—James "Jimmy" Johnson and Catherine Servoss Johnson—was not. In the spring of 1887 he returned to New York while she remained in Iowa. In January 1890 Catherine Johnson petitioned the court for a divorce on the grounds of abandonment, and her husband did not contest it. A skilled carpenter, Jimmy Johnson eventually went into Oklahoma Territory, building bridges for the Southern Kansas Railway (a forerunner to the Santa Fe). In 1907 he homesteaded a section of land near the present town of Gage, Oklahoma, and invited his daughter, her husband, and their children to join him. Johnson sweetened the offer with the promise of a house and a half- section of land. The couple's decision to accept Johnson's proposition eventually resulted in Flora White's extended yearly visits to Oklahoma and the transmission of her papers there following her death.

WRITING A STORY OF AFRICA

Flora White's correspondence remains the most enduring record of her two-year residence in the Cape Colony. It was this collection of letters that prompted Margaret Malone's request to White's executor that her papers be reclaimed from John Haynes Holmes and shipped to relatives in Oklahoma. It is therefore appropriate to consider the way in which nineteenth century women recorded their travel experiences, and the form in which their writing was shared in a wider audience.

In "Travel Writing and Gender," Susan Bassnett wrote that while most male travel writers appeared to have publication in mind when they began to record their thoughts on paper, many women did not.[94] Although some women's travel writings were clearly conceived as monographs, many others were composed as letters, diaries, or sketches. Schriber noted that many middle- and upper-middle-class American women (especially in the Northeast) recorded their travel experiences in diaries and letters, and some of these writings found their way into books. Between 1830 and the end of the century, 195 books of travel were written by U.S. women, 27 before the Civil War and 169 after.[95]

Flora White's writing on her experiences from the Cape Colony likewise found its way into a national magazine and an edited book—first through her fictional short story, "Zan Zoo," published in 1891 in *Harper's New Monthly Magazine*.[96] Later, in 1906, the same story appeared in *The Heart of Childhood*, a collection of "novelettes" edited by William Dean Howells (who served as editor of the *Atlantic Monthly*) and Henry Mills Alden (who was editor at *Harper's*). Reflecting a widespread practice stemming from discrimination against women writers, the author of both the short story and novelette is listed as "George Heath," a pen name for Flora White.[97] In the voice of a male narrator (Heath), White tells the story of a "handsome Caffre girl" whose name is the story's title.[98] (Note: *Caffre*, variously spelled *Caffre, Cafire, Kafir*, or *Kaffir*, is a term Europeans applied to Bantu-speaking people in southern Africa. Although it was widely used from the sixteenth through the early twentieth centuries, it is considered offensive today.)

"Zan Zoo" is a sympathetic portrayal of a young girl who has no parents to look after her. She is not well suited to her new kitchen job on a Boer farm and incurs the wrath of her mistress, Mrs. Beer, who is concerned that Zan be "broken in." As a result of Mrs. Beer's repeated attempts to exert control, Zan—who delights in the natural world of the out-of-doors—becomes "sulkier and sulkier" on the job.[99] Eventually Mrs. Beer, (who bears a resemblance to Mrs. le Roux) whips the girl with a lash, covers her sores with an irritant, and keeps her indoors in a "hot, close, and filthy" room.[100] The immediate cause of the whipping is Mrs. Beer's belief, based on footprint evidence, that Zan picked figs off a tree that were intended for supper. In accusing Zan, Mrs. Beer is acting on evidence supplied by Jacob, a "colored" boy whose ancestry is part "Hottentot."[101] The creation of his character attests to White's awareness of racial/social stratifications and tensions that existed in the Cape Colony during her residence there.

Footprints are persuasive to Mrs. Beer because Zan Zoo has six toes on each foot, a rare characteristic called polydactyly that occurs in persons of African descent more often than in Caucasians (3.6–13.9 cases per thousand births in the former, as opposed to 0.3–1.3 per thousand births in the latter).[102] It is an idiosyncrasy of which Zan Zoo is very proud. Although Flora White, throughout her educational career, championed the safeguarding of children's unique characteristics (in keeping with the views of Westfield principal John W. Dickinson), she is clearly showing in the story that individual differences can produce painful results.

In the plot line, George Heath rescues Zan from her abusive situation and takes her to his native New England. There she has no connection to the plant and animal life "of her own dear veld."[103] As the autumn leaves fall from the trees and the New England winter begins to close in, Zan Zoo's life spark begins to dim. The narrator recounts that "the brave little heart, which had never feared a living thing, was stricken with terror at the sight of the whole world dead, and the thought that she could never feel again the soft earth under her or hear the birds sing, or see the bushes' blossoms. . . . What was life to her now?"[104] Unable to withstand the New England winter, she dies and leaves a distraught narrator who regrets his misguided attempt to save her:

> I cursed myself that I had not been born a woman, or with a woman's sense. To have let her die by inches without a vestige of life or brightness about her, all the time complacently flattering myself that I, her savior, her rescuer, embodied all earthly happiness for her. But my enlightenment came too late. The wee spark of life could not be fanned into a flame.[105]

The story concludes when the narrator returns Zan's body to her beloved veld.

The fictional account is interesting on several levels. First, it supports Blanton's view that although Western women who traveled abroad exhibited traces of both Eurocentrism and racism, some who went to colonial environments also showed sympathy for subjugated people. Blanton suggests this stemmed in part from women's position outside the dominant patriarchal structure at home and abroad. Blanton's view is supported by the implied criticism of "Zan Zoo's" self-reproaching white male narrator who admits to believing he had all the answers and deserved to control the destinies of others. Although the narrative suggests that George Heath lacked "a woman's sense," White is not suggesting that all women make good decisions, or even that she identifies with all women. The fictional Mrs. Beer, for example, is a white female character who exhibits a profound lack of judgment and empathy. Flora's letters home also ascribe many negative characteristics to Mrs. le Roux, a real Cape Colony woman with whom she lived. Since White's letters communicate a strong desire to leave the Cape Colony before she comes to resemble a *vrau* (the common term for a female homemaker in this settler society), it is accurate to say that Flora identified with other educated white women who were from the United States. While she maintained a strong affinity for New England, she felt a kinship with women from other regions, as evidenced by her positive comments about Mrs. Babcock and Mrs. Martin from Chicago, and Mrs. Riddell from New Orleans.

It is interesting to note that Zan Zoo's beating for allegedly picking figs closely resembles a White family story concerning Flora's "bound" brother Joseph. As previously noted, young Joseph White reportedly received a beating from his master for picking a berry on the way to church in what was perceived as a violation of the Sabbath. It was an incident that would not have occurred had Joseph's family not lost status due to the death of his father. Flora White was familiar with the story and may have used it in a different context to illustrate the vulnerability of unprotected children. It is also conceivable that, given the marginalized status of persons in the Cape Colony who were not of European descent, White witnessed the mistreatment of children of color while she resided there. "Zan Zoo" depicts a world in which both white men and women mistreat children who are not of European ancestry. In one scene, for example, a white man sits on a wagon holding a long whip. Sometimes the cattle feel the sting of his lash; at other times he directs the whip at a young Bantu-speaking boy.

Finally, "Zan Zoo" emphasizes the differences between the Cape Colony and New England—differences that White experienced over a span of two years and that were sufficiently great to cause the death of her fictional heroine. That Zan thrived on the veld, faced oppression from her Boer mistress, and died in New England due to the misguided assumptions of her male savior—all reflect White's understanding that privilege and oppression are contextualized, and tenuous. This recognition did not dissuade White from future travel, however. She used the proceeds from the sale of "Zan Zoo" to *Harper's* to fund another trans-Atlantic trip, this time to Sweden in the summer of 1891.

CONCLUSION

Flora White's two years in the Cape Colony were important to her quest for agency and her personal and professional development. The Paarl First Class Public School gave her experience with different kinds of students than she had previously taught. For example, she had all-male classes at the Paarl, with boys possessing cultural perspectives that differed from her own. The Paarl school experience helped White to be more sensitive to the broad range of backgrounds and abilities that students bring to a classroom, as evidenced by her handling of the brilliant Eugene Marais, a boy of Huguenot ancestry who resented English rule. Whereas the "Statement of the Theory of Education in the United States of America" (signed by her father's cousin Joseph White and other leading educators) had cast women teachers in the role of "managing the education of the child while it is in a state of transition from caprice to rationally regulated exercises of the will," White proved her ability to handle student needs at any point along that continuum. [106] She was able to address a desire for caprice with imaginative, hands-on learning activities that delighted children while exhibiting a sophisticated understanding of literature that benefited an older, high-achieving student. Since, by White's own description, a lack of stimulation caused her to focus on her students, she came to regard them as being valuable *in themselves*. White also began to look for ways to meet student needs outside existing systems, for example, by sharing Marais' poetry with a wider audience.

Flora White derived other benefits from her Cape Colony experience. Traveling across the Atlantic built confidence. She drew on the social capital she acquired in the Esty home at Amherst and the Episcopal church at Springfield, and she used it in upper-middle-class environments in the Cape Colony. There—for the first time—White envisioned herself in an administrative role in a school, an option not available in Springfield. During the period between Mr. le Roux's departure and the arrival of the new principal, White gained administrative experience by assuming some of his duties. She also likely had more autonomy at the Paarl than she would have enjoyed in an urban, public school in the United States that operated on an industrial model. This is because the Paarl First Class Public School lacked the bureaucratic structure of a large U.S. public school district, and Mr. le Roux afforded her the opportunity to make professional decisions, as seen in their discussion of leadership of the girls' school. Even when White encountered an *other* in the Cape Colony that she had no desire to emulate (like Mrs. le Roux), the interaction was helpful in White's self-definition by letting her know what she *didn't* want to be—in this case, a *vrau*. White's perception that energy was lacking in the Cape Colony caused her to increase her focus on active learning when she returned home. Perhaps most important, traveling to the Cape Colony helped White look for ways to share her voice with wider audiences.

Flora White left the Cape Colony with the intention of founding an independent school in Springfield, Massachusetts. Among her possessions as she set sail were two thank-you notes from boys she had taught at the Paarl who summed up her student-centered approach. One wrote, "I thank you very much for your good instructions you have given me in school & another thing that I want to tell you is that, that you have learned me to behave in school for at first you yourself know that I had no manners to behave in school."[107]

A second boy expressed a wish that White would fulfill through her distinguished career. He wrote, "Dear Miss White we thank you very much for all the trouble you have taken to teach us. . . . If you perhaps intend teaching again in America I hope that you may take it up as diligently as you have done it here."[108]

NOTES

1. Flora White to Harriet M. White and Mary A. White, n.d. August 1885, Flora White Papers, private collection.

2. Flora White to Harriet M. White and Mary A. White, 30 August 1885, Flora White Papers, private collection.

3. Mary Suzanne Schriber, *Writing Home: American Women Abroad, 1830–1920* (Charlottesville, VA: University Press of Virginia, 1997), 2.

4. Ibid.

5. Casey Blanton, *Travel Writing: The Self and the World* (New York: Routledge, 2002).

6. Beatrice Bijon and Gérard Gacon, eds., *In between Two Worlds: Narratives by Female Explorers and Travellers, 1850–1945* (New York: Peter Lang, 2009).

7. Alison Blunt, *Travel, Gender and Imperialism: Mary Kingsley and West Africa* (New York: Guilford Press, 1994).

8. Schriber, *Writing Home*, 21.

9. Ibid., 20.

10. Ibid.

11. Ibid.

12. Drew Keeling, "Transatlantic Shipping Cartels and Migration between Europe and America, 1800–1914." *Essays in Economic and Business History* 17 (2012): 195–196.

13. Amanda Porterfield, *Mary Lyon and the Mount Holyoke Missionaries* (Oxford: Oxford University Press, 1997).

14. Lamin Sanneh, "Christian Missions and the Western Guilt Complex," *The Christian Century* (1987): 331–334.

15. Flora White to Harriet M. White and Mary A. White, 6 August 1885. Flora White Papers, private collection.

16. Flora White to Harriet M. White and Mary A. White, 5 August 1885, Flora White Papers, private collection.

17. Flora White to Harriet M. White, 1 August 1885, Flora White Papers, private collection.

18. Flora White to Mary A. White. n.d. August 1885.

19. Flora White to Harriet M. White, 6 August 1885. Flora White Papers, private collection.

20. The Particular Baptists were one of two major Baptist groups in England, the other being General Baptists. Particular Baptists were Calvinists who practiced believer baptism and particular (as opposed to general) atonement.

21. Flora White to Harriet M. White, 2 August 1885, Flora White Papers, private collection.

22. Ibid.

23. Ibid.

24. Ibid.

25. Ibid.

26. Flora White to Harriet M. White and Mary A. White, 4 October 1885, Flora White Papers, private collection.

27. Flora White to Mary A. White, 28 February 1887, Flora White Papers, private collection.

28. Flora White to Harriet M. White and Mary A. White, 3 August 1885, Flora White Papers, private collection.

29. Ibid.

30. Ibid.

31. Flora White to Harriet M. White and Mary A. White, 30 August 1885.

32. Ibid.

33. Readers may recognize that White was the "belle of the ball" on the *Spartan* and wonder if she exhibited such behavior earlier in her life. Unfortunately, there are no records to document how White previously interacted with others in social settings. One clue may exist in her novel, *Bloodroots in the Wake of Circumstance*, in which the main character is a bright, inquisitive, creative young girl.

34. Flora White to Harriet M. White and Mary A. White, 30 August 1885.

35. Ibid.

36. Ibid.

37. Henry Wadsworth Longfellow, *The Song of Hiawatha: An Epic Poem* (Chicago: M. A. Donahue, 1898).

38. Flora White to Harriet M. White and Mary A. White, 30 August 1885.

39. Flora White to Harriet M. White and Mary A. White, 4 October 1885; Flora White to Harriet M. White, 9 August, 1886, Flora White Papers, private collection.

40. Flora White to Mary A. White, 28 February 1887.

41. Flora White to Harriet M. White, 20 March 1887, Flora White Papers, private collection.

42. Flora White to Harriet M. White and Mary White, 8 May 1887. Flora White Papers, private collection.

43. Leonard Thompson, *A History of South Africa* (New Haven and London: Yale University Press, 2000), 33.

44. Ibid.

45. Nigel Worden, *Slavery in Dutch South Africa* (Cambridge: Cambridge University Press, 2010), 3.

46. Thompson, *A History of South Africa*, 36.

47. Worden, *Slavery in Dutch South Africa*, 42.

48. Ibid., 41, 43.

49. Thompson, *A History of South Africa*, 36.

50. Ibid., 38.

51. Richard Elphick and Rodney Davenport, eds., *Christianity in South Africa: A Political, Social, and Cultural History* (Cape Town: Creda Press, 1997).

52. Thompson, *A History of South Africa*, xxi.

53. Ibid., 55.

54. Flora White to Harriet M. White and Mary A. White, 4 October 1885.

55. Flora J. White, "The Boers of South Africa in Their Social Relations," *Journal of Social Science* 38 (1901): 177–188.

56. Ibid., 177.

57. Ibid., 177.

58. Ibid., 187.

59. Ibid., 186.

60. Flora White to Harriet M. White and Mary A. White, 14 November 1885, Flora White Papers, private collection.

61. Flora White to Harriet M. White and Mary A. White, 17 September 1885. Flora White Papers, private collection.

62. Flora White to Harriet M. White, 6 June 1887. Flora White Papers, private collection.

63. Ibid.

64. Ibid.

65. Flora White to Harriet M. White, 9 August 1886. Flora White Papers, private collection.

66. Flora White to Harriet M. White, 20 March 1887. Flora White Papers, private collection

67. Flora White to Harriet M. White and Mary A. White, 23 May 1886. Flora White Papers, private collection.

68. Thompson, *A History of South Africa*, 110.

69. White, "The Boers of South Africa," 176.

70. Flora J. White, "Reply to Mr. Johnson," *Unity* 127(7) (1941), 119.

71. Flora White to Harriet M. White, 9 August 1886.

72. Flora White to Mary A. White, 25 December 1885. Flora White Papers, private collection.

73. Flora White to Harriet M. White, 25 November 1886. Flora White Papers, private collection.

74. Ibid.

75. Flora White to Harriet M. White, n.d., Winter 1887, Flora White Papers, private collection.

76. Flora White to Harriet M. White, n.d., August or September 1886. Flora White Papers, private collection.

77. Flora White to Harriet M. White and Mary A. White, 23 May 1886. Flora White Papers, private collection.

78. Ibid.

79. Ibid.

80. Ibid.

81. Conrad Reitz, "The Tragic Genius of Eugene Marais," (1980), http://www.caans~acaen. ca/Journal/issues_online/Issue_II_1_1980b/Reitz.pdf.

82. Flora White to Mary A. White, 28 February 1887. Flora White Papers, private collection.

83. Flora White to Mary A. White, 19 September 1886. Flora White Papers, private collection.

84. Ibid.

85. Flora White to Mary A. and Harriet M. White, 6 March 1887. Flora White Papers, private collection.

86. Ibid.

87. Grace Moyer Share, conversation with author, August 7, 2003.

88. Flora White to Harriet M. White and Mary A. White, 6 June 1887. Flora White Papers, private collection.

89. Pearle Tanner, "Heath and Its Families," in *Sesquicentennial Anniversary of the Town of Heath, Massachusetts, 1785–1935*, ed. Howard Chandler Robbins (Heath, MA: Heath Historical Society, 1935).

90. "Looking Back over Centuries White Family First Mentioned in 1333," *The Franklin Press and Shelburne Falls News* (Franklin County and Shelburne Falls, MA), May 2, 1929, 1–3.

91. Flora White, "Life Facts of Flora White and Family Recorded Mar. 18, 1939," Heath Historical Society, 10.

92. "J. D. White Life History," n.d. Flora White Papers, private collection.

93. Paul R. Amato and Shelley Irving, "Historical Trends in Divorce in the United States," in Mark A. Fine and John H. Harvey, eds., *Handbook of Divorce and Relationship Dissolution* (New York and London: Routledge 2006), 45.

94. Susan Bassnett, "Travel Writing and Gender," in Peter Hulme and Tim Youngs, *The Cambridge Companion to Travel Writing* (Cambridge: Cambridge University Press, 2002), 225–241.

95. Schriber, *Writing Home*, 2.

96. George Heath, "Zan Zoo," *Harper's New Monthly Magazine* 83 (1891): 345–355.

97. William Dean Howells and Henry Miller, eds. *The Heart of Childhood* (New York: Harper & Brothers, 1906).

98. Heath, "Zan Zoo," 345.

99. Ibid., 348–349.

100. Ibid., 350.

101. Ibid., 346.

102. Carla Novick, M.D., "Polydactyly of the Foot," *Medscape Reference: Drugs, Diseases & Procedures*, http://emedicine.com/article/1260255-overview#a0199.

103. Heath, "Zan Zoo," 351.

104. Ibid., 354.

105. Ibid., 354–355.

106. U.S. Bureau of Education, "A Statement of the Theory of Education in the United States of America as Approved by Many Leading Educators," U.S. Government Printing Office (1874), 19.

107. John Van Breda to Flora White, 15 June 1887. Flora White Papers, private collection.

108. Isaac Roos to Flora White, 16 June 1887. Flora White Papers, private collection.

Chapter Four

The New Education

When Flora White in 1887 envisioned a new school with "a doz. or so chairs and 1 or two low tables . . . in place of desks," she recognized a need to change the physical components of the classroom to accomplish major pedagogical reform.[1] Nine years later a young man named John Dewey would visit Chicago's school supply stores with a similar hope of finding furniture suited to the needs of young children. After a series of frustrating conversations with salesmen who were unable to accommodate his request, Dewey spoke to one dealer who summed up the problem: "You want something at which the children may *work*; these are all for *listening*."[2]

After Dewey founded his laboratory school at the University of Chicago in 1896, visitors frequently remarked that it did not look like a school at all. In 1928 Harold Rugg and Ann Shumaker summed up the general reaction:

> Is this a schoolhouse, this great, sunlit home? These cheerful rooms—walls colorful with children's paintings, floors spotted with bright rugs, light, movable tables and comfortable chairs—are these classrooms? Groups of children engaged in animated conversation—are these classes? Is this the assembly room of a school, or is it a children's theater?[3]

Rugg and Shumaker concluded that the new school was "different in atmosphere, housing, furniture . . . in its basic philosophy and psychology; . . . [and] in the role that it assigns to pupil and teacher initiative.[4]

The same year Dewey founded the laboratory school, Flora White pressed NEA members for a classroom atmosphere that also differed from that of traditional schools. Instead of pushing students into "dreary brick buildings on small plots of ground," White wanted to situate them in classrooms with "'[a] handful of children, not more than fifteen, with plenty of space and air and sunlight, doing things they love to do, making things they love to make, coming to this happy spot by no compulsion but of their own will daily."[5]

White had an opportunity to implement some of her ideas when, immediately upon her return from the Cape Colony in 1887, she established a private day school in Springfield "to demonstrate progressive methods of education."[6] She, her sister Mary, and their mother lived at 60 School Street, where the Springfield City Directory listed Flora's occupation as teaching "private school." The City Directory for 1889–1892 shows that both Flora and Mary White were teaching at Miss White's School at 60 School Street. Harriet White died at that address in March 1892, and the White sisters' names are absent from the City Directory, beginning in 1893.[7]

A newspaper article written late in Flora White's life gives the name of only one pupil at the Springfield private school—a name also documented by White's great niece, Grace Moyer. The student was Archibald Galbraith (Harvard 1899), who, as an adult, taught at three boys' preparatory schools before becoming headmaster of Williston Seminary (later Williston Academy) in Easthampton, Massachusetts. The exact dates of Galbraith's attendance at Flora White's new private school are unclear. A local history states that Galbraith began attending school at age two in San Diego (where his father was a contractor engaged in building railroads). The same source adds that Galbraith entered the Springfield (MA) public schools in 1886 at age nine and later graduated from Springfield High School.[8] This description does not indicate whether Galbraith attended any other schools between the time he entered the public system and graduated from it. In fact, Flora White was in the Cape Colony when Galbraith first enrolled in the Springfield public schools, and he was only fifteen when the White sisters closed their private school.

The two documents that suggest Galbraith studied under Flora White are important. They show that, although primary teaching was seen as "women's work" (as reflected in the 1874 "Statement" signed by Secretary Joseph White and other chief school officials), Flora was instructing at least one older boy in Springfield, as she had in the Cape Colony.[9] White's association with Galbraith continued after the closing of her Springfield school. In 1905 he married Helen Ecob McIntosh, a Smith alumna trained in Froebel's kindergarten pedagogy. The couple had two sons, the first of whom was born in 1907 in Concord, when the Whites operated their home school there and Galbraith taught at the nearby Middlesex School for boys. According to Grace Moyer, Flora and Mary White taught the Galbraith children—presumably in their school's lower department, which accepted young boys.[10] Upon leaving Concord, Archibald Galbraith served as Williston's headmaster from 1919 to 1949, stressing "the finest values of traditional education" coupled with instruction geared to individual student needs.[11]

Beyond the references to Galbraith, no class lists, lesson plans, or school catalogs are extant for Miss White's School in Springfield. The only existing visual images of the interior of 60 School Street during this period are professional funeral photographs taken in Harriet White's room where she died. While it was the custom among many Victorians to photograph deceased relatives, the pictures of Harriet White's room do not include her bed or body. However, the sepia-toned photographs are revealing in two respects. First, the furniture in the spacious room reflects a middle-class lifestyle—with a tufted velvet loveseat, shelves with an ample supply of books, hurricane lamps, an eclectic mix of chairs reflecting early American and Victorian tastes, draped tables, a bust, a decorative plate, and rugs. The room also contained family photographs on the mantel and desk, and one large photo portrait of Harriet White centered over the fireplace. The decor suggests the Whites had risen above poverty and improved their social status. This is noteworthy since most biographies of women founders of U.S. progressive schools depict women of middle- to upper-middle-class backgrounds.[12] Inasmuch as Isaac Esty bequeathed a number of household items to the Whites, it is likely that some of the furnishings came from his home. A second revelation in the photograph is the Whites' attitude toward interior light. Two windows are shown in Harriet White's room, one with the formal draping typical of the Victorian era. The other is not draped but, rather, has a full-length blind and short curtain in the lower quarter of the window, presumably for privacy. It would appear that the window treatments in the room are in keeping with Flora's preference for allowing sunlight to permeate the home/school.

Even with the absence of teaching materials from Miss White's School in Springfield, Flora White's quest for agency through a new pedagogy is documented in her speeches, published writing, and professional affiliations during this period. The sources place her in the formative period of the progressive education movement and, more specifically, the *child-centered* strand of progressive education,[13] the evolution of which is detailed by Rugg and Shumaker and also by William J. Reese.[14]

Some twenty-first-century scholars criticize historians of progressive education for overlooking the contributions of women to the movement. Alan R. Sadovnik and Susan F. Semel write that "histories of progressive education tend to be histories of great men"—including theorists John Dewey, William Heard Kilpatrick, Harold Rugg, George Counts, or their opponents.[15] Sadovnik and Semel add that Diane Ravitch also "contributed to this trend" by attributing the founding of child-centered schools in the early twentieth century to "upper middle-class parents, rather than the women founders of these schools."[16]

However, the earlier account of Rugg and Shumaker suggests the importance of unnamed women practitioners who, like Flora White, experimented with teaching methods in real school settings in progressive education's formative period. The authors note that between 1900 and the First World War, there was "a growing body of theory but little practical application" of child-centered education. Rugg and Shumaker pose and answer a key question in order to credit the contributions of these [women] practitioners in helping to create child-centered schools in the United States:

> Where in the American school system could it start? Not easily in the great body of public schools, committed to mass education and domineered over by the disciplinarian conception. Not truly even in the laboratory schools of the new schools of education that were springing up all over the country, for they were immersed in a veritable slough of technique—the investigation of intelligence, the analysis of the learning processes in the school subjects, and the statistical study of school practice.
>
> No, the movement for a freer type of education had to be launched almost altogether from outside the school system. It came, after the preparatory years, essentially from laymen, parents of means desiring the best in the way of schools for their children, and *enthusiastic free-lance teachers* (emphasis added).[17]

This chapter presents White's ongoing quest for agency as she moved beyond primary school teaching, founded an innovative private school, challenged gender stereotypes, and contributed to important educational reforms in a society undergoing the Second Industrial Revolution.

A CURRICULUM FOR AN INDUSTRIAL ERA

Herbert M. Kliebard writes that by the 1890s, the "educational center of gravity" in the United States had shifted "from the tangible presence of the teacher to the remote knowledge and values incarnate in the curriculum."[18] With the growth of cities, the school no longer served as the visible presence of a cohesive community. Rather, the school mediated between the family and "a puzzling and impersonal social order" created by industrialization and immigration.[19] Traditional family life, where it existed, appeared inadequate for preparing young people for a complex, technological world.

By the 1890s, there was a growing demand for secondary education in the United States, where roughly half of high school graduates entered college.[20] In 1892—amid high school principals' complaints that differing college admissions requirements made it difficult to prepare students for higher education—the NEA appointed a Committee of Ten to study the issue under the leadership of Harvard president Charles W. Eliot. According to Kliebard, the committee's initial focus on college entrance requirements "almost inevitably . . . became imbedded in broader matters of principle, such as the extent to which a single curriculum, or type of curriculum, would be desirable in the face . . . of large numbers of students, [and] . . . a different type of student."[21] The committee's report the following year recommended four different courses of study in high school (Classical, Latin-Scientific, Modern Languages, and English), each of which should be accepted for college admission. The report also recommended making no curricular distinction between students preparing for college and those preparing for "life," inasmuch as a good education for life was "the proper preparation for the rigors of college studies."[22]

The Committee of Ten's report generated criticism. Flora White appears to have offered her objection when she told the NEA in 1896, "Let us not stand like the witches of Macbeth, throwing into the cauldron of the school curriculum every sort of dismembered organ we can pelf, believing that some power potent will be generated in the broth."[23] Late in life, when commenting on the original reason for establishing the Committee of Ten, White recalled that she "made it clearly understood that [Miss White's Home School in Concord] was an experiment in educational values; that it stood upon the merits of its theories and would be in no way dominated or influenced by college requirements." White added, "My pupils however had no difficulty in passing college examinations."[24]

One of the Committee of Ten's most vociferous critics was a prominent educator who would play an important role in Flora White's career. He was Granville Stanley Hall, a pioneering psychologist who in 1892 became the first president of the American Psychological Association. Hall believed that decisions on what to teach should be made according to the natural order of child development.

Like White, G. Stanley Hall (1844–1924) grew up in a small farming village in Franklin County, Massachusetts. He left his home town of Ashfield (some twenty miles from Heath) to attend Williston Seminary for one year in nearby Easthampton. He then entered Williams College and, following graduation, attended Union Theological Seminary from 1867 to 1869. Studying at Harvard under William James, Hall was the first American to receive a PhD in psychology. He also studied experimental psychology in Germany under Wilhelm Wundt. In 1880 President Eliot invited Hall to lecture at Harvard, an appointment that eventually led to Hall's first major research in child study—an 1883 article titled "The Contents of Children's Minds." With the help of four trained kindergarten teachers, Hall attempted to identify the experiences children had in common before they entered school. He was surprised to find that, for example, 65 percent of the children interviewed had no concept of an ant and 55 percent did not know that wooden objects came from trees.[25] Hall concluded that teachers should make no assumptions about what children know upon entering school. He also believed that the order in which children acquire concepts depends on their environment. Hall became the leader of the *developmentalists* in the child-study movement.

G. Stanley Hall scaled back on his study of children when, in 1885, he accepted an appointment in psychology at Johns Hopkins University. Within a few years he became president of Clark University in Worcester, Massachusetts, and renewed his interest in child study after a personal tragedy. In the spring of 1890, Hall's wife and eight-year-old daughter were accidentally asphyxiated, leaving him with a nine-year-old son. Meanwhile, Jonas Clark, the university's wealthy benefactor, began to withdraw his support for the institution. Following a period of grief, Hall returned to child study with "a new sense of promise."[26] He assessed the growing interest among professional educators and began to view child study as scientific psychology as well as an exciting pedagogical endeavor. In 1894, the charismatic Hall announced at the annual meeting of the NEA, "Unto you is born this day a new Department of Child Study."[27] According to one biographer, Hall believed child study would benefit the teacher "to make her forever young, sympathetic, and professional."[28] Hall also contended that child study "should be preeminently the woman's science."[29] He was supported by enthusiastic teachers who gathered data on their students' physical growth, psychological development, and sexual maturation. They were bolstered by upper-middle-class club women with the education, intelligence, and leisure to devote to the cause. Flora White supported Hall, as evidenced by the fact that she advocated "sane and conscientious child study" in her 1896 paper for the NEA.[30]

G. Stanley Hall identified the chief goals of child study to be promoting child health, assisting the teacher by involving as many sensations as possible, and achieving what he termed "child psychological unity"—or discovering the child's personalities.[31] Influenced by Charles Darwin and Herbert Spencer, Hall reflected a belief in the theory of recapitulation, which held that the development of individual humans occurred in stages reflecting their ancestors' evolution. Child study advocates identified a series of developmental stages (infancy, childhood, youth, adolescence), each with its own unique characteristics and psychology. Hall urged teachers to individualize instruction according to children's needs and interests, rather than stifling their natural impulses as he believed was the case in traditional schools. To child study advocates, the needs of children could be met by free play, healthful exercise, and oral instruction, while the needs of youth called for intensive instruction in reading, writing, and arithmetic.

Although Flora White would later distance herself from Hall, he gave her a strong endorsement in 1898 when she established her Concord school. Hall wrote:

> For some years of personal acquaintance with Miss Flora J. White and knowledge of her educational ideals and large competency for her work, I am confirmed that her school at Concord can be heartily commended to parents for its

general methods and scope, and for the devoted personal attention each pupil is sure to receive.[32]

MOTOR AND MANUAL TRAINING

Flora White returned to the United States from the Cape Colony believing she had witnessed a pervasive lack of energy there. The observation led her to the conclusion that physical activity was an important part of education. In her 1896 speech to the NEA, White stated that many U.S. children had limited opportunity for movement at school, being "compelled to sit for five long hours each day, with what motor activities?—these movements of the fingers with pen and pencil, movements of the tongue in forming words, straining of the eyes over blurring, swimming black and white signs. . . ."[33] She further asserted that "We are cowardly and niggardly in our spending of energy, because we have turned our backs on nature, and yet find no system of economics to help us."[34] In an apparent reference to her travel to the Cape Colony, White suggested that an organism was strengthened by expending energy in the face of challenge:

> I have noticed in certain countries beyond the Tropics, trees that have impressed me with their grandeur and vigor, and then some morning I have gone forth and found them lying in the dust with helpless, upturned roots, windblown. Sun and shower had fondled them. With no obstacles to overcome, no winters to resist, no rocks to upturn, they had put forth a rank, showy, ineffective verdure, a growth in appearance but not in strength.
> We want no wind-blown characters.[35]

Writing in 1939, White recalled that, upon returning to Springfield, she became an "advocate" for a "new type of Educational Training involving bodily activity"[36] that she called *motor training*, an apparent reference to the development of fine- and gross-motor skills.

Although Flora White's interest in developing fine- and gross-motor skills would lead her to instruct girls in gymnastics and sports, it also contributed to her pioneering work in teaching girls woodcrafts. In so doing, White challenged gender stereotypes because woodcrafts were widely regarded as male activities, just as needlecraft and embroidery were seen as appropriate female pursuits. White's involvement in woodcraft instruction should be understood in the context of growing support for manual training in the United States during the late nineteenth and early twentieth centuries.

As early as 1870, Joseph White—Secretary of the Massachusetts State Board of Education and first cousin of Flora's father—implemented the Massachusetts Drawing Act, the first effort of a state to compel public schools to teach drawing. Supported by citizens wishing to decrease reliance on European draftsmen, the act required populations over ten thousand to provide free industrial or mechanical drawing for citizens over fifteen years of age. [37] While some U.S. citizens wanted to lessen European influences in their country, others looked across the Atlantic for ways to reform their educational system. According to David J. Whittaker, it was "glaringly apparent" that the U.S. apprentice preparation did not meet existing needs, and employers' organizations, labor unions, and educational theorists began to look to Europe for alternatives. [38]

During the Philadelphia Centennial Exposition in 1876, Victor Della Vos, director of the Moscow Imperial Technical School, attracted attention by exhibiting a system of industrial training designed to move people quickly from farm labor to industrial jobs. Inspired by what became known as the Russian System of Industrial Arts, engineering instructor Calvin Woodward founded in 1879 the Manual Training School at Washington University in St. Louis. Woodward discovered that his students had trouble thinking in three dimensions and needed simple wood models to illustrate complex mechanical problems. Accordingly, he introduced a three-year secondary program with a curriculum divided between mental and manual labor. John Runkle, President of the Massachusetts Institute of Technology, likewise began a program of industrial shops in schools and established a School of Mechanic Arts for students who wanted to pursue industrial work rather than engineering. Runkle also promoted the inclusion of industrial education in the general high school curriculum. Beyond these initiatives, private manual training schools proliferated in cities throughout the United States during the late nineteenth century.

Of particular relevance to Flora White's life was another exhibit at the 1876 Philadelphia Centennial Exposition. Otto Salomon, a Swedish citizen, presented a system of wood handcrafts—called *slöjd* in Swedish, and *sloyd* in English. The Scandinavian word meant "craft" or "manual skill." [39] Solomon's system, known as Educational Sloyd, had a developmental purpose, in contrast to the economic purpose promoted by Della Vos. The educative aspects of Salomon's system appealed to Flora White.

Otto Salomon were born in Göteborg, Sweden, to a Jewish family that had migrated from the Germanic states. His uncle, August Abramson, was apprenticed as a youth to a hardware merchant in Göteborg and, over time, became "founder and owner of one of the most extensive businesses in Sweden." [40] In 1868 Abramson purchased an estate at Nääs—an action that would have been prohibited prior to 1860 when Swedish law prevented Jews from acquiring property in rural areas. In 1869 Abramson lost his wife, a popular opera singer who died at age thirty-seven. Having no progeny, he invited his nephew Otto to live at Nääs and assist him on the estate. Salomon's parents were relatively affluent. After grammar school, he spent four months at the Technological Institute in Stockholm and eight months at

Ultuna Agricultural Institute near Uppsala; however, he did not complete either course of study. Salomon was largely self-taught as a teacher and educator.

Over a period of years, the two men introduced their system of Swedish handcrafts to the world. *Slöjd* had evolved in rural Sweden where—until the late nineteenth century—people spent long winter evenings making wooden household and farm utensils to supplement the family income. When industrialization transformed Swedish society, and work and school were removed from the home and institutionalized, support grew for promoting home industries by teaching young people traditional Swedish handcrafts. Dehumanizing factory conditions had eroded worker morale, and the incidence of alcoholism among Swedes was increasing. A contributing factor was the widespread production, sale, and use of *brännvin*, a brandy made from potatoes that was distilled legally in the home and widely regarded as a form of currency. To combat this social problem, the Swedish government passed laws restricting the home distillation and sale of alcohol and also provided funds for establishing private slöjd schools to develop skilled workers and reaffirm the values of good citizenship. August Abramson became an early supporter of this effort. In 1868 he founded a slöjd folk (neighborhood) school and four years later established a slöjd work school for boys on his estate. Six years later Abramson and Salomon began a slöjd training school for girls. Their curriculum included a broad range of studies that separated craft work along gender lines—wood-slöjd, turnery, wood-carving, or saddlery for boys and weaving, spinning, knitting, sewing, and cookery for girls. By 1886 the girls' and boys' schools had merged. Abramson and Salomon closed the school in 1888 to devote full attention to training teachers in slöjd methods.

Abramson and Salomon had already been experimenting for a number of years with slöjd training for teachers. Although they initially planned to train artisans to be slöjd instructors, Salomon modified that approach when he visited Uno Cygnaeus in Finland in 1877. Cygnaeus, father of Finnish folk schools and pioneer in educational arts and crafts, persuaded Salomon to organize slöjd on an educational rather than an economic basis, and incorporate it into the elementary curriculum. Following the visit, Salomon began a scientific study of slöjd as a means of education. He developed five-week courses for Swedish teachers and in 1882 discontinued the artisan training program. Salomon also dropped other forms of slöjd in favor of wood-slöjd. Eventually he offered four courses for teachers annually—each lasting six weeks—as well as two summer courses for men and women, a spring course for women, and a winter course for men. He called the program the Seminarium for Teachers.

At first glance, training in traditional Swedish handcrafts would seem an unlikely point of departure for reforming schools in an industrializing country. However, beneath his conservative appearance Salomon had ideas about education that were deemed "progressive, even radical."[41] He persuaded teachers that handcrafts were a critical medium for transforming the elementary school and moving away from mass education methods that emphasized rote memorization of "superficial" knowledge.[42] While Salomon carried on slöjd instruction at Nääs—urging individualized learning and independence of thought and action—Abramson maintained good relations with the conservative Swedish king, Oskar II, and other influential Swedes. Aware that, as Jews, their actions might be met with suspicion in Lutheran Sweden, the two men wanted to demonstrate they were good citizens. Showcasing the country's handcrafts helped to deflect criticism that might have otherwise been aimed at their school.

Salomon borrowed ideas from John Amos Comenius and John Heinrich Pestalozzi as well as other theorists including John Locke, Jean Jacques Rousseau, Friedrich Froebel, Christian Gotthilf Salzman, and Herbert Spencer. Salomon also read in their own languages the works of educators and philosophers who favored physical activity as a means of formative education. He believed that, in addition to placing too much emphasis on rote learning, elementary schools shortchanged children by requiring them to spend too much time at desks without physical movement. The core of education, he felt, was developing a child through his or her own learning. Salomon articulated several principles of educational slöjd:

1. To instill a taste for and an appreciation of work in general.
2. To create a respect for hard, honest, physical labor.
3. To develop independence and self-reliance.
4. To provide training in the habits of order, accuracy, cleanliness and neatness.
5. To train the eye to see accurately and to appreciate the sense of beauty in form.
6. To develop a sense of touch and to give general dexterity to the hands.
7. To inculcate the habits of attention, industry, perseverance and patience.
8. To promote the development of the body's physical powers.
9. To acquire dexterity in the use of tools.
10. To execute precise work and produce useful products.[43]

Salomon's curriculum consisted of a series of eighty-eight woodcraft exercises of increasing difficulty (later reduced to sixty-eight) that were designed to incrementally develop the student's physical and cognitive skills. Like Comenius, Salomon believed children learned systematically by developing a series of foundational concepts on which others could be built. Slöjd students began instructions with the simplest and most concrete representations of an idea. Subsequent lessons progressed in logical order toward higher levels of difficulty and abstraction. The resulting work products were a series of models of everyday household items that students created from wood. Students were supposed to accurately reproduce the models by working at their own speed, with the teacher acting as a guide but not interfering in the work process. Salomon encouraged teachers to know their students throughout the process, and to develop a knowledge base in crafts as well as theoretical subjects so they could understand each child's mental, physical, and moral development. As educational slöjd began to enjoy international appeal, Salomon also encouraged followers to develop model series that were relevant to various cultures in which slöjd was taught.

THE NÄÄS EXPERIENCE

In May 1891, Flora White wrote her mother from the *SS Gilbert* as she traveled across the Atlantic from New York to Copenhagen toward her final destination at Nääs, Sweden, near the city of Göteborg. While her Springfield school was closed for the summer, White planned to spend the vacation period studying slöjd at the Seminarium for Teachers with educators from all over the world. The publication of "Zan Zoo," the short story White sold to *Harper's*, had generated the funds to purchase transportation to Europe, and the coursework was free. Although four thousand Swedish teachers and fifteen hundred teachers from other countries would eventually study at the Seminarium between 1880 and 1907,[44] Flora White was nevertheless a trail blazer, being one of only twenty-seven Americans to receive instruction there by 1893.[45]

White reported from the ship, "We have had such gloriously beautiful days but so cold one could not write on deck and staying below was out of the question." Her comment likely suggests a reluctance to mingle with migrants in steerage. She added, "[T]oday we are in the iceburg [*sic*] region and the fog is so dense and the cold so bitter and the decks so wet that one must stay below willy nilly—so I am taking it out in a nice lazy morning in bed writing to you."[46]

Upon arriving in Nääs, White used glowing terms to describe the grounds of the estate of August Abramson, where the Seminarium was located. She wrote to her mother and sister Mary, "How am I ever to tell you about all the loveliness here?"[47] According to White, the estate grounds displayed "Nature at its best," since the two men "have the good taste of leaving her [Nature] alone[,] really believing that God's sense of beautiful is truer & his expression of it nobler than man's."[48]

Flora White's correspondence described the layout of the Seminarium for Teachers. She noted, "There are about 6 or 8 houses connected with the school—very pleasant—built in sort of seaside style only better. We all take our meals in one house. It is about 2 min. walk for me. Everything is exquisitely simple—dainty—and fresh. I have a very pleasant room all to myself . . . and window that gives me a lovely view."

She also detailed the work schedule:

> We work from 8 o'clock a.m. to ½ past 4 p.m. with ½ hour intermission for lunch—but during these hours we have exercise in the Ling system of gymnastics twice a day and interval of a few minutes in which we are obliged to leave the work rooms. We have to stand at our work which is rather hard but the rooms are so pleasant and the views so lovely when we look up that nothing seems a hardship.[49]

Salomon was concerned about the posture of Seminarium students given the long periods they spent standing in uninterrupted work. Therefore, he incorporated gymnastics instruction developed in Sweden by Pehr Henrik Ling (1776–1839). Originally designed to produce medical benefits for athletes, Ling gymnastics emphasized the integration of perfect bodily development and muscular beauty. Today Ling is credited with introducing calisthenics and with inventing wall bars, beams, and the box horse. His gymnastics were eventually adopted by school systems in the United States, United Kingdom, and Japan.

Each day at Nääs, Salomon supplemented the six to seven hours of practical handcraft work carried out by the teachers with one to two hours of theoretical lectures and discussions. Offering classes in more than one language, Salomon exposed teachers to a variety of subjects including educational history, handcraft teaching methods, psychology, morals, and hygiene. He hoped the teachers would develop their students' will, morality, and interests as they learned to solve problems at increasingly higher and more complex levels.

In a letter to her mother and sister Mary, White described how Salomon insured that students learned correct slöjd procedures without undue interference with their work:

> There is such a fine fellow that works near me—Captain of our Slöjd room— who cannot speak anything but Swedish but who has managed by smiling and watching my work and various signs in mutual language of all nations to be extremely friendly and kind. It is charming to see how anxious he is that work should all go right. The Captain of the room is one of the students who has been voted in that position by the other pupils & it is his duty to keep us in order etc. that is to see that we stop work at the proper time & are ready to begin in time & put our tools in the right places. The work is delightful. I enjoy it more & more every day. Everybody here has such an appetite after their work—we are all quite ready for our 4 meals a day.[50]

White also reported gender issues that surfaced during her summer at the Seminarium. She wrote, "There are about 3 times as many gentlemen as ladies here—We do everything together except eating. I think it a very funny plan to separate us then."[51] Occasionally White was confronted with gender assumptions that offended her, as when she wrote, "There is a big, fat jolly German here who thinks we are all very unwomanly to be doing this work. He writes much against slöjd of this kind for woman in the 'Zeitung' at home. Of course we are all against him in spite of his jolly face and charming ways which he is always entertaining us with."[52]

One Seminarium participant in 1891 suggested the school's benefits extended beyond the skills acquired and the lovely surroundings. Hjalmar Berg wrote, "Nääs is a good Slöjd school, and much besides. It is the meeting place of leading teachers of all degrees and all nationalities, for common work, and for the interchange of ideas. Professors, inspectors, secondary and elementary teachers, women as well as men, there meet on common ground as comrades."[53]

A ROMANCE INTERRUPTED

White's letters to her sister Mary show that during her summer at the Seminarium she became romantically involved with a male teacher to whom she only refers with the common Swedish first name of Nils. Flora White wrote:

> He [Nils] is such a splendid fellow[,] May. I just long to have you know & love him. His chief virtue is loving me which he does thoroughly and satisfactorily but he has plenty of others. He has the kind of face that makes everyone say at once what a fine fellow that must be & let me tell you that everything was practically settled between us before we had ever spoken to one another at all. That sounds dreadfully romantic and scandalous but it is quite true.[54]

Later White wrote her sister about a conversation with a Swedish woman who was studying at the school:

> She wanted to know what I thought of him [Nils]. I told her that he seemed a very agreeable fellow. "He is very clever [,]" she said "& I can tell you that he likes you very, very much." Of course I was duly surprised—We had been engaged about a fortnight then. Dearest, darling sister I shall be with you so soon—Nils wishes he were you when I get there. He sent his love to you the other day.[55]

Later White described a visit to Stockholm with Nils:

> I have been out with Nils the whole afternoon. We walked through the parks— peeked into his room—took dinner outdoors to the accompaniment of an ex-

cellent band. . . . We are having such a nice time together—you cannot think—
We are going to a concert together this evening. . . . Nils and I have talked so
much about you today darling & you gave him your love and he returned it
with interest. . . . He is so good so good—you cannot think how good.[56]

White's letters discuss her sadness when Nils was away, her plans to
return to Massachusetts, and his intention to come to the United States. They
also describe factors that would make it difficult for him to relocate (his
father's lack of support, Nils's position as the oldest of nine children, and
poor prospects for a Swedish teacher in the United States). White's correspondence, however, gives no indication she wanted to remain with Nils in
Sweden. For example, one week before her departure for the United States
she wrote her sister, "It seems such a little time now before I go home—Ah!!
But I have had such a beautiful summer & I would not have it out of my life
for a great deal." White told her sister that she and Nils were continuing to
write every few days, adding, "I have so much to talk to you about."[57]

Having fallen in love after entering her career, Flora White appears to
have made a choice to continue to live as a single person. According to Sara
M. Evans, it was a "stark choice" for educated U.S. women during the late
nineteenth century "between the traditional domesticity of marriage and a
career of paid work."[58]

In 1939 Flora White published a poem titled "Amour" that uses sexual
imagery, perhaps reflecting her summer romance in Sweden. The poem begins with a description of a fire with red flames reaching upward. (In the
original, undated manuscript White says the fire is "throbbing forth desire,"
words that are absent in the published poem.) In both the original and published versions "a life-begetting flame" is detonated and quickly fades into
darkness, with only a brief afterglow. White likens the fire's intensity, sudden eruption, and disappearance to love, which is—by its nature—short-
lived.[59] "Amour" provides the only clue on the outcome of Flora's relationship with Nils, since the White sisters' correspondence stopped when Flora
once again resided in Springfield.

PHYSICAL CULTURE

Harriet White died in March 1892, only seven months after Flora's return
from Sweden. The following year, the White sisters left Springfield so Flora
could promote slöjd and physical activity on a larger scale. John W. Dickinson—former principal of Westfield Normal School and then Secretary of the
Massachusetts State Board of Education—invited her to open "the department of motor-training" at Westfield.[60] White decided to "give up private
school" and accept the appointment because of the "acute" need to acquaint
teachers with "new methods."[61] Between 1893 and 1895, she taught slöjd

and physical culture to largely female classes in the teacher training program at Westfield where she enjoyed the use of a well-equipped slöjd room and gymnasium. Her physical culture classes included Ling gymnastics three times per week, and theory, physiology, and teaching methodology. The offerings were consistent with Jennifer Hargreaves's and Patricia Vertinsky's definition of physical culture as "activities where the body itself—its anatomy, its physiology, and importantly its forms of movement—is the very purpose, the raison d'être of the action."[62]

Flora White's promotion of active learning at Westfield represented a change of direction from the time when the Massachusetts State Board of Education reinforced a cult of invalidism among the institution's primarily female student body. For White, physical fitness became a lifelong commitment. She would write:

> The narrow chest, the flexing knee, the helpless hand, are uncultivated. Ignorance of the uses of the body is ignorance, and is less to be excused and more to be deplored than lack of knowledge in our politest literature. The primal, natural self-expression of which all other forms grow is the act. We choose, then for our youth, "more life, and fuller."[63]

White's correspondence indicates that even when she was taking Ling gymnastics classes in Sweden, she was already becoming comfortable with a new standard of female beauty that reflected physical well-being. During the summer of 1891 she wrote a letter to her sister Mary to report, "Nils . . . tells me that his father has changed his mind and thinks I must be all that can be desired in the shape of a young woman."[64]

Criticism of female athleticism and fears of the resulting bodily changes were expressed not only by lay people but by many medical and scientific authorities of the period. For example, Dudley Sargent, M.D. (1849–1924), who directed physical training at Harvard for forty years, worried that athletics were making women too masculine by broadening their shoulders, narrowing their hips, and enlarging their necks and hands. In 1899, Arabella Kenealy, M.D., published the essay, "Woman as an Athlete," in which she described the foolish athleticism of a woman named Clara who "bartered" womanly qualities "for a mess of muscle."[65] Eight years later University of Chicago sociologist William I. Thomas wrote that women needed to exercise, but "athletics were beyond their physical capacity." He argued that a woman's reproductive function resulted in early arrested development, and that she "resembles the child and the lower races, i.e., the less developed forms." According to Thomas, this was "a very striking evidence of the ineptitude of women for the expenditure of physiological energy through motor action."[66]

During her employment at Westfield, Flora White's professional work drew the attention of Francis Parker (1837–1902), who attended one of her lectures. As a student at the Humboldt University of Berlin, Parker had been exposed to the new pedagogical methods of European theorists. When he became superintendent of the Quincy, Massachusetts, public schools, Parker revised the elementary curriculum—replacing drill, recitation, and memorization with a new pedagogy built on children's natural curiosity in the world around them. After meeting with success in Quincy, Parker accepted a district superintendency in Boston where his innovative approach failed to gain traction in the large, bureaucratic system. In 1883 he became principal of the Cook County Normal School in Chicago where he once again successfully implemented the "new education."[67] Parker replaced textbooks with materials developed by students; reorganized the curriculum with integrated subjects; and oversaw a process of embedding formal academic study in the child's physical, social, and personal environment. When John Dewey joined the faculty of the University of Chicago in 1894, he enrolled his children at Francis Parker's School. Dewey also credited Parker with being the father of progressive education. Although Francis Parker asked Flora White to head a department at the Cook County Normal School, she declined because she had so recently accepted the Westfield appointment. When she did leave that position in 1895, she continued her work in physical culture by becoming associate principal of the Posse Gymnasium in Boston.

Baron Nils Posse is remembered for his contribution to the introduction of Ling gymnastics to the United States. Born to a Swedish noble family, he graduated from the Royal Military School in Stockholm and completed two years of study at the Ling Royal Central Institute. Following graduation, Posse and his wife—the former Rose Moore—settled in Boston where they hoped to generate interest in Swedish gymnastics. In 1888 Boston philanthropist Mary Hemenway (1820–1894) invited Posse to offer gymnastics instruction to teacher volunteers in the city, in the hope of eventually incorporating Swedish gymnastics into school systems throughout the United States. Hemenway—the descendant an old New England family—was the daughter of one of the wealthiest merchants in New York City and the wife of a successful Boston merchant who died in 1876. She funded a number of philanthropic pursuits in the area of physical education and home economics. With Posse as the teacher, Hemenway established the Normal School of Gymnastics in Boston; however, in 1890 he left to establish, with his wife, the Posse Gymnasium in the same city. Flora White completed a summer course of study at the Posse Gymnasium and in 1895 became associate principal of the school. According to White, Posse continued to handle the medical department of the gymnasium, while she handled educational matters. The *Posse Gymnasium Journal* notes that White lectured "on psychology and pedagogics, besides taking care of most of the practical work."[68] Nils

Posse died in 1895, shortly after White began her employment there. Baroness Rose Posse continued to operate the gymnasium; however, his death—coupled with White's suffering "an acute attack of appendicitis" requiring hospitalization, surgery, and "a period of bed rest"—resulted in her departure from the Posse Gymnasium in search of new employment.[69] The quest would lead her from Boston to Concord, with an interlude in Heath.

CONTEXTUALIZING FLORA WHITE

Flora White returned to Massachusetts from the Cape Colony with the goals of supporting active learning and creating a classroom environment based on the needs of pupils. In so doing, she situated herself squarely in the child-centered camp of the early progressive education movement where she attracted the attention of luminaries G. Stanley Hall and Francis Parker. Choosing "more life, and fuller" for her students and herself, she first worked with her sister in their private school in Springfield, and then at Westfield Normal School and the Posse Gymnasium. White made important contributions to the "preparatory years" of progressive education, which—according to Rugg and Shumaker—suffered from an abundance of theory but little data from practical implementation. During this period Flora White also furthered the cause of educational slöjd, which sought to prepare students for the new industrial order while avoiding the problems of the mass education evident in many public school settings. White was one of the first Americans—and one of the very earliest U.S. women—to participate in the slöjd training offered at Nääs to international educators.

When White is placed chronologically with other woman founders of child-centered schools, it is clear that she was on the cutting edge of the movement. Among the women featured in Sadovnik and Semel's *Founding Mothers and Others,* Charlotte Hawkins Brown founded the Palmer Institute in 1902; Marietta Johnson founded the Organic School in 1907; Margaret Naumburg opened the Children's School in 1914; Caroline Pratt founded the City and Country School in 1914; and Helen Parkhurst opened the Dalton School in 1920. By comparison, Flora White founded her child-centered schools in Springfield and Concord, Massachusetts, in 1887 and 1897, respectively. Although she was a contemporary of John Dewey (who was born in Vermont in 1859), his work was conducted at the University of Chicago and then at Teachers College. Rugg and Shumaker would therefore place Dewey's work in the "laboratory schools of the new schools of education" and not with the "enthusiastic free-lance teachers" like White. A closer look at Francis Parker's life, however, reveals that he and Flora White shared some interesting commonalities.

Like White, Francis Parker hailed from New England, being born in Piscatauquog, New Hampshire, in 1837. He attended a village school and aspired to enter an academy for boys. However, when Parker was seven his uncle bound him out to a farmer because the boy's father—a man of modest means—had suffered an early death. Like Flora White's brother Joseph, Parker was poorly educated as a bound boy. However, whereas young Joseph White remained in a binding agreement until he was twenty-one, Parker was able to leave his master at age thirteen to live with his sister in Mount Vernon, New Hampshire. He enjoyed developing an intimate understanding of the flora and fauna around Mount Vernon, as young Flora White would later enjoy the natural world at Heath. When Parker was a young adult he discovered—as White did—that he lacked the credentials and money to pursue his professional aspirations. He became a principal in Carrollton, Illinois, and then served in the Union Army in the Civil War, where a bullet injured his vocal cords and ended his military career. (Parker received the title of Lieutenant Colonel during his convalescence.) He then became a principal in Dayton, Ohio, and head of Dayton Normal School. Despite his strong performance, Francis Parker received criticism from his colleagues for his limited formal education.

Parker felt he could enhance his educational credentials through European study—as had Horace Mann, one of Parker's heroes. Utilizing a small inheritance from his aunt, Parker went abroad to study in Germany, Holland, Switzerland, Italy, and France. Like Flora White, he was strongly influenced by his exposure to the ideas of Comenius, Rousseau, Pestalozzi, Froebel, and Herbart (who advanced the discipline of psychology before William James). Parker drew from many sources: Comenius's ideas about natural learning; Rousseau's child-centered philosophy; Pestalozzi's notion that education was an active process that needed a subsequent educative act; Froebel's emphasis on the whole child; and Herbart's belief in placing emphasis on a single subject. According to Semel and Sadovnik, Parker translated the important findings from his European study into five general principles:

(1) learning by doing, (2) the generation of power through concentration and correlation of subjects, (3) child and community-centered education to create citizens for the democratic society, (4) education of the whole child for character development and not just for the acquisition of knowledge, (5) education through concrete experiences in a natural environment.[70]

One could speculate on the degree to which Parker's and White's child-centered education was influenced by an intimate knowledge of bound children whose growth was limited by forced conformity to adult needs. One might also conjecture what Flora White's professional future might have been if she had accepted Parker's job offer. Apart from her possible concern that a premature resignation from Westfield could alienate the Secretary of the State Board of Education and other Massachusetts officials, a permanent location to Chicago would have been challenging, given her attachment to New England. By 1899 Parker had resigned from the Cook County Normal School (with most of his teachers) to start the Chicago Institute Academic and Pedagogic, the foundation of the Francis Parker School. Its founder, Anita McCormick Blaine (daughter of the inventor of the McCormick reaper), was a woman of great wealth who had served on the Chicago Board of Education. It was Parker's hope that the private school would be a model for common schools.

In the context of the "new education," or the formative period of the progressive movement, Flora White clearly emerges as an innovator—a characterization she would have welcomed, and a role she regarded as life-enhancing. At age eighty-seven, in a newspaper interview, White looked back on the last decade of the nineteenth century and derived satisfaction from the fact that she was, professionally, on the cutting edge. Her pride was not limited to school matters, however. After discussing her educational accomplishments, she informed the journalist, "But there is something more . . . I was one of the first persons in this part of the United States to have my appendix removed."[71]

NOTES

1. Flora White to Mary A. and Harriet M. White, 6 March 1887, Flora White Papers, private collection.
2. Harold Rugg and Ann Shumaker, *The Child-Centered School* (New York: Arno Press and *The New York Times*, 1969), 1.
3. Ibid., 2.
4. Ibid.
5. Flora J. White, "Physical Effects of Sloyd" (paper presented at the annual meeting of the National Education Association, Buffalo, NY, July 1896), 4.
6. Flora White penned this note on the last page of her hard-bound copy of the *Sesquicentennial Anniversary of the Town of* Heath. Flora White Papers, private collection.
7. Michele Plourde-Barker to author, 24 August 2004. Flora White Papers, private collection.
8. John H. Lockwood, *Western Massachusetts: A History 1636–1925*, www.ebooksread.com/authors-eng/john-h-john-hoyt-lockwood/western-massachusetts-a-history-1636–1925-volume-3-kco.shtml.
9. Joel Perlmann and Robert A. Margo, *Women's Work? American Schoolteachers 1650–1920* (Chicago: University of Chicago Press, 2001), 1.
10. Grace Moyer Share, "Identification of People" (written in 1986), Flora White Papers, private collection.
11. Archibald V. Galbraith, *Some Objectives of the Endowed Preparatory School* (Easthampton, MA: Williston Academy, 1967), 1–4.
12. Alan R. Sadovnik and Susan F. Semel, eds., *Founding Mothers and Others: Women Educational Leaders during the Progressive Era* (New York: Palgrave, 2002), 256.
13. Susan F. Semel identified three major strands of progressive education that called for reforms along child-centered, social efficiency, and/or social reconstructionist lines. See Susan

F. Semel and Alan R. Sadovnik, eds., *"Schools of Tomorrow," Schools of Today: What Happened to Progressive Education* (New York: Peter Lang, 1999), 9–10.

14. William J. Reese, "The Origins of Progressive Education," *History of Education Quarterly* 41 (2001): 1–24.

15. Sadovnik and Semel, *Founding Mothers and Others*, 253.

16. Ibid.

17. Rugg and Shumaker, *The Child-Centered School*, 48–49. Despite Rugg and Shumaker's acknowledgment of women practitioners' contributions, the marginalization of this group continued as progressive education evolved. Using gender as a category of analysis, Diana Moyer notes that while men were sometimes included among child-centered educators, women were not identified as social reconstructionists. The former group were viewed as having a narrow, individualist focus, while the latter were depicted as promoting social justice. See Diana Moyer, "The Gendered Boundaries of Child-Centred Education: Elsie Ripley Clapp and the History of US Progressive Education," *Gender and Education* 21 (2009): 531–547.

18. Herbert M. Kliebard, 1987. *The Struggle for the American Curriculum, 1893–1958* (New York and London: Routledge, 1987), 1.

19. Ibid.

20. Ibid., 10.

21. Ibid.

22. Ibid., 12.

23. White, "Physical Effects of Sloyd," NEA paper, 3.

24. Flora White to Anne Halfpenny, 17 June 1940, Westfield State College.

25. John Cleverley and D. C. Phillips, *Visions of Childhood: Influential Models from Locke to Spock* (New York: Teachers College, Columbia University, 1986), 50.

26. Dorothy Ross, *G. Stanley Hall: The Psychologist as Prophet* (Chicago: University of Chicago Press, 1972), 260.

27. G. Stanley Hall, "Child Study," 1894, 173–179, as quoted in Dorothy Ross, *G. Stanley Hall*, 288.

28. Ross, *G. Stanley Hall*, 289.

29. Ibid., 260.

30. White, "Physical Effects of Sloyd," NEA Paper, 6.

31. Ross, *G. Stanley Hall*, 289.

32. The endorsement appears in White's nine-page school informational booklet, a copy of which is in the collection of the P.V. M. A. Library, Deerfield, Massachusetts. See *Miss White's Home School*, 1900, 7.

33. White, "Physical Effects of Sloyd," NEA Paper, 3.

34. Ibid., 6.

35. Ibid.

36. Flora White, "Life Facts of Flora White and family, Recorded Mar. 18, 1939," Heath Historical Society, 4.

37. Paul E. Bolin, "The Massachusetts Drawing Act of 1870: Industrial Mandate or Democratic Maneuver?" in *Framing the Past: Essays on Art Education*, ed. Donald Soucy and Mary Ann Stankiewicz, Reston, VA: National Art Education Association, 1990).

38. David J. Whittaker, *The Impact and Legacy of Educational Sloyd* (London and New York: Routledge, 2014), 97.

39. Hans Thorbjornsson, "Otto Salomon (1849–1907)," *Prospects: The Quarterly Review of Comparative Education* 24 (1994), 1.

40. "Abramson, August." *The Jewish Encyclopedia*, http://www.ljewishencyclopedia.com/articles/621-abramson.

41. Thorbjornsson, "Otto Salomon" 2.

42. Ibid.

43. Ibid., 4.

44. Thorbjornsson, "Otto Salomon," 1–11.

45. Salomon, Otto, *The Theory of Educational Sloyd* (Boston: Silver Burdett, 1900), 147–148.

46. Flora White to Harriet M. White, 20 May 1891. Flora White Papers, private collection.

47. Flora White to Harriet M. White and Mary A. White, 31 May 1891. Flora White Papers, private collection.
48. Ibid.
49. Flora White to Harriet M. White and Mary A. White, 31 May 1891. Flora White Papers, private collection.
50. Flora White to Harriet M. White and Mary A. White, 13 June 1891. Flora White Papers, private collection.
51. Ibid.
52. Ibid.
53. Salomon, *The Theory of Educational Sloyd*, xi–xii.
54. Flora White to Mary A. White, 2 August 1891. Flora White Papers, private collection.
55. Ibid.
56. Flora White to Mary A. White, 16 August 1891. Flora White Papers, private collection.
57. Ibid.
58. Sara M. Evans, *Born for Liberty: A History of Women in America* (New York: The Free Press, 1989), 147.
59. Mary A. White and Flora White, *Poems by Mary A. White and Flora White* (New York: Paebar, 1939), 27. The original manuscript is included in the Flora White Papers, a private collection.
60. Flora White to Anne Halfpenny, 17 June 1940.
61. White, "Life Facts," 5.
62. Jennifer Hargreaves and Patricia Vertinsky, eds., *Physical Culture, Power, and the Body* (New York: Routledge, 2007).
63. Flora J. White, "Physical Effects of Sloyd," *Sloyd Bulletin* (1899), 7.
64. Flora White to Mary A. White, 16 August 1891.
65. Arabella K. Kenealy, "Woman as an Athlete, 1899," in *Out of the Bleachers: Writings on Women and Sport*, ed. Stephanie L. Twin (Old Westbury: Feminist Press, 1979), 43.
66. Stephanie L. Twin, 1985. "Women and Sport," in *Sport in America: New Historical Perspectives*, ed. Donald Spivey (Westport, CT: Greenwood Press, 1985), 202.
67. Wayne J. Urban and Jennings L. Wagoner Jr. *American Education: A History* (New York and London: Routledge, 2009), 216.
68. "Here and There," *Posse Gymnasium Journal* 3(1895): 10.
69. White, "Life Facts," 6.
70. Semel and Sadovnik, "*Schools of Tomorrow*," 30.
71. "Poetess, Educator Lives Quietly in Retirement," *Greenfield Gazette and Courier* (Greenfield, MA), July 14, 1947: 6.

Chapter Five

Visionary Women

Several months before her death, Pauline Agassiz Shaw (1841–1917)— widely reputed to be the wealthiest woman in Boston—penned the following message to her children: "I had too much. You will have too much—and it will require great effort, with God's help, to determine 'to give' rather than 'to hold,' and to think deeply as you spend to spread for progress and welfare rather than for 'pleasure' . . . or mere temporary amusement."[1]

The statement summed up Shaw's commitment to philanthropy, which included her support of educational slöjd. Three years before Flora White studied at Nääs, Shaw established a Sloyd Training School in Boston that would be an important influence in the White sisters' lives. The school's founding was described by its director, Gustaf Larsson, a Swedish citizen and graduate of the Seminarium for Teachers. He recalled arriving in Boston on July 1, 1888, with the goal of interesting "school boards and other promoters of education" in educational slöjd.[2] Like Francis Parker and Baron Nils Posse, Larsson discovered the importance of finding a philanthropist to fund his idea—and like Parker and Posse, his philanthropist would be a woman. Although he intended to stay in the city for a short period of time, Larson was introduced, within one week of arrival, to Pauline Agassiz Shaw. A member of a fledging group supporting Froebel-inspired public kindergartens, Shaw wanted to start a new program at the North Bennet Street Industrial School on the city's North End, where she served as board president. Shaw immediately hired Larsson to teach in two of her private summer schools. Years later Larsson recalled his early interaction with the philanthropist:

> After painstaking and thorough observation Mrs. Shaw became convinced that slöjd was founded on the same principle that underlies the kindergarten system, namely, that the mental and moral growth of the human being must be the

first consideration of *every* teacher and that occupation, whether of mind or hands, must serve only as a means to the end.[3]

Larsson remained in Boston for the rest of his life where he directed the Sloyd Training School located in the North Bennet Street Industrial School building. Over the next three decades he and Shaw created and implemented a program that introduced educational slöjd to over four hundred of Boston's kindergarten and elementary teachers at the training school. As early as 1903 Larsson estimated that the school's graduates had influenced thirty-four thousand students across the United States.[4]

Shaw and Larsson's approach to learning by doing was in keeping with Flora White's interest in motor activities, and she became involved in the Sloyd Training School after returning from Nääs. During that period Mary White served as the Sloyd Training School's Associate Principal;[5] Flora graduated from the institution in 1897 and also authored an article in *The Sloyd Bulletin,* a publication of the school.[6] Although Flora had already learned slöjd techniques at Nääs and had taught slöjd at Westfield, she may have enrolled at the Boston School for one—or a combination of three— reason(s): to understand how slöjd could be adapted to the United States; to gain an additional credential since she lacked a bachelor's degree; and/or to network with proponents of the new education who visited the school.

THE BENEFACTOR

Pauline Agassiz Shaw (1841–1917) was born in Switzerland, the youngest child of famed scientist Louis Agassiz and Cecile Braun. Pauline's mother died when she was seven years old, and the young girl lived with her grand-mother until age nine. She then joined her father at Cambridge, Massachu-setts, where he was a professor at Harvard University. When Pauline was eleven, her father married Elizabeth Cabot Carey, founder of Radcliffe Col-lege for Women and its president for eight years. At age nineteen, Pauline Agassiz wed Quincy Adams Shaw, a copper mining heir and financier. It was a marriage that lasted nearly fifty years.

Much of Pauline Shaw's early philanthropy was an outgrowth of the work of Elizabeth and Mary Peabody, who—inspired by the theories of Froebel— initiated the first experiment in public kindergarten in the United States. Shaw was so taken by their methods of instruction that she founded a kinder-garten for her own children and those of her neighbors. When the Boston School Committee ceased funding the Peabody sisters' kindergarten, Shaw funded thirty-one free kindergartens throughout the city, many of which were situated in public school buildings. Eventually the Boston School Committee took over fourteen kindergartens, and the program became an integral part of the school system. Given this record of accomplishment, it is not surprising that in 1880—when G. Stanley Hall wanted to study children entering first grade in Boston's public schools—he was financed by Pauline Agassiz Shaw. Four of Shaw's kindergarten teachers acted as Hall's investigators.

In 1885, Shaw contracted with the Boston public schools for manual training classes at the North Bennet Street Industrial School for three hundred students from local grammar schools. She expressed her vision of what the classes would accomplish:

> I hope we shall carry on the work this year beyond what it has been and each year strengthen its usefulness in some way. . . . The whole boy should be sent to school and not part of him; it is not enough to train the intellect alone . . . but the eye and the hand are together the most trustworthy leaders of the brain; the eye must no longer say to the hand "we have no need of thee."[7]

According to Lawrence A. Cremin, by 1890 U.S. slöjd proponents believed that "if the ordinary activities of the kindergarten could be joined to *slöjd* at the elementary level and tool exercises or homemaking in the secondary school, the result would be an orderly progression of manual work to parallel intellectual activities throughout the twelve-year period of general education."[8] Properly balanced, these proponents believed slöjd had the potential of offering popular schooling to meet the demands of the industrial era.

Shaw's contract with the Boston public schools was a natural outgrowth of her experiment two years earlier in Prevocational Training for North End grammar school students. As the name implies, these classes developed manual dexterity rather than emphasizing skills for a specific vocation.

Shaw chose a neighborhood with an interesting history in which to fund her slöjd program. The North End—once a center of Boston's commercial, social, and intellectual activity— was home to many historic sites that Americans had long associated with the birth of the United States. The neighborhood had been a fashionable place of residence and the location of the original North Church where Increase and Cotton Mather dominated the pulpit. By 1721 the steeple of a new church in the North End (later called *Old North Church*) acted as a beacon to ships in Boston Harbor. The neighborhood was also home to Paul Revere, who in 1775 was instructed to ride to Lexington and Concord to warn Patriot leaders of advancing British troops. However, the North End began to decline following the American Revolution when nearly one-third of Boston's residents vacated the city for England or eastern Canada.[9] The rapid growth of shipping and mercantile trades reshaped the neighborhood, as did immigration and industrialization.

By the time Larsson arrived in Boston, the North End was "one of the most densely populated areas of the world."[10] The residents were new immigrants, largely from southern Italy, who had no prior experience living in an industrialized, urban environment. According to a history of the North Bennet Street Industrial School, neighborhood families "were crammed into two and three room apartments in poorly lit tenements. Residents shared plumbing facilities and the streets were littered with refuse from human and animal waste. Disease was rampant, and contaminated food abounded."[11]

By 1889, Shaw had brought slöjd teachers to the North Bennet Street Industrial School. Two years later, Gustaf Larsson became head of the slöjd program there, a position he held until his death in 1919. In addition to instructing students, Larsson trained teachers and published a quarterly journal on the principles of educational slöjd. While following the basic concepts he learned at Nääs, Larsson adapted Otto Salomon's program for a U.S. environment. Due to Shaw's financial support, instruction at the Sloyd Training School was free for nearly twenty years.

Educational slöjd and other programs at the North Bennet Street Industrial School were intended to address concerns about new immigrants, who natives of the Bay State had regarded with skepticism (and sometimes hostility) since the 1830s. Even well-educated Massachusetts citizens viewed new immigrants from a deficit perspective, focusing on what the families *failed* to provide their children. In 1889, Francis Parker described recent Eastern European immigrants in Boston: "[H]undreds of parents turn their children out into the streets in the morning to care for themselves, while they, by selling fruit, grinding organs, begging, or even worse, strive to eke out a miserable existence."[12] In this context, some educational reforms gained popularity as compensatory programs for perceived family deficits. According to Marvin Lazerson, while kindergarten initially catered to affluent citizens in Massachusetts, its most important support eventually came from those who cast it "as an institution of the urban slum."[13] With its emphasis on learning by doing, the early kindergarten movement had stressed its universal applicability to all children. In late nineteenth-century Massachusetts (where poverty and immigrants were regarded as synonymous) kindergarten had strong appeal because it recognized children's need for activity and play while introducing order in their lives. The words of the editor of *Century Magazine* demonstrate such cultural bias by observing that kindergarten was "our earliest opportunity to catch the little Russian, the little Italian, the little German, Pole, Syrian, and the rest and begin to make good American citizens of them."[14]

In this environment, Flora White contended that the purpose of education was to help youth achieve "More life, and fuller."[15] Toward that end, the physical, mental, and moral effects on a human being were inseparable, since "Man is a unit. . . . [H]e has no mentality that is not physical and moral, no morality that is not mental and physical, no physical activity that is not mental and moral."[16] Here White's ideas were consistent with Shaw's belief in teaching the "whole boy."[17]

According to White's reminiscences, she delivered lectures at the Sloyd Training School on "the physical basis of psychology,"[18] alternating every other week with the lectures of Harvard professor William James, who had published *Principles of Psychology* in 1890.[19] At the time, James was applying his philosophical principles to pedagogical practice in a manner he later set forth in *Talks to Teachers on Psychology: And to Students on Some of Life's Ideals.*[20] James depicted the child as a behaving organism with a mind that assisted him in adapting to life. The purpose of education, James felt, was to organize the child's powers of conduct to prepare him for his social and physical milieu. As a starting point of instruction, James suggested the teacher should awaken and broaden the child's interests while training his will to sustain attention to productive thought and ethical action. James also thought the teacher should inculcate good habits to free the child to act as an intelligent being and, whenever possible, subject his ideas to practical testing. First and foremost, he believed the job of the teacher was to turn the "sensitive, impulsive, associative, and reactive organism" of the child into purposeful, thinking adult who would *fully apply individual talents in the struggle to achieve a better life*" (emphasis added).[21]

Despite the support for educational slöjd from such prominent Massachusetts residents as Pauline Agassiz Shaw and William James, the movement had its critics. G. Stanley Hall and Francis Parker expressed concern that slöjd was "hypermethodic and tyrannic" because students created their handcraft projects from course models.[22] The two men advocated more creativity and training in "the powers of imagination," increased coordination between manual training and art, and the use of a project method of instruction.[23] Other educators opposed manual training in the lower grades in general. The best-known advocate of this position was William Torrey Harris, a Connecticut native and former superintendent of the St. Louis public schools. Harris resided in Concord, Massachusetts from 1880 until 1889, when he left the state to become U.S. Commissioner of Education. He warned that teaching carpentry to a child gave him a limited knowledge of himself and of human nature. Teaching a child to read, on the other hand, offered him a key to all human wisdom.

Flora White's unpublished lectures include a manuscript she originally titled "Manual Training and Manual Education" and later changed to "Child Training and Education." In the lecture, White asserted that when training occurs, someone chooses a predetermined standard and then works with the learner toward attainment of that standard. The "most perfect training," White argued, would therefore consist of "the most perfect conformity to the best standards." This would mean "the most complete surrender of individual idiosyncrasies." She added that although training has its place in education, it does not constitute the whole of education, which involves growth. White told her audience, "Let us admit . . . that whenever we attempt to train. . . .we

ourselves inevitably impose limitations upon those with whom we work."
Growth, by contrast, exercises itself in ways "we cannot predict, the height to
which . . . we cannot guess." Noting that one could train a soldier but not a
poet, White recommended that youth be allowed to "live in the world of
nature, the artist world, the poet-world, the world in which it may create."[24]

Writing in the *Sloyd Bulletin*, Larsson contended that slöjd was distinguished from other forms of manual training in several respects:

1. In aiming at ethical rather than technical results, and at general organic
   development rather than special skill.
2. In employing only pedagogically trained teachers.
3. In using rationally progressive courses of exercises applied on objects
   of good form which are also of special interest and use to the worker.
4. In striving after gymnastically correct working positions, and in encouraging the use of both the left and right sides of the body.
5. In giving each individual opportunity to progress according to his
   particular ability.[25]

Unfortunately for Larsson, developments were occurring in the United States
that minimized the chance that educational slöjd would be thoroughly understood and appreciated. In public schools "a new class of administrators" was
emerging with training in scientific management procedures developed in
factories.[26] Their support of a narrow conception of manual training was
reinforced by businessmen who wanted "practical trade training" to free
them from increased union regulation of apprenticeships.[27] Cremin notes that
in the end, "talk about a liberalizing balance between manual and intellectual
activities became increasingly academic."[28]

Gustaf Larsson died in 1919, two years after Pauline Agassiz Shaw. The
Sloyd Training School continued to operate a successful program until 1921,
and today educational slöjd is seen as a forerunner to technology education in
the United States. [29] According to Hans Thorbjornsson, an estimated one
hundred thousand U.S. schoolchildren received instruction in the American
version of slöjd. At one point, John Dewey—"intrigued" by Larsson's pro-
motional efforts—offered Otto Salomon three hundred dollars to give a series of lectures on educational slöjd at the University of Chicago. Salomon
was unable to accept because he had to lead summer courses at Nääs. Gustaf
Larsson was, however, successful in getting Dewey to lecture at the Sloyd
Training School in Boston.[30]

Although slöjd is not a household word, the movement in which Flora
White invested much energy is noted in the annals of educational history, and
its effects are still apparent today. In 1890 Charles Kunou, a Scandinavian
immigrant and fellow student of Larsson's at Nääs, established a slöjd department at the Throop Polytechnic Institute, now the California Institute of

Technology. His student Ella Victoria Dobbs completed a slöjd course there and became the supervisor of handwork for the third and fourth grades in the Los Angeles schools. Dobbs taught at Throop and became supervisor of manual work for the public schools in Helena, Montana. Later she pursued an interest in creative expression and studied at Teachers College at Columbia University. Dobbs subsequently accepted a position at the University of Missouri where she completed research on her master's thesis, "The Manual Arts as an Illustrative Factor in History and Geography." In addition, she wrote teaching methods textbooks and became a major figure in art education. Dobbs promoted the idea that handwork could be used as a teaching method (which she called "expressional handwork") and taught as a subject matter (which she called "technical handwork").[31] In so doing, she echoed the balance of intellectual and manual work envisioned by Larsson, White, and supporters of the Sloyd Training School.

THE HEALER

Writing in 1939, Flora White recalled that while she and her sister Mary resided in Boston, they "boarded for many months" with Dr. Grace Wolcott, who became their physician and close friend.[32] Like Flora White, Dr. Wolcott emphasized education and physical well-being in her professional work. Wolcott's home, and likely her medical office, were located at 68 Marlborough Street in Boston's Back Bay neighborhood. A graduate of the Medical College of Pennsylvania, Wolcott pursued postgraduate study at the Philadelphia Polyclinic and then in Vienna and Paris. She began her Boston medical practice in 1884 and, the following year, helped to create the Trinity Dispensary for Women in the city. It was "the first dispensary ever established for evening service," with the goal of providing working women with medical care without a loss of time or wages.[33] The dispensary grew out of the Girls Industrial Club of Trinity Church (where Rev. John Cotton Brooks's brother, Phillips Brooks, was the longtime rector), which invited several of Boston's women physicians to lecture on hygiene and advise patients on health problems. Before long, Dr. Wolcott and her colleague, Dr. Lena V. Ingraham, expanded the staff to include six physicians, some of whom were specialists. In addition to medical services, the dispensary offered weekly lectures on dress, as well as evening classes in calisthenics. During 1891—in an effort to provide medical care to the same clientele—Dr. Wolcott became a founder of the Vincent Memorial Hospital, a freestanding hospital for women, where she was Chief of Staff. In 1940 it became the gynecology service of Massachusetts General Hospital. Today the Vincent Department of Obstetrics and Gynecology at Massachusetts General exists as a legacy of Grace Wolcott's pioneering work.

As a result of her friendship with the White sisters, Grace Wolcott visited Heath and in 1903 began innovative work there in occupational therapy for women. Utilizing a 1793 home that had been refurbished and enlarged (which Wolcott named *Myrifield*) she established an "occupational camp for nervous patients" that was, according to the *Boston Medical and Surgical Journal,* one of the first efforts of its kind.[34] "Boston's best-known men physicians" frequently sent women to Heath where, under Dr. Wolcott's care, they received therapy in the form of gardening, chair-caning, and weaving in the bucolic setting of western Massachusetts. The patients were inspired by Wolcott, "a deeply religious woman," to adopt "a new and better way of life." She urged them "to become useful members of society, to live sanely, and to find joy in living in the country and in the study of Nature."[35] Her medical skills were reportedly augmented by exemplary personal traits. Contemporaries described Wolcott as possessing "[s]trength mated with tenderness, faith and joy, boundless courage, unstinting devotion, [and a] glowing personality."[36]

Grace Wolcott retired from her practice at Vincent Memorial Hospital in 1912 and continued as a consulting physician and member of the hospital's board of managers. She died suddenly at Heath in 1915 at age fifty-seven. According to one source, her life ended "with a swiftness and directness characteristic of all she did."[37] Dr. Wolcott had an important influence on Heath because some of her loyal patients became enamored of the town and bought homes there after leaving Myrifield. The most noted woman in this group was Ethel Lyman Paine, who grew up in Trinity Church in Boston where Phillips Brooks was her family's "greatest influence" and "dearest friend."[38] She was a descendant of Robert Treat Paine, a signer of the Declaration of Independence.

NO PLACE LIKE HOME

Grace Wolcott was one of several people who purchased property at Heath through a connection with Flora and Mary White. A local history points to "The Era of the Summer People" that began when the White sisters returned to Heath in 1896, and continued with their recruitment of interesting, accomplished, and idiosyncratic people as summer residents who eventually formed an intellectual community.

Although the sisters held a special fondness for Heath throughout their lives, their interest in returning was likely piqued when the town celebrated its centennial. Heath was incorporated on February 14, 1785; however, the centennial committee concluded that natives of the town, "remembering the snow drifts of Winter[,] would prefer to celebrate the occasion among the halcyon Summer days."[39] The centennial event was therefore scheduled for

August 19, 1885, when Flora White was en route to the Cape Colony. Family records show that, despite her absence, she carefully read the published centennial book and corrected, amplified, and underscored portions of the text by penciling notes in the margins. The book contained a full discussion of the role of White family members in the founding and development of Heath (especially Colonel Jonathan and Asaph White). It also noted Joseph White II's service in representing the town in the Massachusetts state legislature. The book named the twenty-three Heath natives (all male) who, since 1785, had graduated from college; additionally, it listed fifty-three "Ladies from Heath" who had studied at "Higher Seminaries." Included were Hattie, Mary, and Flora White of the Westfield Normal School. Also highlighted were the names of "Ladies from Heath . . . [who] Married Lawyers," "Ladies from Heath . . . [who] Married Clergymen," and "Ladies from Heath . . . [who] Married Physicians."[40] The assumption here was that women achieved vicariously through the accomplishments of their husbands

To celebrate Heath's first one hundred years, the Congregational Church was "hastily decorated," with the stars and stripes bearing the word *WELCOME*. The program included a scripture reading from a Colonel Jonathan White's 154-year-old Bible, a procession, vocal and instrumental music, and a dinner. The speeches included a "Historical Address" and talks titled "Our Brave Soldiers—Cheers for the Living; Tears for the Dead," "Fort Shirley," and "The Development and Influence of New England Ideas."[41] Although the centennial book provided census data showing a dramatic decline in Heath's population over the years, one orator, Dr. Theron Temple, delivered an address titled "Heath—Once Prosperous; What Shall Her Future Be?" Reflecting cultural and racial biases and hope for a turnaround in the town's decline, he told the audience:

> I predict that . . . we shall again see on these hills, flocks and herds more numerous than at any time in the past. Liverpool, London and Glasgow have thrown open their markets to you, and every year their agents are coming directly to your doors to purchase the products of your farms. . . . But the most important product of these quiet country homes will be, in the future, as in the past, noble *men* and *women* whose characters and morals are untainted by the vices of our great cities: Christian men and women who . . . shall go out to educate and Christianize the ignorant and the heathen of the lands who have come to our own shores, completing at home what they so nobly begun [*sic*] in other climes, and among the savage tribes of America; and whose labors and memories, like theirs, shall bless mankind, and be stored among the most previous treasures of succeeding generations.[42]

A local history notes that although Heath's centennial was largely a "homespun affair" without the benefit of a historical society, the arrival of Flora and Mary White in 1896 changed the character of future town celebrations.[43] The White sisters "were colorful, enterprising, and energetic, and they were organizers."[44] In 1899–1900 they collaborated with other residents to form the Heath Historical Society, with Flora serving on the executive committee. This gave the sisters an "outlet"—and, with the organization's sponsorship, they planned and promoted "Old Home Week" at Heath in 1902, 1903, and 1909, "with a dizzying program of activities."[45]

The Whites' primary objective in returning to Heath was to buy the land their forebears had farmed on Charlemont Hill. Despite what Flora called her "passionate desire" to purchase the old family farm, the owner "refused to sell."[46] Instead, the sisters made an initial purchase of a half-acre of land and buildings from another of Heath's old farms. They named the property Plover Hill from the upland plover that nested there. Flora reported that she and her sister kept Plover Hill as a summer home for "about forty years."[47] A local history notes that—besides Plover Hill and "property elsewhere"—the sisters bought additional land where they employed a series of tenant farmers.[48] Writing in 1939, Flora White explained that she and Mary used the house at Plover Hill as a center for small camps for girls. The additional farmland provided supplies for their camp and school.

Another returning Heath native was Felicia Emerson Welch (1828–1916), who in 1897 became the sisters' near neighbor and the first of the "summer people" to arrive after the Whites.[49] The oldest daughter of Heath's physician (and Laura Emerson's sister), Felicia Welch had resided in Athens, Ohio, with her husband John, a justice of the Ohio Supreme Court. Following his death in 1891, she moved to Amherst to live with her mother and sisters. When the Heath Historical Society was founded, Felicia Welch became its first vice president. The president was Edward Payson Guild, a summer visitor in the home of his mother Amelia and uncle, Henry K. Smith. Mr. Smith donated a number of articles to the society's collection and became its first custodian.

The Heath Historical Society was incorporated as a nonprofit organization in 1902; however, even before its founding Felicia Welch purchased twenty acres of land and donated it to the society to "get the ball rolling."[50] The acreage included the site of Fort Shirley, one of a line of forts built to protect English colonists as England and France fought for empire during the mid-eighteenth century. Welch reported that the initiative for organizing the society came from the White sisters.

TOWN OF THE UNUSUAL

Despite Flora and Mary White's fondness for Heath, it was too remote a location for a day and boarding school. While Mary stayed in Boston for "a year or two" as associate principal of the Sloyd Training School, Flora founded a school in another place of historic significance—Concord, Massachusetts.[51]

Concord had a nonconformist history. Ralph Waldo Emerson (1803–1882), its most famous resident, had proudly observed that Concord differed from other Puritan settlements in that it had no "witch trials, ghost sightings . . . [or] the whipping of Quakers through the streets."[52] When on April 19, 1775, British regular troops tried to confiscate military supplies the Provincial Congress had stored at Concord, its North Bridge became the site of the beginning of the American Revolution as the local militia opened fire on the soldiers. Emerson immortalized the event by writing the "Concord Hymn," which extoled the farmers who "fired the shot heard round the world."[53] In 1875 the town commissioned a statue by Daniel Chester French that became Concord's landmark—a Minuteman, or revolutionary patriot who responded to crises on short notice.

Concord was further defined by Henry David Thoreau (1817–1862), a former schoolmaster and lifelong resident of the town. The son of a pencil manufacturer, Thoreau summed up a single year in his own life as "Made pencils in 1844."[54] The following year he went to Emerson's property bordering Walden Pond on the outskirts of Concord in an effort to live simply; however, he was interrupted and incarcerated for failure to pay a poll tax. Thoreau reflected on the experience in "Civil Disobedience" (published in 1849) as well as in *Walden* (published in 1854). His writing criticized the U.S. government for tolerating the existence of slavery and engaging in the war with Mexico in 1846. Thoreau was not alone in this view. When the United States gained vast amounts of Mexican land at the war's end, a national debate ensued on whether slavery should exist in the new territory. (This was the same debate in which Flora White's father engaged in 1850 when he supported Charles Sumner's election to the U.S. Senate.) In Concord, many residents wanted to contain slavery or abolish it altogether. One prominent abolitionist was Franklin B. "Frank" Sanborn (1831–1917), a young Harvard graduate recruited by Emerson to teach at a private school his children attended. Sanborn rented half of the double house at 50/52 Belknap Street that Flora White would later select as the location of Miss White's Home School.

In 1859, Sanborn was one of the "secret six"[55]—the only people with advance knowledge of radical abolitionist John Brown's plan to raid the federal government arsenal at Harper's Ferry, Virginia, to supply guns to slaves.[56] Sanborn met with Brown at his Belknap Street residence in May 1859, just months before the raid. Following the attack on the arsenal, Brown was captured, tried, and hanged—a martyr to the abolitionist cause. Sanborn fled to Canada but, at Emerson's request, returned to Concord.

On April 3, 1860, U.S. Senate deputies entered Sanborn's home (then on Sudbury Road in Concord) and removed him to face charges as Brown's accomplice. A crowd of townspeople (including Emerson) surrounded them and stopped the arrest. Concord resident Annie Whiting aided resistance efforts by boarding the deputies' carriage, consuming all available seating space with her full skirt. She refused to move, thereby preventing the deputies from placing Sanborn in the carriage. Meanwhile, Sanborn's lawyer hurried to the home of abolitionist judge Ebenezer Rockwood Hoar to obtain a writ of habeas corpus. He gave it to Concord's deputy sheriff who demanded that the Senate deputies surrender their prisoner. When they refused, the deputy sheriff empowered the one hundred fifty men and women present to act as a *posse comitatus*. Approximately twenty men among the group pursued the Senate deputies out of town.

Four days later *The New York Herald* reported that Concord residents had unanimously adopted a resolution stating, "Concord remains where she was on the 19th of April, 1775, and there she will remain forever."[57] A second resolution asserted that "resistance to tyrants is obedience to God."[58] The charges against Frank Sanborn were eventually dropped. Forced to close his school during the U.S. Civil War, Sanborn turned his attention to writing and co-founding the Concord School of Philosophy with Transcendentalist leader Amos Bronson Alcott, father of Louisa May Alcott. (The two men had financial backing from William Torrey Harris.) In 1893, Sanborn and Harris co-authored *A. Bronson Alcott: His Life and Philosophy*. Sanborn pursued the cause of social reform by establishing the American Social Science Association, of which he and Harris were officers. Sanborn became a friend of Flora White when she moved to Concord and involved her in the American Social Science Association. She presented a paper on the Boers of South Africa at the organization's annual meeting in 1900.

The thwarted "kidnapping" of Frank Sanborn became part of Concord's lore. Over time, the town counted additional distinguished residents in its population including kindergarten pioneer Elizabeth Peabody and authors Louisa May Alcott and Nathaniel Hawthorne. According to Elizabeth Gregg, editor of *The Letters of Ellen Tucker Emerson,* "Important people lived at Concord, not only literary people . . . but also distinguished jurists, congressmen, educators, inventors, and horticulturalists." By the last quarter of the nineteenth century, Concord had evolved into "a prosperous place of progressive farmers and comfortable commuters [to Boston], who supported schools, library, and lyceums with enthusiasm and kept up with the advances of the age."[59] At the same time, Concord retained its nonconformist image. As late as 1938 *The Boston Globe* called it the "'Town of the Unusual'— quaint, homelike and placid as it looks. The town where all kinds of movements have started, ever since that affair at Concord Bridge in 1775."[60]

Even before Flora White came to Concord, she drew from Emerson in describing her educational philosophy. In 1896 she reminded her NEA audience of Emerson's observation that "The heart and sinew of man seem to be drawn out of him. . . . Our age yields no great and perfect persons. The rugged battle of fate where strength is born we shun. . . . We are parlor soldiers."[61] In an undated, unpublished speech White also showed admiration for Thoreau by noting, "Thoreau was truly great and very right in refusing to make another pencil after having acquired the ability to make one well. In that single act of his was concretely lived as much philosophy as Emerson ever wrote."[62]

When White founded her Concord school in 1897, most of the town's famous residents no longer lived there. (*The New York Times* cited Frank Sanborn, 1831–1917, as the last survivor of an era.) Nevertheless, with a well-educated citizenry, a reform tradition and—as White noted—"charming surroundings of wood, field, and river," Concord appeared to be a promising location for a progressive school.[63]

Flora White left no written record of the process by which she decided to found Miss White's Home School in 1897 in Concord. Since she was not independently wealthy and lacked the backing of a philanthropist, the school needed to draw affluent families who could afford the annual tuition of $100 for day pupils and $600 for boarding students, the equivalent of $2,910 and $17,400 today.[64] With good rail access, Concord had the advantage of being well situated to draw boarding students from Boston (twenty miles away, or thirty-five minutes by train), New York (two hundred miles away), and Philadelphia (three hundred miles away). One possible explanation for the school's location may be the close friendship that existed between Pauline Agassiz Shaw and Ellen Tucker Emerson (1839–1909). A daughter of Ralph Waldo Emerson, Ellen resided in Concord where she acted as an organizer and hostess of the town's public dances and social events. Additionally, Flora White was close to the Emerson family of Amherst and Heath, who may have provided a helpful introduction. Whatever the sequence of events, Ellen Tucker Emerson taught dance at Miss White's Home School after its founding, and Louisa May Alcott's great-nieces and great-nephews were also students there.[65]

SOME GOOD NAMES

Flora White had been instructed since childhood on the value of a good family name. As early as 1898 she promoted her school by getting endorsements from people whose positive name recognition would attract applicants. She received (and shared) letters of support from two individuals who were well known in ecclesiastical and academic circles. The first was the Reverend E. Winchester Donald, D.D., Rector of Trinity Church in Boston where Grace Wolcott was an active member. (One source described him as being born and educated in New England, which allowed him to understand the region's "Puritan ideals.")[66] A second letter of endorsement was provided by Massachusetts native G. Stanley Hall, president of Clark University in Worcester. In her early school publications, White included testimony from Donald and Hall along with the names, job titles, and locations of ten additional references. Eight of the ten were male; nine out of ten had graduated from college. Six references in the group were New England natives; the others were born in New York (2), Pennsylvania (1), and Ireland (1). Four of White's references are discussed in previous chapters—John W. Dickinson, formerly the principal of Westfield State Normal School and Secretary of the Massachusetts State Board of Education; the Reverend John Cotton Brooks, Flora's Springfield rector; Dr. Thomas M. Balliet, superintendent of the Springfield Public Schools; and Dr. Grace Wolcott, pioneering physician in women's health and the Whites' close friend. The remaining six people included Dr. Benjamin Kendall Emerson, Professor of Geology at Amherst College and author of the genealogy titled "The Emerson Family;" Dr. Frederick Wilcox Chapin, a physician who practiced in Springfield, Massachusetts; David White, Flora's cousin and a member of the U.S. Geological Survey in Washington, D.C.; the Reverend Wallace MacMullen, pastor of Park Avenue Methodist Episcopal Church in Philadelphia; Dr. Charles Hanford Henderson, an educator, lecturer, and writer on technical education who was living in Philadelphia; and Helen Putnam Wadleigh Hoar, a Concord resident and mother of two sons. She was married to the prominent attorney and civic leader, Samuel Hoar, whose father—abolitionist judge Ebenezer Hoar—became United States Attorney General under Ulysses S. Grant. Helen Putman Wadleigh Hoar's own father served as U.S. Senator from New Hampshire. The Hoar and White families had an interesting historical connection in that John Hoar, a founder of Concord, negotiated Mary Rowlandson's release from the Algonquin tribes during her 1676 captivity.

Flora White's Concord school building had historic as well as architectural importance. Miss White's Home School was located in a two and one-half story, wooden clapboard structure that the Massachusetts Historical Commission lists as significant for its combination of Federal, Greek, and Colonial Revival architecture. Constructed around 1815 as Concord's largest store, it was moved from Main Street to its present location on Belknap Street in 1844 and converted to a double house. When the White sisters acquired the building they gave it a "radical update" by changing the entry, placing classrooms at the rear of the structure, and adding a wing.[67] Given the new pedagogy that White would introduce, the "radical update" was metaphorical as well as physical, as discussed in the next chapter.

It is useful, when considering the founding of Miss White's Home School, to compare Flora's actions in 1897 with her imagined school a decade earlier. Of particular interest are the thoughts she shared with her mother and sister Mary before leaving the Cape Colony to return home. Flora wrote, "I care more about a plot of ground than the house. . . . I can't explain to you now the tremendous importance in my mind of the plot of ground if our school becomes what I want it to become. . . . I want the school rooms a part of the house or at least joined to it in some way when we have our own."[68]

Flora White was able to combine the sisters' home and school at 50/52 Belknap Street, as she had done in Springfield. However, her plan for a plot of ground seems to have evolved in the face of practical realities and her strong attachment to Heath. Although the White sisters were able to utilize the woods, fields, and river around Concord for the sort of active and natural life they wanted to encourage, property was much more expensive there than in western Massachusetts. Additionally, many families who sent their daughters to Miss White's Home School wanted to extend the experience beyond the academic year and into the summer. Flora White hoped she could own a very special plot of ground—the ancestral farm of the White family. When that hope was not realized, the sisters purchased other land, thereby shaping the summer experience they could offer, and eventually changing Heath itself. Plover Hill Camp for Girls became a landmark in the town and a regular part of the White sisters' educational program.

Despite her disappointment over the White family farm, Flora expressed considerable enthusiasm in describing (in a camp booklet) Plover Hill's location on an "open upland" eighteen hundred feet above sea level in full view of "Greylock and the Housatonic Range on the west, Monadnock on the east, and the rolling hills of Buckland and Ashfield on the south."[69] White reported that the air was "cool and bracing, and the water, which comes from deep-seated springs, . . . remarkably pure." She promised "thoroughly hygienic and health-giving" surroundings at Plover Hill camp, with access to a woodland with many "brooks and winding paths." Finally, White wrote that the camp had "a variety of fine old trees—beeches, elms, oaks, and maples—scattered over it, and here and there forming small groves available for recreation."[70] It was an impressive plot of ground.

CONCLUSION

Flora White's period of residence in Boston and her return to Heath included important experiences that suggested women's roles in society could be expanded. Although women were largely absent from the top of the organizational charts in educational institutions where White had worked, she came into close contact with women who made important organizational and societal contributions from a variety of vantage points. Pauline Agassiz Shaw was a visionary philanthropist who used her family wealth to improve the education of immigrants in Boston. White's neighbor, Felicia Emerson, acted strategically and proactively to ensure that the Heath Historical Society came into being and had important work to do. (Fort Shirley, which Welch purchased, eventually became the site of archaeological excavations conducted by Yale University and the University of Massachusetts.) Grace Wolcott identified a need for poor and working-class women to receive medical care and found a way to provide it without causing them to lose wages when they were ill.

Given the marginalization of women in Flora White's world, it is not surprising that she chose to primarily list male endorsers with good names to attract applicants to her largely female school. However, it is also very revealing that White included some women on the list of references, an indication of the impact she believed they were capable of having. The strategy was successful. Late in life, White would look back to the days when she ran her school in Concord, deeming it to be a "marked success," and the "climax" of her educational work.[71]

NOTES

1. Norma Hoffman, "Pauline Agassiz Shaw, 1841–1917: A Forgotten Visionary," *AFFIL-IA* 15 (2000): 361.

2. Gustaf Larsson, *Sloyd* (Gustaf Larsson, 1902), 17.

3. *Pauline Agassiz Shaw; Tributes Paid Her Memory at the Memorial Service Held on Easter Sunday, April 8, 1917 at Faneuil Hall*. Boston, privately printed, 43.

4. Sarah Henry and Mary A. Williams, *North Bennet Street School: A Short History* (Boston: Chadis Printing, 1987), 20.

5. Flora White, "Life Facts of Flora White and Family Recorded Mar. 18, 1939," Heath Historical Society, 6.

6. Flora J. White, "The Physical Effects of Sloyd," *Sloyd Bulletin*, 2 (1899): 5–10.

7. Henry and Williams, *North Bennet Street School*, 13.

8. Lawrence A. Cremin, *The Transformation of the School: Progressivism in American Education, 1876–1957* (New York: Alfred A. Knopf, 1969), 33.

9. Guild Nichols, "North End History: Boston's First Neighborhood," www.northendboston.com. For more information on colonists who remained loyal to the crown, see Maya Jasanoff, *Liberty's Exiles: American Loyalists in the Revolutionary World* (New York: Vintage Press, 2012).

10. Henry and Williams, *North Bennet Street School*, 9.

11. Ibid.

12. Francis Parker, "The Kindergartens of Boston," *Kindergarten Magazine* I (March 1889), 334–335, as reported in Marvin Lazeron, "Urban Reform and the Schools: Kindergartens in Massachusetts, 1870–1915," *History of Education Quarterly* (1971): 124.

13. Lazeron, "Urban Reform and the Schools," 118.

14. Ibid., 117–121.

15. White, "The Physical Effects of Sloyd," *Sloyd Bulletin*, 6.

16. Ibid., 2, 6.

17. Henry and Williams, *North Bennet Street School*, 13.

18. White, "Life Facts," 5.

19. William James, *Principles of Psychology, with Introduction by George A. Miller* (Cambridge: Harvard University Press, 1983).

20. William James, *Talks to Teachers on Psychology: and to Students on Some of Life's Ideals with introduction by Gerald E. Myers* (Cambridge: Harvard University Press, 1983), 114.

21. Ibid.

22. Hans Thorbjornsson, "Otto Salomon (1849–1907)," *Prospects: The Quarterly Review of Comparative Education* 23 (1994): 8.

23. Ibid., 9.

24. Flora White, "Child Training and Education," n.d., Flora White Papers, private collection, 1–11.

25. Gustaf Larsson, "Letter to Sloyd Graduates," *Sloyd Bulletin* 2 (1899): 4.

26. Lawrence A. Cremin, *The Transformation of the School*, 34.

27. Ibid., 33.

28. Ibid., 34.

29. *New Hampshire Technology Education Curriculum Guide* (Concord, NH: New Hampshire Technology Education Association, 2001), 3.

30. Hans Thorbjornsson, "Swedish Educational Sloyd: An International Success," *Tidschrift*, (2006): 19–23; Doug Stow, "Nääs: Placing the Hands at the Center of Education," *Woodwork* (2008): 63.

31. June E. Eyestone, "The Influence of Swedish Sloyd and Its Interpreters on American Art Education," *Studies in Art Instruction: A Journal of Issues and Research*, 34 (1992): 34–35.

32. White, "Life Facts," 16.

33. "Transactions of the Forty-first Annual Meeting of the Alumnae Association of the Woman's Medical College of Pennsylvania" (Philadelphia: Alumnae Association of the Woman's Medical College of Pennsylvania, 1916): 35.

34. Ibid.; "Grace Wolcott, M.D." *Boston Medical and Surgical Journal*, 173 (1915): 791.

35. "Transactions of the Forty-first Annual Meeting," 35.

36. "Grace Wolcott, M.D.," 792.

37. Ibid.

38. Sarah Cushing Paine and Charles Henry Pope, eds. *Paine Ancestry: The Family of Robert Treat Paine, Signer of the Declaration of Independence* (Boston: Printed for the Family, 1912), 319.

39. Edward P. Guild, ed., *Heath, Mass. Centennial, Aug. 19, 1885* (Boston: Advertiser Publishing Company, 1885).

40. Ibid., 142.

41. Ibid., 1–148.

42. Ibid., 111–112.

43. Edward Calver, *Heath, Massachusetts: A History and Guidebook* (Heath, MA: Heath Historical Society, 2009), 189.

44. Ibid.

45. Ibid.

46. White, "Life Facts," 11.

47. Ibid.

48. Calver, *Heath, Massachusetts*, 188.

49. Ibid.

50. Ibid., 189.

51. White, "Life Facts," 6.

52. Concord, Massachusetts: American History through Literature, http://www.endnotes.com/american-history-literature-literature.concord-massachusetts.

53. Ralph Waldo Emerson, "Concord Hymn, 1837," in *Early Poems of Ralph Waldo Emerson* (New York: Thomas Y. Crowell, 1899).

54. Sherman Paul, ed., *Walden and Civil Disobedience by Henry David Thoreau* (Boston: Houghton Mifflin, 1960), xiii.

55. The others were Dr. Samuel Gridley Howe, a Boston physician and husband of Julia Ward Howe, who wrote "The Battle Hymn of the Republic;" Thomas Wentworth Higginson, a Worchester, Massachusetts Unitarian minister and Transcendentalist; Theodore Parker, a Boston Unitarian minister and Transcendentalist; Gerrit Smith, millionaire antislavery philanthro-

pist from Peterboro, New York; and George Luther Sterns, an American industrialist and merchant.

56. Franklin B. Sanborn Papers, Georgetown University.

57. *New York Herald*, April 7, 1860.

58. Ibid.

59. Edward Jarvis, *Traditions & Reminiscences of Concord, Massachusetts, 1779–1878* (Concord, MA: Library Corporation, Concord Free Public Library, 1993), xlii.

60. A. J. Philpott, "Mary O. Abbott's Sculptures on Exhibition in Concord," *Boston Sunday Globe*, May 29, 1938.

61. Flora J. White, "Physical Effects of Sloyd" (paper presented at the annual meeting of the National Education Association, Buffalo, New York, July 1896).

62. Flora White, "Growth and Education," n.d. Flora White Papers, private collection.

63. *Miss White's Home School*, 1900. Concord, MA, 4.

64. Ibid., 5.

65. Miss Pickwick, "Girl about Town," *Daily Oklahoman*, February 9, 1941.

66. Joseph N. Blanchard, D.D. "A Sermon in Memory of E. Winchester Donald, D.D., LL.D. Late Rector of Trinity Church, Boston, Preached in Trinity Church Sunday Afternoon, November 20, 1905" (Boston: Printed for Trinity Church, 1905).

67. Josiah Davis Store, 50/52 Belknap Street, *Survey of Historical and Architectural Resources, Concord, Massachusetts*, vol. 1. Boston: Massachusetts Historical Commission, form 94.

68. Flora White to Mary A. White and Harriet M. White, 6 March 1887. Flora White Papers, private collection.

69. *Plover Hill Camp for Girls in Charge of the Misses White* (Boston: Todd Printer, 1907), 2.

70. Ibid.

71. Flora White to Anne Halfpenny, 17 June 1940. Westfield State College.

Chapter Six

A Redeemer

The 1897 founding of Flora White's Concord school was her most ambitious exercise of agency until that time. She had left public school teaching, started her own small private school, and improved her pedagogical and physical skills in Springfield, Boston, and abroad. Now White was assuming responsibility for developing a curriculum, equipping a school facility, hiring faculty, cultivating parents, selecting students, and keeping the enterprise afloat financially. Her own late-in-life assessment that Miss White's Home School was a marked success and the peak of her career suggests she accomplished those goals. White's recollections are supplemented by statements of her former pupils in oral interviews conducted by Renee Garrelick in the 1970s.

"The White's were a very interesting pair of ladies and as I think now, they were very progressive," recalled Elizabeth Darling Babcock (1905–1995), a former student at Miss White's Home School. Babcock explained that the White sisters' young pupils "did a great deal of acting out in whatever we were learning. . . . Whenever we had pageants or performances, it was a very serious thing."[1]

Babcock's 1977 description was a testimony to Flora White's pedagogy, which she demonstrated even in traveling as a young teacher by organizing *tableaux* on a ship bound for Cape Town, and preparing boys in the Cape Colony for a pageant performance on King John. White believed she introduced a new type of education to Concord, and would have appreciated the progressive label Babcock bestowed on her. In a 1941 newspaper interview, White recalled Concord's initial reaction to the "motor activities" in her curriculum. *The Daily Oklahoman* reported, "Boys who formerly had sworn at Latin and Greek, spent such long hours at Flora's school in the delight of motor activities that their mothers declared—'Miss White and her new courses have ruined home life in Concord.'"[2]

121

English instruction at Miss White's Home School also generated comment. Adeline Eveleth Cabot (1899–2007)—another former student and a member of the Smith College class of 1923—reported to Renee Garrelick that Miss White's was "a remarkable school." She added, "I had the most wonderful grounding in English literature that anyone could possibly have."[3] Cabot's comment brings to mind Flora's intensive study of English literature during her youth under the direction of Isaac Esty and her mother.

Despite her apparent success, White remains largely unrecognized as an early contributor to the formative period of progressive education. However, primary and secondary sources show current understandings of the period are fraught with inaccuracies and omissions resulting from the rivalries of male theorists, the marginalization of women as educational practitioners, and the eventual prominence of John Dewey in the progressive education movement. These sources suggest a need to cast a wider net in studying people involved in the formative period of progressive education, including White.

QUESTIONS OF INFLUENCE

An important piece of historical evidence is a 1900–1901 informational booklet on Miss White's Home School that is now part of the collection of the Pocumtuck Valley Memorial Association Library and the Historic Deerfield (Massachusetts) Library. It is one of two such publications of the school that are extant today, the other being the 1906–1907 booklet that belonged to Flora's niece Catherine White and is now privately held in Flora White's archive. The 1900–1901 booklet announces the philosophical principles of Miss White's Home School:

> This school is an effort in the direction of organic education, and is founded in the belief that a healthy, active organism is the first requisite for a healthy, active mind.
>   Regime, physique, and bodily alertness are considered pre-eminent as factors of education.[4]

Although present-day readers may be unfamiliar with the term *organic education,* it is interesting that in 1900 White felt no need to define it for her public, apparently expecting they would understand its meaning. The term is attributed to Charles Hanford Henderson of Philadelphia (1861–1941), an early rival of John Dewey.[5] Henderson taught physics and chemistry in Philadelphia prior to his 1893 appointment as principal of the city's Northeast Branch of the Manual Training School. He subsequently lectured on manual training at Harvard in 1897–1898 and was appointed headmaster of Brooklyn's Pratt Institute, a trade school with a developing emphasis in art and design. Henderson's name appears in both booklets as an endorser of Miss

*organic education
preceding Marietta Johnson*

White's Home School. In 1907, by his own account, Henderson was present when Marietta Johnson opened a school emphasizing organic education in Fairhope, Alabama.[6]

Writing in 1896, Henderson observed, "A progressive education would be one in which the educational process [is] being constantly readjusted to meet . . . changing conditions."[7] He advocated an educational program that would address the physical, intellectual, and moral needs of children. Noting that children are inherently curious, Henderson suggested they want "to be employed . . . with something that interests *them*, not something that interests mamma or papa, or the teacher."[8] He actively promoted his views by giving public lectures in Boston on organic education—first in 1897 at the Sloyd Training School and then in the winter of 1899 at the Industrial School Hall, in a ten-lecture series sponsored by Pauline Agassiz Shaw. Henderson continued to promote organic education during the fall of 1899 in a lecture series at Griffith Hall in Philadelphia and in 1902 when he published a book, *Education and the Larger Life*, featuring a chapter titled "Organic Education."[9] In presenting this concept, Henderson envisioned all parts of the human organism operating together as a fundamental condition for success. (Some educators—from Henderson's lifetime up to the present—have used the term, *whole child*, to illustrate this phenomenon.) The book generated strong sales that were sustained over time, surprising both the publisher and Henderson. In 1914 he published a sequel titled *What Is It to Be Educated?* that was designed to offer "concrete and practical" approaches to his ideas.[10]

After the publication of *Education and the Larger Life*, Flora White continued to use the term, *organic*, in her school's 1906–07 booklet that stated, "This school was founded in the belief that a healthy, active organism is the only sure foundation for a healthy, active mind."[11] Perhaps to assure parents who might hesitate to place their children in what White acknowledged was an experimental school, she added:

> [This school] has been described as a new departure in education, but it is rather an effort to retain in its grasp that which has in all ages been recognized as the best in education.
>
> It considers, as did the schools of Greece, that good physique and bodily vigor are indispensable to mental activity; and it therefore provides a training [that is] organic, vital, [and] permanent.[12]

Given the statements in White's school booklets, it is surprising that Jeroen F. Staring wrote in 2013 that "only one reformer—Marietta Johnson of Fairhope, Alabama—dared to found a school, its core curriculum sailing under the flag of Henderson's organic education."[13] (Johnson's school founding date of 1907 was a decade after Flora White's.) It is also surprising that some current publications of the State of Alabama fail to mention Henderson when discussing theoretical influences on Marietta Johnson. On one hand Johnson's memoir, *Thirty Years with an Idea* (published by the University of Alabama Press in 1974), clearly credits New York pediatrician Nathan Oppenheim and Henderson as major influences in her pedagogy and school program. Yet the current *Encyclopedia of Alabama* reports that Johnson's ideas were shaped by Oppenheim's *The Development of the Child*, as well as Jean Jacques Rousseau, Friedrich Froebel, and John Dewey.[14] No mention is made of Henderson, nor is his name included in a *University of Alabama News* article that attributes Johnson's theoretical influences to Rousseau, Froebel, and Dewey.[15]

In her memoir, Marietta Johnson details the circumstances that led to the founding of the School of Organic Education. In 1902, Johnson—a former supervising teacher in a Minnesota normal school—moved with her husband Frank to the utopian community of Fairhope, Alabama, on Mobile Bay. Like many residents of Fairhope, the Johnsons were socialists, and the community was established according to the single-tax theory of Henry George, author of *Progress and Poverty*.[16] Johnson's memoir describes how she radically altered her pedagogy after reading Nathan Oppenheim's 1898 book, *The Development of the Child*, and then Henderson's *Education and the Larger Life*. She wrote:

> Henderson, in his epoch-making book . . . presented a most constructive criticism of life and education. He not only agreed with Oppenheim as to the nature of the growing child and the insistence that the adult's supreme responsibility is to supply the right conditions of growth, but suggested a practical program—life-giving to body, mind, and spirit.
>
> This idea took possession of me and I could not rest until I had started a school.[17]

Prior to encountering Oppenheim's and Henderson's books, Johnson had operated in a professional environment where "The Curriculum was sacred!"[18] She discovered she "had been forcing children 'way beyond their powers . . . [and] had practically been maiming their minds and emotions." She concluded the entire system in which she taught "went directly contrary to the natural needs of the child."[19] Johnson's assessment resembles Flora White's statement in an undated manuscript: "[S]chooling—falsely called education—disregards the laws of growth, begins its work from the outside, induces, directs, restrains, [and] satisfies itself only by making child-life into a dwarfed image of adult life."[20]

However, Fairhope, Alabama was very different from Concord, Massachusetts—especially in the quality of its public education. In a 1978 interview, Concord resident Laurence Eaton Richardson reported the "high standing" of Concord schools in the early twentieth century "was exceeded only by that of the schools of Quincy."[21] Alabama, on the other hand, was still struggling to build a viable system of public education when the Johnsons arrived there. They and other Midwestern transplants soon discovered that Fairhope's public schools compared unfavorably to schools in their previous communities. With the support of one Fairhope couple who offered to provide twenty-five dollars per month for expenses, Johnson opened a free school for six young pupils. She even recruited students with disabilities who could not attend public schools. Neither she nor White, however, had student bodies that were racially diverse. While Miss White's Home School existed largely on student tuition and fees, Johnson gained the financial support of Joseph Fels, founder of Fels Naptha Soap Company, who funded single-tax initiatives throughout the United States. Fels's philanthropy allowed Johnson to relocate the School of Organic Education to a better facility and draw children of well-to-do families in the Northeast and Midwest who were interested in progressive education. (Two of Margaret Mead's sisters enrolled at the school, as did Upton Sinclair's son who—like some other well-to-do students—attended only during the winter when their parents were vacationing in the South.)[22] The school afforded students an opportunity for physical exercise, nature study, music, handwork, storytelling, dramatizations, and games. They were led into reading, writing, arithmetic, and geography not through coercion, but by their desire to know.

Eventually Marietta Johnson made "society friends" from Greenwich, Connecticut, who invited John Dewey to visit the School of Organic Education in December 1913.[23] He had left the University of Chicago for Teachers College/Columbia University in New York, and was working with his daughter Evelyn on a book on experimental schools (published in 1915 as *Schools of To-morrow*). Although Evelyn conducted all school visits but one in preparation for the book, John Dewey made the trip to Fairhope. He brought his fourteen-year-old son Sabino, who attended the School of Organic Education for a week and wanted to stay.

In the preface to *Schools of To-morrow*, John Dewey noted that the schools presented in the book "were chosen more or less at random; because we already knew of them or because they were conveniently located." He added they did not begin to represent the efforts of "sincere teachers" in schools "growing up all over the country" where efforts were underway to "work out definite educational ideals."[24] Most of the schools presented in the book were located in the Midwest or New York, where the Deweys had lived.

Marietta Johnson's school was the first to be featured in *Schools of To-morrow*. Its presentation constituted the entire second chapter, immediately following a chapter (presumably written by Dewey) on the teachings of Rousseau. Dewey described the School of Organic Education as an experiment in Rousseau's principles, making no mention of Henderson. Dewey wrote, "To this spot [Fairhope] during the past few years students and experts have made pilgrimages, and the influence of Mrs. Johnson's model has led to the starting of similar schools in different parts of the United States."[25] Even before the publication of *Schools of To-morrow*, Dewey reported on his visit to Fairhope, suggesting the School of Organic Education continue as an "experiment station" so its method could "spread and permeate the rural schools of the county and then of adjacent counties."[26] There is no mention of Henderson in the written record of Dewey's report.

Some scholars noticed the omissions. Writing in 1961, Lawrence A. Cremin observed that Marietta Johnson "undoubtedly" borrowed the term *organic education* from Charles Hanford Henderson.[27] (In the bibliography, Cremin also cited *Education: A History*, a 1946 book by A. Gordon Melvin that portrayed "the [Francis] Parker-Henderson-Johnson stream as the authentic stream of progressive education").[28] Moreover, Joseph W. Newman suggested in 1999 that Dewey did not acknowledge Henderson's work in organic education because the two men were rivals.[29] In 2015, Thomas Fallace and Victoria Fantozzi likewise noted that Dewey failed to mention Henderson in *Schools of To-morrow*.[30] It is important to point out, however, that Dewey went *beyond* the omission these scholars discussed, actually implying in the book that the term, organic education, was *Johnson's*. (Dewey wrote, "She calls her methods of education 'organic' because they follow the natural growth of the pupil.")[31]

Given Dewey's professional activities in 1902, he was in all probability aware of the publication of *Education and the Larger Life* and its chapter titled "Organic Education." From 1894 to 1904 Dewey was Chairman of the Department of Philosophy, Psychology, and Pedagogy at the University of Chicago. He also directed the faculty of the school of education and served as editor of *The Elementary School Teacher*. During this period, Henderson's writings were cited in numerous professional publications ranging from general education and industrial education journals, to official reports and religious magazines.[32] Moreover, *The New York Times* highlighted the connection between Henderson, organic education, and Marietta Johnson shortly before her Greenwich friends invited Dewey to visit Fairhope. On March 16, 1913, the *Times* ran a full-page article on Johnson's school under the headline, "Founder of Organic Education Tells of New School." A subheading stated, "Mrs. Marietta I. Johnson of Fairhope, Ala. Discusses a System of Developing the Latent Powers of Children and Points Out Weaknesses of Prevailing Methods of Teaching." The *Times* reporter wrote a brief introduction and then recorded Johnson's words for the remainder of the article in which she credited Oppenheim's book and then Henderson's for influencing her pedagogy and program. Johnson stated:

> The next step in my process came when I procured Dr. Henderson's "Education and the Larger Life." This is a remarkable contribution to our educational science. It puts the whole interest upon the doer, not upon the thing he does.

Knowledge, itself, is of no value, unless the person can profit by it, and in consequence, there is much useless knowledge in the world. We all know that. Yet, despite our knowledge of it, we suppress the child in every way, almost, that he may "learn."[33]

It is difficult to imagine that John Dewey, a New York resident, would have been unaware of the *Times* article; however—even if that were the case—Dewey's own writing clearly documents his knowledge of Henderson's prior work in organic education. In October 2015—five months after the release of *1915* *Schools of To-morrow*—Dewey published a piece in *School and Home Education* in which he responded to William C. Bagley's criticisms of his new book. Dewey denied the allegation that *Schools of To-morrow* focused on his "disciples" who put his theories into practice. He answered Bagley by writing, "So far as Mrs. Johnson's Organic Education is not the result of her own public school experience, it is inspired by the writings of Dr. Hanford Henderson."[34] It would appear that Dewey neglected to appropriately credit his rival in a book with a large readership but used Henderson's name to sidestep criticism in a publication with a smaller circulation.

Following the publication of *Schools of To-morrow*, Marietta Johnson became increasingly identified with John Dewey rather than Charles Hanford Henderson. This is evident in Alabama publications, previously mentioned, that cite Dewey as an early influence while failing to mention Henderson. (In *The Transformation of the School*, Cremin noted that "Mrs. Johnson read other works [in addition to Oppenheim] that helped her in formulating her ideas, among them *Education and the Larger Life* by C. Hanford Henderson, the scientist-headmaster of Pratt Institute in New York, and some early pamphlets of John Dewey.")[35] Henderson's legacy was also diminished by misspellings of his name in Marietta Johnson's memoir, completed shortly after her death in 1938 and housed at Teacher's College prior to its 1974 publication by the University of Alabama Press. While Johnson named Henderson as being—along with Oppenheim—a key influence on her pedagogy and school program, his name was repeatedly appeared in the text as C. *Manford* Henderson. The misspelling was replicated in George Allen Brown's Memoir of Marietta Johnson, published at the eighteenth annual meeting of the Alabama Historical Association and again in *Thirty Years with an Idea*. According to Brown, Marietta Johnson stated, "It was when she studied 'Education and the Larger Life' by Charles Manford Henderson that she felt she had something practical upon which to start, and with her *own* small boys, she began to experiment."[36]

Schools of To-morrow initially underwent nine printings, and after 1915 Dewey's prominence grew. Henderson never came close to equaling his former rival's influence. By Marietta Johnson's own acknowledgment, Dewey's support helped her raise funds for her school, and she became one of the first U.S. women educational leaders to gain recognition for twentieth-century reform efforts. Half a century later, Lawrence Cremin recognized Johnson's pioneering work in *The Transformation of the School*. He called the School of Organic Education "easily the most child-centered of the early experimental schools."[37] As early as 1919, Johnson became a founding member and one of five speakers at the first meeting of the Progressive Education Association (PEA), which became the most influential voice for child-centered pedagogy in the United States.

The reader might wonder why, if he was reluctant to give credit to his rival Henderson, Dewey would offer unqualified praise to Johnson, even suggesting organic education was *her* term. The answer may lie in the prevalent, binary view of gender that placed men in the role of theorists and women in the role of practitioners. As a woman, Johnson was never a threat to Dewey's prominence as an educational thinker, as Henderson was in 1915. (The early importance of the two men is suggested in a 1920 *Washington Times* article that claims progressive education began with Dewey and the Laboratory School at the University of Chicago, and with Henderson's manual training experiments and writing.)[38] The theory/practice dichotomy that marginalized women's contributions to educational thought over time (both before and after Dewey) has been explored by feminist scholars from Jane Roland Martin to Susan Douglas Franzosa.[39] They demonstrate the dichotomy is a false one, inasmuch as the women who experimented with new educational practices were also informing theory. It is noteworthy that, over one hundred years after the founding of Marietta Johnson's school, scholars have continued to discuss the degree to which her contributions to educational thought may have been marginalized. An example is Jerry Aldridge and Lois McFayden Christiansen's 2013 book, *Stealing from the Mother: The Marginalization of Women in Education and Psychology from 1900–2010*. The authors note that "many of the progressive ideas Marietta developed have been basically ignored or attributed to John Dewey."[40] Other scholars have explored Dewey's views that both empowered and marginalized women in such works as Charlene Haddock Seigfried's edited book, *Feminist Interpretations of John Dewey*[41] and Francis Maher's essay, "John Dewey, Progressive Education and Feminist Pedagogies: Issues of Gender and Authority."[42] In examining the historiography of gender and progressive education, Kathleen Weiler observed that "when Dewey addressed the situation of women, he never seems to have considered the idea that 'man' was a privileged location."[43] Weiler concluded that Dewey "dealt unevenly" with "different representations of women, and most frequently ignored the question of gender altogether."[44]

Charles Hanford Henderson died in 1941. Five years later Melvin wrote that Henderson, a superb writer who was "modest to a fault," was "[o]ne of the greatest educators of the twentieth century" who, "far from being heralded from the housetops, was almost forgotten even before his death."[45] In 1914 Henderson opened Marienfeld, an open-air school in Samarcand, North Carolina. (The school had the same name as a pioneering boys' camp Henderson founded in Chesham, New Hampshire. There he concluded that camp was necessary to keep some students from experiencing summer learning loss.) After moving to the South, Henderson remained there for the rest of his life, retiring in Tryon, North Carolina, and spending winters in Daytona Beach. It is likely that the White sisters first met him when he was lecturing at the Sloyd Training School in Boston. Beyond having an interest in educational theory, they operated a camp for little boys at Heath called Cross Lots and would have had an additional reason for interest in Henderson's work.

Even though Miss White's Home School was founded well before Marietta Johnson's, it would be virtually impossible to determine who established the *first* school to operate under the principles of organic education. However, given the information in Flora White's school booklets, the connection between organic education and the slöjd movement, and the interest in the new education in New England and elsewhere, there are compelling reasons to revisit school founders in the formative period of progressive education, in order to better understand the movement. It is noteworthy that at the turn of the twenty-first century, when historians began to explore the contributions of women progressive educators, the lack of sources caused scholars to begin their research with women who had been associated with John Dewey. After all, they had to start *somewhere*. While this effort produced important scholarship, it also had a limiting effect. Of the female founders depicted in Alan R. Sadovnik and Susan F. Semel's edited book, *Founding Mothers and Others: Women Educational Leaders during the Progressive Era,* most had a connection to Dewey. Among the book's founders who established schools before 1935, none were situated in New England. In view of the region's prominence in the history of education—and the evidence left by Flora White—there are likely other women leaders in that region whose stories would be useful to scholars. If, as Dewey suggested, educational experimentation was occurring all over the United States, historians would be well advised to explore experimental schools that existed across a broad geographical area.

WHITE'S PROGRAM OF STUDY

The two booklets from Flora White's Concord school provide important details about all aspects of its program. Founded as Miss White's Home School for Children, it was usually called Miss White's Home School or sometimes Miss White's Home School for Girls. Flora likened it to "a refined, well-ordered family, each member of which is expected to show careful consideration for others."[46] She informed prospective parents that the school's "happy home" ambiance "eliminates the dangers of the large boarding-school, and provides a natural, wholesome atmosphere for growing girls and boys." White added, "Parents who would not ordinarily send their children from home feel entire confidence in placing them in this school."[47]

The 1900–1901 booklet states the school is "organized for girls" but would consider exceptions, especially when a family wanted to place "two or more children" in the same school.[48] The 1906–1907 booklet is more definitive on admission requirements: the school accepted girls under seventeen as day and boarding students and boys under twelve as day students "provided they are unquestionably desirable as companions and pupils."[49] Parents and guardians who were not known to Flora White were asked to submit references with applications.

In 1900–1901, the entire enrollment of Miss White's Home School was limited to twenty, including a maximum of eight boarding students. Six years later, the booklet simply stated, "The number is limited, in order that each pupil may receive the individual attention necessary to the utmost progress, but is sufficient to give stimulus and natural competition."[50] In 1906, Miss White's Home School was comprised of three departments—Lower, Intermediate, and Upper. Intermediate students paid 25 percent more tuition than Lower department pupils; Upper department students paid 50 percent more than the rate charged for Miss White's youngest students.

Although very little information remains on White's faculty, she assured parents that "The teachers in all departments are of established reputation and marked ability."[51] Secondary sources document two teachers from Miss White's Home School: Edith F. Whitney, who graduated from Radcliffe in 1898 and taught at the Concord school in 1900; and Myrtle Anne Ball, who had both a B.A. and M.A. from Lawrence College when she taught at Miss White's Home School from 1907 to 1909.

The teachers taught a curriculum that had a "[u]nity of purpose" focusing on a "definite preparation for higher education and for life." Academic subjects included English, three foreign languages (Latin, German, and French), mathematics, and science, with each program of study drawing on the prior year's instruction—and "in every case [being] adapted to the pupil to meet the demands of her highest development."[52] White noted that the study of English took "precedence of all other linguistic studies."[53] Looking back in 1977, Adeline Eveleth Cabot concurred, recalling that the instruction she received in Latin and mathematics did not compare to the teaching of English literature. She reported:

> We read poetry and had Latin and math. These were taught by a lovely lady named Miss Emma Smith, who did all the translations for us so that I really

didn't learn that much about Latin and math but had a wonderful grounding in English literature. Mr. Allen French gave us a course in art in the early Italian painters with pictures which was also very good.[54]

French was an author, historian, antiquarian, and Concord resident who held degrees from MIT and Harvard. His course was in keeping with the school's offering of "Informal talks upon Art, Music, and Literature by eminent persons" that made an "interesting and valuable addition to the regular school course."[55] Students could receive special instruction in piano, violin, singing, advanced drawing, and dancing."[56] This appealed to students like Elizabeth Darling Babcock, who said music was a "lifelong interest" that inspired her to become a violinist and founding member of the Concord Orchestra.[57] School booklets extolled the "historic and literary" associations of Concord and attested to their "stimulating" effect on young students.[58] As a young girl, Babcock had a strong sense of Concord's historical and literary past, as confirmed by an entry in the diary she kept as an eight-year-old: "Sunday, Mr. Sanborn came to dinner today. He was not invited but that is all right if you are a sage."[59] (She was referring to Frank Sanborn, a founder with Bronson Alcott of the Concord School of Philosophy, who was defended by Concord townspeople after supporting John Brown's raid on Harper's Ferry in 1859.)

An important emphasis of Miss White's Home School was motor training in which "Games, Sloyd, and Gymnastics (both educational and corrective) form[ed] an integral part of the school work."[60] Flora White claimed to offer a quality of motor training that could not be obtained elsewhere. She gave special attention to "the development of physique," a priority made possible by a "well-equipped" school gymnasium[61] that White directly supervised and incorporated into the program as "a fundamental part of the school life."[62]

Just as Marietta Johnson's students studied geography in the "woods, fields, streams and bay" and worked on manual arts,[63] so Miss White's Home School utilized the "wood, field, and river," in Concord that provided "constant attractions to out-of-door life."[64] The White sisters also operated an optional summer program at Plover Hill in Heath where girls could be active indoors and outdoors. They could play basketball[65] or make use of ropes, a climbing ladder, and other apparatus for indoor gymnasium work. They could also enjoy hiking in the hills, for which they were instructed to bring "stout walking boots."[66] Throughout the experience, the girls followed an energetic regimen in a natural setting. A typical day at Plover Hill began at 6:30 a.m. with breakfast, an hour of gardening, and a domestic science lesson. The girls then gathered on the veranda for an hour's Shakespeare study, after which they had a gymnastics lesson and a game of basketball. In good weather they might have a picnic on the cliffs. Next was lunch and a rest, followed by their choice of an afternoon outing—for example, a cross-country walk to the top of a neighboring hill or a visit to the woods "to secure twigs for their rustic work." The girls had free time after supper, which was followed by constellation study and "telling the myths associated with them."[67] It was a regimen that directly countered warnings from the medical and scientific community that young women should be limited in their physical and intellectual pursuits.

AN AWKWARD ENDORSEMENT

If Marietta Johnson worried about maiming children through false pedagogy, Flora White also had to worry about maiming young women through false assumptions about their nature. Such inferences were especially problematic when voiced by a prominent psychologist and endorser of Miss White's Home School. G. Stanley Hall led the child study movement that attracted Flora White early in her career, and once envisioned that child study would become *the women's science*. When White founded her school in 1897, Hall provided her with a letter of endorsement that appears prominently in the 1900–1901 bulletin. Nevertheless, in 1904 Hall published a two-volume work, *Adolescence: Its Psychology and Its Relation to Physiology, Anthropology, Sociology, Sex, Crime, Religion and Education*.[68] Drawing from evolutionary theory, he argued that the adolescent female was "at the top of the human curve from which the higher super-man of the future is to evolve."[69] He wrote that adolescent girls were very susceptible to reproductive organ damage and should single-mindedly devote themselves to the natural role of motherhood. Hall also argued that the biological differentiation of the sexes at puberty necessitated educational separation during adolescence.

Sixty-five years after the publication of Hall's book, Lawrence Cremin observed that "there is no understanding the present apart from . . . [Hall's] contribution," adding that he "injected into the mainstream of American educational thought some of the most radical—and I happen to think virulent—doctrines of the twentieth century."[70] (Cremin's comment likely stems from the fact that, in addition to studying the differences between men and women, Hall also did work in racial eugenics.) As early as 1903, in an address to the NEA, Hall had quoted medical opinion that women were in danger of excessive brain work that could harm their reproductive function. He said that women primarily had a procreative role and should be spared the "illusory" freedoms promised by higher education.[71] Hall viewed female graduate students at Clark University as "individuals"—that is, they did not represent most women and were the terminal products of evolution since they were both single and childless.[72] (His argument recalled Dr. Edward H. Clarke thirty years earlier, who blamed college education for a variety of female disorders.) Hall reserved special comment for the "bachelor woman" whose "mentality" makes her a "good fellow" and "compassionate in all the broad intellectual spheres." (This, of course, is the category in which he would have placed Flora White.) Hall noted that the bachelor woman had:

> taken up and utilized in her own life all that was meant for her descendents, and has so overdrawn her account with heredity that, like every perfectly and completely developed individual, she is also completely sterile. This is the very apotheosis of selfishness from the standpoint of every biological ethics. [73]

Although such comments would have been hurtful, White did not alienate Hall or drop him as a reference. Given Hall's prominence, she likely assessed the benefit of using his name as a reference for her school. At the same time, White gave no indication of scaling back her efforts to develop young women intellectually and physically to prepare them for higher education. Instead, she appears to have made a decision to feature Hall less prominently in 1906–1907 than in 1900–1901 (before he made his controversial remarks to the NEA or published *Adolescence*). No letter of endorsement from G. Stanley Hall appears in 1906–1907; his name, title, university affiliation, and city of residence are simply included with the other references.

Flora White's correspondence suggests she distanced herself from Hall in other ways. Hall is remembered as a prominent opponent of coeducation, as reflected in David Tyack and Elisabeth Hansot's seminal work, *Learning Together: A History of Coeducation in American Public Schools*. [74] Late in life, Flora White looked back over her career and disagreed with Hall. In a 1940 letter to the president of the Westfield Alumni Association, Flora described Miss White's Home School (which she had characterized in 1900 as being *organized for girls* with young male students attending as *exceptions*). This time, four decades later, White wrote that the school was *coeducational*, without qualification. [75]

Flora White's most telling assessment of G. Stanley Hall's views can be found in her poem, "Redemption," in which she describes a fern growing in the crevice of a rock, under an old maple tree. G. Stanley Hall accompanied White when she found the fern, and she notes that she wrote the poem for him. Composed at an unspecified time, "Redemption" appears in the 1939 publication of *Poems by Mary A. White and Flora White*. [76]

The dedication of a poem is usually an occasion for honoring someone. In this case, however, White names Hall in order to counter his criticism of all women who do not bear children. "Redemption" describes the life cycle of the fern which—unlike other plants—does not flower in order to propagate. It is lovely though it lacks—even scorns—"floweret or fruitage," the female parts of plant reproduction. Instead, the fern reproduces by alternating generations. [77] (While many plants grow to full adulthood straight out of the seed, the fern has an intermediate stage called a gametophyte, with spores being produced on the underside of mature plants. A gametophyte will fertilize itself, or others. Once the fertilization occurs, the adult fern will begin growing.)

By citing a case in nature in which alternating generations reproduce, White answers Hall's accusation of selfishness. She uses verse to explain her own life choice to forego marriage and family and redeem the world through teaching the young.[78]

The poem's title suggests a new interpretation of a traditional view of women that became widely accepted in the United States following the American Revolution. Amid discussions of the role women might play in the new country, domestic life gained political meaning in the ideal of the Republican Mother. Her role was to *redeem* the new nation by educating sons to be moral and virtuous. The ideal persisted well into the twentieth century, reflecting a belief that men did the actual work of politics while women's political role was limited to rearing good citizens.[79] Here White offers a new interpretation by asserting the merit of single women who redeem humankind by educating children. This attitude was reinforced in White's 1941 interview with a reporter from *The Daily Oklahoman* who wrote that succeeding generations of pupils came to Miss White's School so that "now Flora has so many 'children' scattered over the county that her train is met by them in Chicago, Kansas City and all along the route from New England to Oklahoma."[80]

PARENTS AND STUDENTS

In establishing her Concord school, Flora White had to not only consider the needs of children, but also of their parents. This fact is illustrated by the experience of another early progressive educator, Caroline Pratt, upon founding the City and Country School in 1914. Pratt hoped to establish a school for poor immigrant children in Greenwich Village. Although Pratt's offer of free tuition was attractive to families, the parents resisted her desire to incorporate play beyond kindergarten. They believed their children's well-being in the new country depended on success in school, which the immigrant parents understood in traditional terms. When Pratt could not convince them of the importance of exploration and play in learning, she had to look to another segment of the Greenwich Village population—artistic and creative people attracted by low rents for studios and living spaces. With a new parent clientele, the school flourished.

Flora White relied on word-of-mouth recommendations, school booklets, and advertisements in *The Atlantic Monthly* and *The Nation* to reach prospective parents of her Concord school. Although there are no lists of White's parent clientele or student body, a number of primary and secondary sources identify individuals with Flora White and her educational program. Taken together, they offer valuable insights about the milieu of Miss White's Home School.

The school's parents were largely upper-class members of old New England families, prominent Concord residents, or successful professionals who placed a high value on their children's education. For example, Mary Ogden Abbot's mother (Mary Adams Abbott) was a direct descendant of presidents John Adams and John Quincy Adams. The girl's father, Grafton St. Loe Abbott (Harvard 1877), was a lawyer and businessman. The son of a U.S. Congressman, Grafton Abbott's business interests took him "far afield"— even to a chain of sugar properties in Cuba.[81] Mary Adams Abbott enjoyed an active life and at age fifty-six accompanied her daughter on a hunting expedition in Balistan, a mountainous region in the northern part of present-day Pakistan.

Sidney Coolidge (Harvard 1886)—the father of another of White's students—was a direct descendent of President Thomas Jefferson and of entrepreneur Francis Cabot Lowell, who is credited with bringing the First Industrial Revolution to New England. Coolidge was Treasurer of Lowell Bleachery in Lowell, Massachusetts.

Frederick Alcott Pratt, another parent, was the son of Anna Bronson Alcott. (She was Louisa May Alcott's oldest sister who inspired the character Meg in the semiautobiographical novel, *Little Women*.) Frederick Pratt was himself the inspiration for the character Demi in *Little Men*. Pratt and his wife, Jessica Cate Pratt, named their daughter Louisa Alcott after her great-aunt. They were active in establishing the Orchard House in Concord (the family home where Louisa May Alcott grew up) in the famous author's memory.

One father, Frederick Winsor Jr. was well known in education circles. An 1893 Harvard graduate, Winsor founded Middlesex School on the edge of Concord in 1901 and sent at least one daughter (Dorothy) and one son (John) to study with the White sisters. Prior to moving to Concord, Winsor had previously taught at two boys' preparatory schools, including Phillips Exeter Academy. He became headmaster of the New Country School for Boys in Baltimore where he incorporated educational slöjd into the program. Winsor—who also introduced slöjd at Middlesex—hoped his nondenominational school would be distinctive from other New England boys' boarding schools. His mission was to "find the promise that lies hidden" within each student.[82]

Another father, Walter L. Fisher, was the son of the President of Hanover College in Indiana. He was a prominent Chicago lawyer who moved to Washington, D.C., to become Secretary of the Interior under President William Howard Taft. Walter Fisher was married to Mabel Taylor Fisher, "a strong woman who educated her children in the social responsibilities by example and word."[83] Their daughter Margaret attended Miss White's Home School in Concord, as well as Miss Madeira's School in Washington, D.C., and the Francis Parker School in Chicago. Family correspondence reveals "high expectations for success and personal integrity" among the Fishers. Margaret, for example, once received a letter from her older brother Frederick stating, "You know how important achievement is to our tribe."[84]

General Charles Knight Darling (Dartmouth 1885)—Elizabeth Darling Babcock's father—was a prominent Boston lawyer, a veteran of the Spanish-American War, and a Son of the American Revolution. His wife, Elizabeth Holmes Darling, was disaster chairman for the local Red Cross and a member of several women's clubs. She served on the board of the Concord Home for the Aged.

The available biographical information on several students from Miss White's Home School indicates that in later life they distinguished themselves in academia, the arts, and civic leadership. For example, Mary Ogden Abbott was an accomplished artist in several media, especially wood carving. A graduate of the School of the Museum of Fine Arts in Boston, she carved the wooden doors at the entrance to the Department of the Interior in Washington, D.C., Abbott's landscape paintings depicted views of the American West, the western Himalayas, and Mexico. She established a Concord studio that was formerly occupied by famed sculptor Daniel Chester French. From 1920 to 1928, Abbott and her mother traveled throughout the globe, backpacking in the Grand Canyon and exploring Asia, the Middle East, and Europe. Abbott hunted wild game in Kashmir, Ladekh, and Baltisan and shot a jaguar in Mexico that was sent to the Museum of Natural History in New York. A skilled equestrian, she maintained stables in Concord until 1977 when she gave them to the city.

Another student, Mary Lowell Coolidge, attended Miss White's and then the Winsor School in Boston. She graduated from Bryn Mawr and received a PhD from Radcliffe. Coolidge became a professor of philosophy and then Dean of Wellesley College where she was known for her clear thinking and ability to cut to the heart of an issue. An excellent equestrian with a strong aesthetic sense, Coolidge shared Flora White's view that individual differences should be protected and encouraged. This is illustrated by Coolidge's reaction, as an adult, to a physician's order that she limit her use of cigarettes. She calculated her allotment and divided each cigarette into thirds, placing one small segment in a cigarette holder. One Saturday morning, Coolidge overheard a colleague in the Faculty Common Room recalling the idiosyncrasies of former Wellesley professors. As she divided her cigarette and carefully inserted one-third into the slender smoking accessory, Coolidge remarked, "It is a pity that there are no longer any eccentrics on the faculty."[85]

Margaret Fisher, who attended Miss White's Home School, entered the University of Wisconsin at age nineteen and received a degree in economics two years later, writing a thesis on the American labor movement. When asked why she wanted to study economics, Fisher replied that she thought women should be able to make a living. She began working as an architect but later changed direction, following her passion as an abstract painter. Fisher enrolled in the Art Institute of Chicago and also studied at the Art Students League in New York City. Born in 1898, she had several prestigious solo exhibitions late in life including Harvard University in 1973 and the Art Institute of Chicago in 1975. Fisher died in 1990, and a 2003 article offered the following characterization: "In an artistic career that spanned seventy years, Margaret Fisher . . . produced a body of work that reflects the vicissitudes of American modernism even while it resists classification."[86]

Dorothy Winsor (1896–1986) attended Miss White's Home School between the ages of six and twelve and later recalled these years in an interview conducted by her grandson, Rick Zamore.[87] She was related to Ethel Lyman Paine (later Moors) on her mother's side and—like Moors—was a direct descendant of a signer of the Declaration of Independence. Dorothy learned the principles of slöjd from Flora White and maintained a lifelong interest in woodworking. (In 1973 she reported to former college classmates, "I replaced our cellar stairs with a minimum of masculine assistance.")[88] After Miss White's, Dorothy spent a year in Paris and studied in Boston at the school founded by her aunt, Mary Pickard Winsor. She attended Radcliffe College for two years; taught geometry, psychology, and American government at Chamberlayne School in Boston; and in 1922 married Eliot Walter Bisbee, a teacher at Middlesex School. The couple had six children. In 1927 she took an unusual step for a married woman with a large family by returning to college to study history. Her interest in public affairs extended from the international to the local. For example, the May 14, 1942, *Boston Transfer* described her leadership of a Federal Union group that sponsored a pro-United Nations rally in the city.[89] After her husband's death in 1950, Bisbee became founder and director of the Citizens for the Boston Public Schools and president of the local chapter of the League of Women Voters. She expressed pride that her family members had few disagreements despite their large numbers, a claim that was born out when her mother died. The family found a "fair and efficient" way to divide two trunks of silver among the eight grandchildren using a system that was later published in a 1990 issue of *Management Science*.[90]

Henry Howard Brooks, who also spent his early years at Miss White's Home School, studied at the School of the Museum of Fine Arts in Boston and painted at the Fenway Studios in that city. A member of the Guild of Boston Artists, Brooks exhibited at the Pennsylvania Academy of Fine Arts and the Corcoran Gallery in Washington, D.C. He eventually moved to Cape

Cod. Brooks's oil paintings are characterized by a clean, crisp style and strong use of color.

The parents and students of Miss White's Home School were an active and colorful lot. Although the girls were marginalized due to their gender, they had both race and class privilege. School booklets make no mention of free tuition or opportunities for scholarship students. Since White enjoyed neither family wealth nor substantive philanthropic support, she depended on tuition and fees to operate her school. Primary sources describe, however, one student who was not from an elite background: Catherine White, the daughter of Flora's brother Joseph, who lived in Nebraska with her parents and brother Charles (1893–1975). Catherine's older brother, Joseph "David," died of meningitis at age eleven in 1900.

During their marriage, Joseph and Jennie White moved from the town of Pickrell, Nebraska, to nearby Beatrice and then back to Pickrell where they ran a general merchandise store and post office. In 1908 they and their children relocated to northwest Oklahoma. Jennie White's father (James "Jimmy" Johnson) lived there, where he had operated a hotel and saloon in Gage and in 1907 homesteaded a section of land six and one-half miles northwest of the town. The year before Johnson became a homesteader, anti-liquor advocate Carrie Nation came to Gage on a lecture tour and received a "cold reception."[91] Although Johnson was active and colorful, he did not enjoy class privilege. He had owned and operated a hotel on the Erie Canal and worked on construction projects along the Erie Canal and the Southern Kansas Railroad. First coming into Oklahoma Territory in 1897, he saw the semiarid, High Plains environment evolve from open ranch country to homesteads. Johnson would divide the section he homesteaded between his children, deeding the northern half to his son Charles and the southern half to his daughter Jennie. Johnson would also build separate homes for his two children (and their families) on each half section.

Given Joseph White's difficult upbringing—and differences in lifestyle that distinguished Flora from her brother—she was mindful of the opportunities she enjoyed that had not been available to Joseph or his family. When Joseph's daughter Catherine was sixteen, Flora asked to instruct her at Concord during 1907–1908, and her brother agreed. When he visited Miss White's Home School, Joseph White wrote a self-deprecating account of his own background in a tongue-in-cheek description of his sisters and their female dining companions:

> along about supper time they have dinner which is just like supper only you must call it dinner, and then you have to dress for dinner, or as it appeared to me they undress, that is the laidies [sic] do, and there is where I made my first mistake. . . . I naturally thought I must dress as near like them as I could so I put on a clean pair of overall [sic] took off my shirts pulled up my galluses and

I thought I was pretty well fixed except I didn't show quite so much of my front as the ladies. . . . [Later, while the meal was in progress] a person brings for each one an individual bath tub with a slice of lemon in it, well I thought it was lemonade sure enough and drank it all down, and I noticed all the female parties at the table were all looking at me, and one of them said, how primitive and another said isn't it just to [*sic*] sweet for anything and I answered right up and said it wasn't sweet enough and that was what was the matter with it . . . then I discovered I had drunk the wash water.[92]

Although Catherine appreciated the opportunity for exposure and growth at Miss White's Home School, she found the year to be stressful, largely because the backgrounds of her New England classmates differed markedly from her own Nebraska upbringing. One year after returning from Miss White's Home School, Catherine White moved with her family to northwest Oklahoma to the half-section deeded by her Grandfather Johnson. She attended high school for a period of time but dropped out to teach, first in a country school and then in a town school in Gage. She also attended normal school, married, and raised seven children on a farm. She was an avid reader and enjoyed painting with water colors. Her possessions at the time of her death in 1964 included some linen handkerchiefs that Ellen Tucker Emerson penned with Catherine's name, a photograph of her roommate at Miss White's Home School (Mary Williams, the granddaughter of the famous actor Lawrence Barrett), and a Tiffany pin from her classmate, Mary Coolidge.

SELLING MISS WHITE'S HOME SCHOOL

Flora White wrote that the Concord school was sold in 1914 at the request of her sister Mary, who suffered from poor health. The sisters retired to Heath where, for the next twenty years, Flora continued to tutor students in "Boston, Greenfield, Deerfield [Massachusetts] and in California."[93]

The sale of White's Concord school was noted by Porter E. Sargent, who in 1915 published the first edition of *A Handbook of the Best Private Schools of the United States*. Beginning in 1916, he continued to publish an annual edition titled *The Handbook of Private Schools*. Sargent wrote that the Concord School for Girls ("formerly Miss White's") had been taken over in 1914 by Marianna Woodhull (1864–1935).[94] A minister's daughter, Woodhull had worked for two years at Bates College in Maine where she was Professor of Fine Arts and Dean of Women. With an A.B. from Smith and an A.M. from Columbia, her academic credentials surpassed those of Flora White. In 1907, Woodhull had also published a collection of twelve essays titled *The Epic of Paradise Lost*. She had been a teacher in female seminaries in Morristown, New Jersey, and Washington, D.C., and had studied at Oxford University.

Perhaps to minimize the newness of her enterprise and draw on Flora White's reputation, Woodhull also stated in early magazine ads that her school had formerly been Miss White's. In addition, Woodhull advertised her school's founding date as 1897 (when Flora White began teaching in Concord). Porter Sargent wrote that Woodhull's "broad training and social experience enable[d] her to maintain high scholastic standards and a home of quiet dignity, simplicity, and charm."[95] However, by June 1916, Woodhull advertised in *Scribner's* that the Concord School for Girls would be in a new location in September—on a hill overlooking the town with an acreage suitable for a country school. By 1917, Woodhull had introduced a new school name: *Thenford, The Concord School for Girls*. (Thenford had been the ancestral seat of the Woodhull family in England since the sixteenth century.) The difference from Miss White's Home School became more apparent in 1918 when Thenford began to include military drills in its program. By fall 1919, Marianna Woodhull had left Concord to become the dean at William Smith College in New York, a position she held for one year. Beginning in 1919, her school ceased to appear in Porter Sargent's handbooks or in magazines where Woodhull had previously advertised.

After she left William Smith College, Woodhull's career path is unclear. The *Smith Alumnae Quarterly* reported in 1920 that Woodhull was spending the winter in Paris. In 1931 Woodhull notified the same publication that she had moved to Brooklyn to be near her classes at Brooklyn College. At the time she was teaching four evening classes, five nights a week. She also reported teaching a summer class at Hunter College. Woodhull's death was reported in *The San Diego Union* on February 19, 1935, under the headline, "La Jolla Woman Takes Own Life."[96] The paper stated that Woodhull had been worried about financial problems and left a suicide note for her brother. The article made no mention of her work in Concord—only that she had attended classes at Oxford and taught dramatic arts at Hunter College in New York. Marianna Woodhull's tragic circumstances suggest the difficulty women faced in academic careers and in financing a private school.

In 1916—after Woodhull vacated the building formerly occupied by Miss White's Home School—a new Montessori school began at the same address. Maria Montessori had recently made her first, highly publicized visit to the United States. Anne Bixby Chamberlin, a Concord resident, spearheaded an effort to enable Hope Gardner Dillingham to become principal of the Concord Montessori and Elementary School. Chamberlin's actions underscore the findings of Rugg and Shumaker and Ravitch on the importance of upper-middle-class parents in establishing early progressive schools.

Dillingham, a widow in her late thirties who had studied under Montessori in California, opened the school to girls and boys and capped her enrollment at fifty. Although the initiative was successful, Dillingham died unexpectedly in 1920. Philip McFarland notes that, under Dillingham, the Con-

cord Montessori and Elementary School had followed "the educational philosophy of Montessori herself." Its tenets included a belief that children
differ from adults—and begin their learning at birth; that children take a
"natural pleasure in mastering" their learning environment; that they learn
best by playing with "educational toys" in an "open classroom;" that learning
does not involve the "passive acquisition of facts," but rather, "an active
mastery of the ability to do things for one's self;" that an imposed silence and
a lack of movement hampers learning; that children who are given "interesting tasks" will create their own order; that the school should support every
child's right to fully develop his potential; and that the school should be part
of the community, with parents and children alike involved in the educational
process.[97]

With a void in private school opportunities for girls and young women
that had once been filled by Miss White's Home School, Concord residents
set about founding a new school, Concord Academy, which today is regarded
as one of the top secondary schools in the United States.

FOUNDING OF CONCORD ACADEMY

In a 1977 interview, Harold Cabot explained the impetus for establishing a
new school:

> I understand the reason for the founding of Concord Academy was that many
> of the families in Concord didn't want to send their daughters away to board-
> ing school in some other city and never see them. So they decided to start a
> boarding school here that would be both a day school and a boarding school.
> To get top teachers on the faculty, they attracted girls from other cities to come
> as boarders and the Concord girls would be day students. That worked very
> well from everybody's point of view. Of course, it cost much less for a day
> student than for a boarding student.[98]

Harold Cabot served several years as chairman of the Board of Trustees of
Concord Academy. His wife, Adeline Eveleth Cabot, was an alumna of Miss
White's Home School.

Before Hope Dillingham's death, Anne Chamberlin had already identified Grace Harriman, a Radcliffe graduate in her early thirties, who agreed
to administer an upper school for girls who advanced beyond Montessori
instruction. It opened in September 1919 with a faculty consisting of Harriman and one additional teacher. Following Dillingham's death in 1920, the
upper school combined with the Concord Montessori and Elementary School
to form Concord Academy. Although Chamberlin, a woman of means, had
used her personal funds to offset financial shortfalls, the new school needed a
nonprofit corporation, a board of trustees, and more spacious grounds in

which to grow. Chamberlin was hearing impaired and felt she was not well suited for board and committee work. She stepped aside, and a Committee of Twenty—including Helen Wadleigh Hoar, who supported Miss White's Home School—became incorporators of Concord Academy in 1922. Mary Pickard Winsor, founder and principal of the Winsor School in Boston (and Frederick Jr.'s sister), knew "the situation in Concord;" she "heartily endorse[d] the idea," believing "in its prospect of success."[99] Originally founded as a school for girls, Concord Academy became coeducational in 1971.

SCHOOL AND COMMUNITY

In the twenty-two years between the founding of Miss White's Home School and the establishment of the Concord Montessori and Elementary School, Concord parents grew to accept—even appreciate—White's use of motor activities as a legitimate means of education. When Flora White recalled the accusation that she was ruining home life in Concord (by interesting students in games, slöjd, and gymnastics), she believed she was *changing* the town. Although White cannot be credited with the ultimate success of Concord Academy, she helped to prepare the ground for that institution to grow and prosper. It is noteworthy that some of the same families that supported Miss White's Home School were instrumental in establishing Concord Academy. As for the school's educational philosophy, an excerpt from the 1921–1922 catalogue would have pleased Flora White:

> The Academy seeks to adapt its program as far as possible to the needs of each pupil, arousing her interest in her work, and leaving her the greatest degree of freedom consistent with orderly social relations and the atmosphere conducive to the best intellectual growth. The pupils share progressively in the government of the school and in arranging all its activities.
>
> The music will continue to be conducted by a pupil of Mr. Surette. The art is supervised by Mrs. Alice Ruggles Sohier, an artist of recognized standing.[100]

The excerpt is in keeping with White's focus on individual student need, cultivation of pupil interest, emphasis on the arts, and inclusion of eminent persons in the educational program. It echoes sentiments in White's 1906–1907 booklet, which stated, "The pupils grow in their interests, while forming just judgments and exercising self-control, till love of study and fitting conduct becomes habitual. An appetite for knowledge is thus created, while an ability to acquire knowledge is being developed."[101] It is noteworthy that by Concord Academy's second year, it had been "considerably enlarged" to provide—among other features—a "larger yard . . . [to] provide space for athletics outdoors."[102]

Despite these offerings, readers may wonder why—if residents thought Concord's public schools were second only to Quincy's—there was a perceived void that prompted the founding of Concord Academy for girls. The answer is suggested in a 1981 oral interview of Gladys Clark, who graduated from Concord High School in 1910.[103] Although her comments were largely very positive about her public school experience, Clark recalled elementary classrooms of fifty pupils and an eighth grade principal/teacher who intimidated the students. These were the aspects of public education (discussed by David Tyack in *The One Best System*) that caused Flora White to imagine nature weeping at the sight of a school.[104] In addition, the long tradition of private academies in New England contributed to privileged families taking steps to open a new private school when one was not available for their daughters.

Flora White was successful in improving the education of her female students; however, the experience of her niece Catherine shows the intersection of gender and class at Miss White's School. As will be shown, Flora was sensitive to the fact that her relatives could not easily access the school's program. She continued to promote educational opportunity for her brother's progeny, and for all her students. The published views of G. Stanley Hall, a prominent man who had supported White's work, illustrate the profound challenges White faced in promoting girls' physical and intellectual attainment.

In her handling of Hall—and in White's and Marietta Johnson's relationships with Henderson and Dewey—we see the complicated interactions between early women school founders and the powerful male theorists who endorsed them. The women needed the support of prominent men to advance their own careers; however, the support also brought a degree of marginalization. It was a case of two steps forward and one step back.

White's embrace of organic education clearly situates her school in the new education or early progressive education movement, depending on the preferred terminology. In that sense, she is both typical and unusual. White is typical because the early movement occurred largely through individual, isolated experiments like her own. At the same time, White's case is unusual because she embraced organic education well before Marietta Johnson, who became famously identified with that philosophy. The publication of *Schools of To-morrow* one year after the sale of Miss White's Home School likely contributed to a de-emphasis on research efforts outside the Midwest and New York where John Dewey had lived—including White's native New England, the birthplace of Francis Parker, G. Stanley Hall, and Dewey himself. While early progressive ideologies were shared in places of intellectual exchange in Boston such as the Sloyd Training School, scholars of the twenty-first century have placed their primary focus outside the New England region as they have revisited *Schools of To-morrow* and studied women founders of progressive schools who were associated with Dewey.[105]

Flora White's life and career offer a glimpse into the individual efforts that created the progressive education movement in New England. Her story does not end with the sale of Miss White's Home School, however. In keeping with her philosophy of equating education with growth, she approached her retirement at Heath with a renewed focus on growth—her own.

NOTES

1. "Babcock, Elizabeth D.," interviewed by Renee Garrelick, May 16, 1977, Renee Garrelick Oral History Program Collection, Concord Free Public Library. www.concordlibrary.org/scollect/fin_aids/OH_Texts/babcock.html.

2. Miss Pickwick, "Girl about Town," *Daily Oklahoman*, February 9, 1941, C5.

3. "Cabot, Harold and Adeline," interviewed by Renee Garrelick, November 15, 1977, Renee Garrelick Oral History Program Collection, Concord Free Public Library. www.concordlibrary.org/scollect/fin_aids/OH_Texts/cabot.html.

4. *Miss White's Home School*, Concord, MA, 1900, 1.

5. Lawrence A. Cremin and Lydia Comings both attribute the term, "organic education," to C. Hanford Henderson, who used it as early as 1897 when lecturing in Boston. Although in 1894—when speaking to Massachusetts teachers—Felix Adler had expressed a need for "organic education," his use of the term was diametrically opposite that of Henderson, Flora White, and Marietta Johnson (founder of the Organic School in Fairhope, Alabama). Adler envisioned "organic education" as an effort to fit the individual child into society's needs, rather than to base educational decisions on the needs of the child. Still another view of the term (also differing from Henderson, White, and Johnson) was proposed in 1897 by Harriet M. Scott of the Detroit Normal Training School and Gertrude Buck of Vassar College in *Organic Education: A Manual for Teachers in Primary and Grammar Grades*. Referencing Adler but not Henderson, they presented an "organic education" curriculum that identified periods of civilization that were appropriate to children's interests at various grade levels. In the book, Scott and Buck also recommended breaking stories down into their essential points and teaching them to children in a recommended sequence. For purposes of discussion, this book will use the term, "organic education" as it was understood by Henderson, White, and Johnson and by most educational historians. See Lawrence A. Cremin, *The Transformation of the School: Progressivism in American Education, 1876–1957* (New York: Alfred A. Knopf, 1969), 149; S. H. Comings, *Industrial and Vocational Education: Universal and Self Sustaining* (Boston: Christopher Publishing House, 1915), 158; "Educators' Conference at Plymouth," *New York Times*, July 15, 1894; Felix Adler, "Education and Character," *School Journal*, November 3, 1894; Harriet M. Scott and Gertrude Buck, *Organic Education: A Manual for Teachers in Primary and Grammar Grades* (Boston: D. C. Heath, 1897, 1899).

6. Comings, *Industrial and Vocational Education*, 7.

7. Charles Hanford Henderson, "The Aim of Modern Education," *Appleton's Popular Science Monthly* (August 1896), 496.

8. Ibid.

9. Charles Hanford Henderson, *Education and the Larger Life* (Boston and New York: Houghton Mifflin, 1904).

10. Charles Hanford Henderson, *What Is It to Be Educated?* (New York: Houghton Mifflin, 1914), vi.

11. *Miss White's Home School* (Concord, MA, 1906), 1.

12. Ibid.

13. Jeroen F. Staring, "Midwives of Progressive Education: The Bureau of Educational Experiments 1916–1919" (PhD diss., University of Amsterdam, 2013), 26.

14. Cynthia Mosteller-Timbes, "Marietta Johnson School of Organic Education," *Encyclopedia of Alabama*, http://www.encyclopediaofalabama.org/article/h-1863.

15. "Magazine Tells of Marietta Johnson, Visionary," *UA News*, January 2, 2001.

16. In his 1879 best-selling book, George described the disparity between the haves and have-nots and advocated a single tax on land as the solution. Henry George, *Progress and Poverty: An Inquiry into the Causes of Industrial Depressions, and of Increase of Want with Increase of Wealth* (New York: W. J. Lavell, 1879).

17. Marietta Johnson, *30 Years with an Idea* (University, AL: University of Alabama Press, 1974), 9–12.

18. Ibid., 3.

19. Ibid., xi–xii.

20. Flora White, "Growth and Education" (unpublished manuscript), Flora White Papers, private collection, 4.

21. "Richardson, Laurence Eaton" interviewed by Renee Garrelick, January 19, 1978, Renee Garrelick Oral History Program Collection, Concord Free Public Library. www.concordlibrary.org/scollect/scollect/fin_aids/OH_Texts/richardson.html.

22. Joseph W. Newman, "Experimental School, Experimental Community: The Marietta Johnson School of Organic Education in Fairhope, Alabama," in *"Schools of Tomorrow," Schools of Today: What Happened to Progressive Education*, ed. Susan F. Semel and Alan R. Sadovnik (New York: Peter Lang), 69, 75.

23. Joseph W. Newman, "Marietta Johnson and the Organic School," in *Founding Mothers and Others: Women Educational Leaders During the Progressive Era*, ed. Alan R. Sadovnik and Susan F. Semel (New York: Palgrave, 2002), 26.

24. John Dewey and Evelyn Dewey, *Schools of Tomorrow* (New York: E. P. Dutton, 1915), preface.

25. Ibid., 17.

26. "Professor Dewey's Report on the Fairhope Experiment in Organic Education," in *John Dewey: The Middle Works, 1899–1924*, vol. 7 (Carbondale and Edwardsville, IL: Southern Illinois University Press, 1979), 387–389.

27. Lawrence A. Cremin, *The Transformation of the School*, 149.

28. Ibid., 373.

29. Newman, "Experimental School, Experimental Community," 73.

30. Thomas Fallace and Victoria Fantozzi, "A Century of John and Evelyn Dewey's *Schools of To-morrow*: Rousseau, Recorded Knowledge, and Race in the Philosopher's Most Problematic Text," *Educational Studies* 5 (2015): 136.

31. Dewey and Dewey, *Schools of To-morrow*, 23.

32. Some of the publications included *Industrial Education Magazine, Western Journal of Education, Perkins School for the Blind Annual Report, The Craftsman, Dominicana*, and *Report of the Commissioner of Education for Porto Rico*.

33. Davis Edwards, "Founder of Organic Education Tells of New School," *New York Times*, March 16, 1913.

34. "Educational Survey," *School and Home Education* (October 1915): 1.

35. Cremin, *The Transformation of the School*, 148.

36. George Allen Brown, "Memoir: Marietta Johnson and the School of Organic Education," in Marietta Johnson, *30 Years with an Idea* (University, AL: University of Alabama Press, 1974), xii.

37. Lawrence A. Cremin, *The Transformation of the School: Progressivism in American Education, 1876–1957* (New York: Vintage Books, 1969), 148–149.

38. "'Homelike' School Assn. to Meet Here," *Washington Times*, April 8, 1920, 11.

39. Jane Roland Martin, "Excluding Women From the Educational Realm," *Harvard Educational Review* 52 (1982): 133–148; Susan Douglas Franzosa, "'Schools Yet-to-Be:' Recovering the Work of Nineteenth Century Women in Early Childhood Education," *Vitae Scholasticae* 32 (2015): 5–24.

40. Jerry Aldridge and Lois McFayden Christiansen, *Stealing from the Mother: The Marginalization of Women in Education and Psychology from 1900–2010* (Lanham, MD: Rowman & Littlefield Education, 2013), 67.

41. Charlene Haddock Seigfried, ed. *Feminist Interpretations of Dewey* (University Park, PA: Pennsylvania State University Press, 2002).

42. Francis Maher, "John Dewey, Progressive Education and Feminist Pedagogies: Issues of Gender and Authority," in *Feminist Engagements: Reading, Resisting, and Revisioning Male Theorists in Education and Cultural*, ed. Kathleen Weiler, 13–32 (New York: Routledge, 2001).

43. Kathleen Weiler, "The Historiography of Gender and Progressive Education in the United States," *Paedagogica Historica* 42 (2006), 167.

44. Ibid., 175.

45. A. Gordon Melvin, *Education: A History* (New York: John Day, 1946), 328–331.

46. *Miss White's Home School* (Concord, MA, 1900) 2.

47. *Miss White's Home School*, 1906, 4–5.

48. *Miss White's Home School*, 1900, 3.

49. *Miss White's Home School*, 1906, 6.

50. Ibid., 1.

51. Ibid., 3.

52. Ibid.

53. *Miss White's Home School*, 1900, 2.

54. "Cabot," November 15, 1977.

55. *Miss White's Home School*, 1900, 3.

56. *Miss White's Home School*, 1906, 4.

57. "Babcock," May 16, 1977.

58. *Miss White's Home School*, 1906, 6.

59. "Babcock," May 16, 1977.

60. *Miss White's Home School*, 1900, 2.

61. Ibid.

62. *Miss White's Home School*, 1906, 3.

63. Newman, "Marietta Johnson and the Organic School," 28.

64. *Miss White's Home School*, 1906, 5.

65. James Naismith invented basketball in December 1891 at the YMCA Training School in Springfield, MA (now Springfield College). The game quickly gained popularity in the United States and was introduced into Europe by an American studying at the Seminarium for Teachers in Sweden.

66. *Plover Hill Camp for Girls in Charge of the Misses White* (Todd Printer, 1907), 5.

67. Ibid., 3–4.

68. G. Stanley Hall, *Adolescence: Its Psychology and Its Relations to Physiology, Anthropology, Sociology, Sex, Crime, Religion and Education* (New York: D. Appleton Company, 1904, 1907, 1915).

69. Ibid., 1907, vol. II, 561.

70. Lawrence A. Cremin, in Preface to Charles E. Strickland and Charles O. Burgess, *Health, Growth, and Heredity: G. Stanley Hall on Natural Education* (New York: Teachers College Press, 1965), viii.

71. Patricia Anne Vertinsky, *The Eternally Wounded Woman: Women, Doctors and Exercise in the Late Nineteenth Century* (Manchester, UK: Manchester University Press, 1989), 173.

72. Lesley Diehl, "The Paradox of G. Stanley Hall: Foe of Coeducation and Educator of Women," *American Psychologist*, 41 (1986): 15.

73. Hall, *Adolescence*, vol. II, 633.

74. David Tyack and Elisabeth Hansot, *Learning Together: A History of Coeducation in American Public Schools* (New York: Russell Sage Foundation, 1992).

75. Flora White to Anne Halfpenny, 17 June 1940, Westfield State College.

76. Flora White, "Redemption," in *Poems by Mary A. and Flora White* (New York: Paebar, 1939), 30–31.

77. Ibid.

78. Ibid.

79. Sara M. Evans, *Born for Liberty* (New York: The Free Press, 1989), 57–58, 239.

80. Miss Pickwick, "Girl about Town," *Daily Oklahoman*, February 9, 1941.

81. *Harvard Class of 1877, Seventh Report* (Cambridge, MA: Harvard, 1917), 4.

82. Hubert C. Fortmiller Jr. *Find the Promise: Middlesex School, 1901–2001* (Concord, MA: Middlesex School, 2003).

83. John R. Clarke, "Margaret Fisher: An American Modernist," *Woman's Art Journal* 24 (2003): 1, 4.

84. Ibid.

85. Jean Glasscock, *Wellesley College, 1875–1975: A Century of Women* (Wellesley, MA: Wellesley College,1975), 466.

86. Clarke, "Margaret Fisher," 4.

87. Dorothy Winsor Bisbee, interviewed by Rick Zamore, circa 1970.

88. Dorothy Bisbee, email message to John Bisbee, February 29, 2016.

89. Ibid.

90. John Winsor Pratt and Richard Jay Zecklauser, "The Fair and Efficient Division of the Winsor Family Silver," *Management Science* 36 (1990): 1293–1301.

91. Dianna Everett, "Gage," Oklahoma Historical Society, http://digital.library.okstate.edu/encyclopedia/entries/G.GA001.html.

92. Joseph White, n.d., Flora White Papers, private collection.

93. Flora White, "Life Facts of Flora White and Family Recorded Mar. 18, 1939," Heath Historical Society.

94. Porter E. Sargent, *A Handbook of American Private Schools* (Boston: Porter E. Sargent, 1916), 161–162.

95. Ibid.

96. "La Jolla Woman Takes Own Life," *San Diego Union*, February 19, 1935.

97. Philip McFarland, *A History of Concord Academy* (Concord, MA: Concord Academy, 1986), 4–5. For a discussion of how Montessori differed from Froebel, see pp. 68–70 in Gerald L. Gutek and Patricia A. Gutek, *Bringing Montessori to America: S.S. McClure, Maria Montessori, and the Campaign to Publicize Montessori Education* (Tuscaloosa, AL: University of Alabama Press, 2016).

98. "Cabot," November 15, 1977.

99. McFarland, *A History of Concord Academy*, 18.

100. Ibid., 14.

101. *Miss White's Home School*, 1906, 2.

102. McFarland, *A History of Concord Academy*, 12.

103. "Clark, Gladys," interviewed by Renee Garrelick, April 12, 1981, Renee Garrelick Oral History Program Collection, Concord Free Public Library. www.concordlibrary.org/scollect/fin_aids/OH_Texts/clark.html.

104. David B. Tyack, *The One Best System: A History of American Urban Education* (Cambridge, MA: Harvard University Press, 1974).

105. Two examples of books that have made significant contributions to an understanding of early progressive education are Susan F. Semel and Alan R. Sadovnik, eds. *"Schools of Tomorrow," Schools of Today* (New York: Peter Lang, 1999); and Alan R. Sadovnik and Susan F. Semel, eds., *Founding Mothers and Others: Women Educational Leaders during the Progressive Era* (New York: Palgrave, 2002).

Chapter Seven

Doing "Precisely as One Pleases"

After Flora White sold her Concord school in 1914, she became a full-time resident of Heath, where she remained for over twenty-five years. However, she did not settle into the comfortable familiarity of her childhood home to enjoy a restful retirement. Instead, White exhibited what Edward Calver calls a "yeasty" quality of mind, which he defined as "vision and contagious enthusiasm."[1] This recollection of White's sense of purpose was shared by Grace Moyer, who described her great-aunt's penetrating eyes and determined stride. Flora White's final years at Heath were yet another chapter in her quest for agency.

There were reasons White chose to reside at Heath over Concord at this stage of her life. She had achieved a level of financial security that was much improved over that of her widowed mother when the Whites last lived at Heath. Compared to Concord, Heath's abandoned farm houses made it "almost affordable as a summer place for impoverished clerics and scholars" who were among White's friends.[2] Additionally, for all of Concord's forward thinking, there were limits to the new ideas its residents would accept. In a 1977 interview, White's former student Adeline Eveleth Cabot and her husband, Harold Cabot, recalled that a local clergyman had tested those limits during White's lifetime. The Reverend Smith Owen Dexter, called in 1907 by the Trinity Episcopal Church in Concord, "preached against the mill owners over in Lowell and all around." According to the Cabots, Dexter "joined a strike against the management of the mill in Lowell, and some members of the parish who were contributors wanted him fired."[3] This controversy is corroborated by the church's published history, which describes the "sweet and unworldly" minister as a "social activist" whose "political leanings concerned the congregation."[4] Nevertheless, the parish and vestry stood by Dexter, who remained in the post until he retired for health reasons in 1932.

As an Episcopalian who lived in Concord through 1914, White would have been aware of the controversy about Dexter's political beliefs. At Heath, White was free of the responsibilities of being headmistress of a school whose demographic group overlapped Dexter's; there she could pursue her own causes without fear of reprisal. As previously noted, White believed that one of the benefits of advancing age was the freedom to do "precisely as one pleases."[5] Flora and Mary White sought new experiences in their birthplace, acquiring Calver's description as "militant schoolteachers descended from one of the most vigorous of Heath families and with very considerable experience of the world."[6] Newland Smith Jr. adds that the two sisters "were an energetic pair and their interests ranged far and wide over the whole community and over all the world. These interests included education, religion, agriculture, history, social programs, and world affairs."[7]

AN ISOLATED, BRAVE PLACE

The context in which Flora White pursued her agency in retirement is described by Elisabeth Sifton in *The Serenity Prayer: Faith and Politics in Times of Peace and War*.[8] Sifton's father, theologian Reinhold Niebuhr, was an ordained minister in the Evangelical and Reformed tradition. The son of German immigrants who settled in the Midwest, Reinhold Niebuhr served a church in Detroit before joining the faculty of Union Theological Seminary in New York in 1928. Sifton's mother, Ursula Keppel-Compton Niebuhr, graduated from Oxford with an honors degree in theology and history. She won a fellowship to Union and began lecturing in theology at Barnard College in 1940. Both were friends of Flora White.

Sifton spent summers at Heath with her family from the mid-1930s through the mid-1950s; she recalls that it had the "physical contours of a classic New England town" with a library, town hall, white clapboard church, and grocery store with a post office in the back. However, it was "off the beaten track," with "no amenities" that would have attracted "rich urbanites" during the summer. Rather, Heath had "an austere, windswept sweetness, this isolated, brave place." Much of its forest had been cleared for meadows and pastures, and one could see for miles on the open hills. The town's late eighteenth- and early nineteenth-century farmhouses "were handsomely plain in that lonely, heartbreaking way that is the distinctive mark of American frontier architecture." She adds that, apart from the beauty of the land and buildings, Heath's "most striking quality" was "the relative absence . . . of all those banal hypocrisies about money, status, power, and authority that regularly contort and distort social behavior in most places."[9]

Sifton offers a description of Heath's Union Church suggesting significant changes had occurred there since Joseph White II's funeral in 1861. (Flora White faithfully attended Sunday services at the Union Church, despite her involvement with the Episcopal denomination.) No longer limited to Congregationalists, the Union Church became more ecumenical, serving members of several Protestant faiths. The new church did not insist on the orthodoxy that once discouraged independent thinkers like Joseph White II from joining. In fact, a number of Protestant clergy—including those with homes at Heath—were beginning to find ways for Christians of different denominations to talk to each other, and to non-Christians. According to Sifton, such initiatives were part of an effort "to make the world safer and more just," especially in light of the xenophobia and carnage that occurred during and after the First World War. Several clergy who spent their summers at Heath were active in "integrationist, ecumenical, and international church activity."[10] Sifton observes, "Small wonder that later one could find four Heath men as delegates to the founding meeting of the World Council of Churches in Amsterdam in 1948, and two observers to Vatican Council II in 1962."[11]

Despite these changes, some things in Heath remained the same. Sifton explains, "This may sound banal, but to the Heath people character was everything, and they scarcely had to say so. Contrary reticence made it plain."[12] Her description recalls the minister's funeral message to Joseph White II's family that the good name he bestowed on them was preferable to a large inheritance.

AN UNUSUAL SUMMER COLONY

An important part of Flora White's environment was the collective membership of "an unusual summer colony" that convened at Heath each summer.[13] The group began with the early collaboration of the White sisters, their neighbor Felicia Emerson, and Dr. Grace Wolcott. Over time, the colony grew in a manner that recalls Betty G. Farrell's book, *Elite Families: Class and Power in Nineteenth-Century Boston.*[14] Farrell studied the families of prominent men in the textile industry and mapped the development of this regional elite by tracing their kinship networks and overlapping business ties. She notes that her subjects maintained and extended their power by building alliances and sustaining family continuity; moreover, in domestic and social activities women and men worked to preserve the family as an economic institution. At Heath—while her primary focus was not economic—Flora White likewise established alliances and worked to extend the continuity of her family. Networking was an act of agency that came naturally to her, as evidenced by the impressive list of endorsers she assembled for Miss White's Home School in Concord.

As early as 1906, Ethel Lyman Paine of Boston—a patient and friend of Dr. Grace Wolcott—returned to Heath and purchased an old farm. She restored the farm house, which became known as the Manse, and established beautifully landscaped gardens and lawns there. (The Manse was originally the home of Heath's first minister whose second wife was Flora White's paternal great-grandmother.) Over time, Ethel Paine bought additional farm properties and settled farm families on them. In 1915 she married John Moors of Boston, a banker and one of five men who—as members of the Harvard Corporation—ran the oldest university in the United States. Although John and Ethel Moors had an imposing home near Boston and an enormous seaside "cottage" in Cohasset (which John preferred over Heath), Ethel was especially fond of the Manse.[15]

Sifton writes that Ethel and John Moors "were definitely a power couple, as we might say today, although they would have hooted at the idea."[16] Smith describes Ethel Moors as "a proper Bostonian lady . . . most gracious, friendly and interested in other Heath people."[17] To Calver, Moors "had about her the air of distinction and gentility associated with the Back Bay in Edwardian times." Ethel had grown up in Trinity Church in Boston where the rector, Rev. Phillips Brooks, was a close family friend and important influence. As a young woman whose chief interests were the church and "Negro schools," she became, by all accounts, politically active.[18] Calver calls her politics "radical."[19] Sifton describes Ethel Moors as "fiercely radical-progressive" and John Moors as "an enlightened progressive, though not so radical as his wife."[20] To Flora White, Ethel Moors was a "warm-hearted" friend and neighbor of uncommon generosity. White wrote in 1939, "We [Flora and her sister Mary] owe her an unpayable debt materially and spiritually."[21]

Like Flora White and Dr. Grace Wolcott, Ethel Moors was responsible for bringing summer people to Heath during the early twentieth century. For example, she befriended Felix Frankfurter—then a Professor at Harvard Law School and an eminent labor law scholar—whom she met as a result of the prosecution of Italian laborers Nicola Sacco and Bartolomeo Vanzetti. The two immigrants were charged with the murder of a paymaster in South Braintree, Massachusetts. The presiding judge, who referred to the accused men as "those anarchist bastards," was satisfied with the guilty verdict and sentenced them to death.[22] Ethel Moors believed Sacco and Vanzetti were innocent and worked (unsuccessfully) to reverse the conviction. Frankfurter was out of the country during the trial but came home to publicize what he considered to be a gross miscarriage of justice. His exposure of the weaknesses of the Sacco-Vanzetti prosecution earned the Moors' admiration. At Ethel's urging, Frankfurter and his wife Marion—a Smith College graduate and daughter of a Congregational minister—purchased a home in Heath. When in 1939 President Franklin Roosevelt appointed Frankfurter to the U.S. Supreme Court, the couple left Cambridge for Washington but continued to spend their summers in Heath. Frankfurter arrived there every June, accompanied by many boxes of books, and had court papers dispatched to him throughout the summer.[23]

Ethel Moors also recruited the Niebuhrs to Heath. Sifton writes, "I don't know the circumstances under which my parents met Ethel Moors, but they surely involved left-wing politics and surely concerned Harvard, where my father preached several times a year and Mr. Moors was a major force."[24] Sifton notes that Ethel Moors approved of Niebuhr's politics, which were critical of the New Deal until after the 1936 election and then "warily supportive" of President Roosevelt's challenges to political and economic conservatives. Sifton further describes her father (and Moors) as being "philo-Semitic" and "internationalist."[25]

Another Heath summer resident was Susan Trevor Knapp, Ethel Moors's relative who today is regarded as a leading American deaconess of the early twentieth century and a pioneer woman leader in the Episcopal Church. Ethel Moors also convinced her childhood friend, Pauline Cony Smith Drown, and her husband, Dr. Edward Staples Drown—a professor at the Episcopal Theological Seminary (ETS) in Cambridge—to acquire a summer home at Heath. Pauline was the widow of theologian Alexander Viets Griswold Allen (1841–1908); she was also Edward Drown's student, and became his second wife in 1913, which created a scandal at ETS. One Heath history describes Pauline Drown as "an unabashed intellectual (a blue stocking literally and figuratively), with a well stocked mind, a fund of anecdotes . . . [who] had no interest in dress and was tactful only when it mattered."[26]

The Heath colony continued to grow as Edward Drown recruited his colleague Angus Dun to purchase a house in Heath, along with his wife Catherine "Kitty" Whipple Pew Dun, the daughter of a major general and a graduate of Radcliffe College. Angus Dun's New York family was associated with a credit-rating firm that merged to become Dun & Bradstreet. He was a professor at ETS who became dean of the school and in 1944 the Episcopal Bishop of Washington, D.C. Born with a deformed hand and limbs, Angus Dun became paralyzed with polio; further complications led to the amputation of one of his legs. Despite his disabilities, Dun graduated from Yale, where he was elected to Phi Beta Kappa, and later graduated from ETS. Known for his pacifist views, he was a strong proponent of the Ecumenical movement.

Margaret Robbins Malone was also instrumental in attracting people to the Heath summer colony. She was a committed pacifist from a Philadelphia ministerial family and the wife of Dana Malone, who served as Massachusetts Attorney General. In 1917, Margaret Malone's husband died in a riding accident, leaving her with three children. Calver notes, "[J]ust as a chain of summer residents began with the Whites, another began because of her [Malone's] presence in Heath."[27] This chain included Dr. Howard Chandler Robbins, Malone's brother and Dean of the Cathedral of St. John the Divine in New York, and his wife, Louise Robbins, who eschewed a career and conventional volunteer activities to pursue progressive causes.

Other members of the Heath colony were Dr. Lawrence Chapin, a Springfield physician who had been one of the Whites' boarding students (and the son of an early endorser of Miss White's School in Concord), and his wife, Ruth Lamson Chapin. Newland F. Smith, head of the physics department at The Citadel in South Carolina, also joined the group, along with William and Sally Vanderbilt of New York, who were friends of the White sisters.[28] Calver described their activities:

> They came to enjoy the good life and almost of necessity did so within the town. The roads were narrow, unpaved, and steep, and automobiles were primitive. . . . Once here they cultivated elaborate flower gardens. They walked. They went birding. They picked berries. They entertained at morning coffee, noon luncheon, afternoon tea, dinner, often on the spur of the moment. . . . They went to the Union church. They had house guests. And they talked. Some of the talk was brilliant, erudite, and witty; some was gossip; some had to do with coping; a great deal had to do with politics. Some of the men were gifted and prominent in their profession; some of the women had fine minds. A great many were social and congenial.[29]

Apart from the contributions of individual members, Sifton suggests there was an understanding within the summer colony that maintained the group's uniqueness. She notes that "thanks to Aunt Louise [Robbins] and Aunt Ethel [Moors], Heath seemed to be dominated by Harvard pedigrees or by no pedigrees at all." Sifton adds, "No exclusive social functions or patterns defined the summer group—that would have been frowned on, anyway—and we all simply joined in regular Heath activities."[30]

Smith observes that, in an earlier period, the White sisters were famous for their afternoon tea parties where topics of discussion ranged from missionary work in Japan, to economic conditions in Europe, to agriculture in Heath. Their collie Lassie usually attended and amused guests by responding with appropriately enthusiastic barks when asked the question, "What would you do if the Germans were coming?"[31] Beyond the frivolity of such moments, Flora White and her companions made a concerted effort to achieve "more life, and fuller."

Just as, many years earlier, White had urged educators to allow children to "test and do and dare," she claimed that right to her own adult learning in retirement.[32] While they lived at Heath, the White sisters organized an agricultural fair that is still in existence. The inaugural event turned a small profit, which they used to establish the Heath Agricultural Society in 1916. As part of their work with the Heath Historical Society, Flora and Mary White participated in the care and restoration of the South and Center Cemeteries in Heath. As early as 1906, the two sisters successfully applied for the return to Fort Shirley of a 1748 gravestone (for baby Anna Norton, daughter of the fort chaplain) that a Williams College professor had removed as a memento of his research.

In 1921 Flora White produced a Biblical pageant at Heath that evoked the Passion Play at Oberammergau and was covered by the New York and Boston press. The *Drama of David* cast townspeople in lead and supporting roles and was held outdoors in a beautiful setting. The "actors" traveled in horse-drawn chariots described as "disguised dump-carts" that added to the spectacle.[33] The pageant raised money for Near East relief. (Writing in 1939, Flora White noted that one reviewer called the *Drama of David* the "Best religious drama since the *early* days at Oberammergau" and urged that the play be published.)[34] The White sisters gave another pageant on their lawn and repeated it at Northfield, Massachusetts, to raise money for a Historical Society project. Local histories indicate they also produced a Chinese entertainment. These events recalled the dramatic performances of students at Miss White's Home School as well as Flora's direction of *tableaux* on the steamship bound for the Cape Colony many years before.

In this atmosphere, Flora White and her contemporaries were able to achieve agency by initiating their own testing, doing, and daring. While Frankfurter—an agnostic Jew from Vienna—questioned and argued with Protestant clergy who summered at the town, and others experimented with new agricultural practices, Flora White pursued her own interests. She published music and poetry for a national audience[35] and contributed regularly to *Unity*, a Unitarian magazine published by John Haynes Holmes, one of the founders of the NAACP and American Civil Liberties Union.[36] She wrote newspaper articles on history, foreign policy, and public affairs.[37] Throughout these endeavors, Flora White maintained a physically active life, doing a daily handstand until she was nearly seventy.[38]

A SENSE OF FAMILY

By the time White retired at Heath, her sister Mary was the only family member in close proximity. Hattie was deceased; Emma had moved to Washington State many years earlier; brother Joseph had been in Oklahoma since 1908. As early as 1925, Flora White began to recruit additional relatives to move to Heath. She focused on her brother's daughter Catherine, a former student at Miss White's Home School. Catherine was in Oklahoma, living with her husband and children. The family was caught in the midst of an agricultural downturn that might cause them to consider relocating to Massachusetts.

In 1913, Catherine White married Golden Moyer, who twelve years earlier had moved with his family from Nebraska to their new home on the southern Great Plains. His father—a lawyer and former school superintendent—had arrived there in 1900, looking for homesteading opportunities in the area of the Oklahoma Territory known as the Cherokee Outlet. It was a 58 by 225 mile strip south of the Oklahoma-Kansas border, extending from the ninety-sixth meridian to the one-hundredth meridian. Despite the U.S. government's previous promise that the land would be the Cherokees' perpetual outlet to their hunting grounds, the tribe lost that assurance after the Civil War, in which the Cherokees supported the Confederacy. The new treaty allowed the U.S. government to dispose of the Outlet lands. In 1893, the Cherokee Outlet was opened for non-Native American settlement. It was Oklahoma's fourth and largest land run, involving over one hundred thousand people. Although the financial panic of 1893 discouraged long-term settlement of the Outlet, public-domain claims that were abandoned or avoided by earlier homesteaders were again made available in 1898–1902. Golden Moyer's father established a homestead on a quarter-section of land near the small town of Gage, where he practiced law. In 1901, at age nine, Golden and a team of two plow horses broke the virgin prairie sod.

However, his work, and that of thousands of other farmers, contributed to "The Great Plowup" of the southern plains between 1901 and 1930. Unbeknownst to most people at that time, widespread agriculture destroyed the prairie grass that kept moisture in the ground. On the southern plains, thirty-three million acres of grassland—a "web of perennial species" that had "evolved over twenty thousand years"—would be "stripped bare" in just thirty.[39]

During the nineteenth century the Great Plains—including the Cherokee Outlet— were regarded as the "Great American Desert," unfit for settlement due to the foot-deep sod, absence of trees, and shortage of rainfall.[40] However, inventions such as the steel plow, barbed wire fence, and windmill pump suggested the grassland could be converted into small family farms. The popularity of dry farming techniques also contributed to the perception that agricultural production—especially wheat production—could be stimulated there. Farmers in the southern plains eagerly read *Campbell's Soil Culture Manual* in which Hardy Campbell of Lincoln, Nebraska, contended that the real problem in a semiarid climate was not a lack of rainfall but the loss of water through evaporation. He argued that dryland wheat didn't need irrigation. Rather, farmers should plant in the fall when a small amount of moisture would produce sprouts, let the crop go dormant in the winter, allow the spring rains to stimulate growth, and harvest in the summer. Campbell suggested that overturned ground be used for mulch to hold the soil in place and minimize evaporation. He even went so far as to suggest that the act of plowing brought additional rain. The Santa Fe Railroad (the eventual successor to the Southern Kansas Railway) encouraged settlement by printing a progress map showing that the rain line of twenty inches or more annually was moving roughly eighteen miles per year with new towns tied to the railroad. "With scientific certainty," some people made claims that steam from the trains actually "caused the skies to weep."[41]

Although the 1890 census had revealed there was no longer a discernable frontier line in the United States, the southern plains functioned as the land of last chances well into the early twentieth century. In 1923, the government called the southern plains "the last frontier of agriculture" after the 1920 census revealed a majority of Americans were, for the first time in history, living in cities and towns.[42] Americans steeped in the virtues of the yeoman farmer had long associated westward expansion with opportunity for the marginalized. Under the terms of the Homestead Act of 1862, they had the government's promise of free land to those who would live there and "improve" it, reflecting the doctrine of *vacuum domicilium*, which had justified taking land from indigenous people since the European settlement of the New World. For many citizens, the southern plains—including parts of Oklahoma, Texas, Kansas, Colorado, and New Mexico—were regarded as the place hardworking people could still own a farm and achieve the American Dream.

Nevertheless, during the 1920s—when the rest of the United States seemed to be experiencing heady times—farmers were in trouble. They had expanded production and rented or purchased new machinery on credit to feed Europe during the First World War, only to see markets shrink following wartime recovery. To meet their credit obligations, farmers further increased production—thereby creating surpluses that caused prices to drop. By the end of the decade, the stock market collapse and the resulting economic dislocation made credit tight.

The numbers tell the story. In 1910, the price of wheat was 80 cents a bushel; five years later, the price had doubled, and U.S. farmers increased production by 50 percent. When the United States entered the First World War, the government guaranteed a wheat price of $2.00 a bushel through the duration of the conflict. However, by the summer of 1929, the United States had a wheat surplus. (There was also a glut in Europe, especially as Russia recovered from the war and resumed its wheat exports.) According to *New York Times* reporter and Pulitzer Prize winner Timothy Egan, "every town along the rail lines of the southern plains sprouted a tower of unsold wheat, stacked in piles outside grain elevators."[43] Wheat prices headed downward, to $1.50 a bushel, then below a dollar, then 75 cents a bushel. Farmers had a choice: they could cut back and hope that prices would rise, or plant more wheat to make the same money on a higher crop yield. Throughout the southern plains, the overwhelming response was to plow up more sod.

Golden and Catherine Moyer were caught in the middle of these difficult economic times. Prior to their marriage, both had completed a normal school course and worked as teachers. They taught in Laverne, Oklahoma, the year they were married, and for the next two years Golden taught and served as a school superintendent in May and Fargo, Oklahoma. He built a two-room house on a quarter-section of land eleven miles from the small town of Gage, which allowed him to teach during the winter and return to the farm in the summer. Over time, he added two bedrooms by relocating and remodeling an abandoned schoolhouse. During the 1918 influenza epidemic the couple moved permanently to the country in the hope of isolating their young family.

It was in the midst of the post-World War I agricultural downturn that Flora White in 1925 arranged for Golden Moyer to become the teacher at the one-room Heath Center schoolhouse located just west of her home. The Moyers' "extended visit" began August 1, 1925, when Catherine, Golden, five children ranging in ages from ten to one, along with their dog Jiggs, left the family farm in Oklahoma for Heath, Massachusetts. [44] The Moyer children included Golden Jr. (b. 1915); Grace (b. 1916); Joseph "Joe" (b. 1918); Dorothy (b. 1920); and Herman (b. 1924). Before they departed Oklahoma, the Moyers rented their farm to a young couple, Alfred and Dixie Hammock.

Traveling in an Overland touring car, the Moyers visited relatives and friends at points along the way. They spent the night at campgrounds, with the parents and infant Herman sleeping on cots under a homemade, canvas tent. The other children and Jiggs slept in the car. Grace reported that apart from the brick Lincoln Highway, they saw virtually no paved highway west of Chicago. Heading east, they visited Niagara Falls and made a brief sojourn into Canada. Seeing more and different trees than they had ever encountered, and—for most family members—gazing on mountains for the first time, the Moyers entered Massachusetts on the Mohawk Trail Highway.

When they arrived at Heath, Flora and Mary White allocated most of the first floor of their home to their visiting relatives and built an additional bedroom over part of their "wood and spring" house to further accommodate them. According to Catherine, the Moyers had five freshly painted rooms downstairs—the entire first floor except for the parlor, which they could use on special occasions—as well as a bedroom and bath upstairs. Catherine reported that there was hot and cold running water in the house. Grace gave a sense of the entire property by reporting that the "wood and spring house was attached to the kitchen area, and adjoined by the milk house, [and] then the hay barn before reaching the car and implement storage." She added, "From there you entered the animal barn." [45]

At the time of the Moyers' arrival, Flora and Mary White were living at Plover Hill (1/4 mile east of their home) caring for a few boys, with the help of a cook and a housekeeper. When autumn turned the trees brilliant colors, the sisters moved to the second floor of their home, which had been converted to an apartment. Grace observed, "All at once the population of Heath was cut in half. The summer people went back home."[46]

Two of the boys the Whites kept at Plover Hill were Robert Gilpin Ervin Jr. ("Bobby") and Henry Nichols Ervin ("Skip"), sons of Robert Ervin of the Harvard class of 1913, and Frances Quincy Nichols Ervin, a former student at Miss White's Home School. Bobby was in the White sisters' care for three years. In a letter he wrote as an adult, he explained that his mother had been an intellectually gifted but socially difficult girl whose prior educational experience had been at a Catholic convent school in France. After sending Frances Nichols to the White sisters, Bobby's maternal grandmother was impressed with the way they handled her daughter. When Bobby appeared to be an even more difficult child, Frances Nichols Ervin sought advice from *her* mother. The practical grandmother figured that if the White sisters could succeed with Frances, they could also handle her grandson.[47] Bobby's wife, Catherine Ervin, reported that her husband "adored" the Whites and especially enjoyed the nature study that was a central part of his curriculum at Heath. Catherine Ervin stated further that the White sisters "were very strict but did it in a way that Bobs [an adult nickname] didn't resent."[48] The characterization recalled a speech in which Flora described a boy with a mind that an "orthodox school" regarded as chaotic. If the school simply *trained* the boy's mind, White reasoned, he would become resentful. Instead, the school should accept the chaos of the boy's mind as *normal*, and let him "test and do and dare."[49]

Grace Moyer recalled that she and all of her siblings got along with Flora, who believed the children's parents did not reprimand them enough. Grace added that Flora was very strict with the children she kept. On one occasion, Flora took Grace, Bobby, and Skip out to pick blueberries. They played instead. Flora required Grace to tell her mother that she hadn't done her duty, and it made a strong impression. The anecdote underscored Sifton's observation that character meant everything to Heath people.

The schoolhouse at Heath Center consisted of one room and enrolled twenty-two students in grades one through eight. Golden Moyer taught three of his own children: Golden Jr. in sixth grade, Grace in fifth, and Joe in third. Dorothy, who was only four years old when they arrived at Heath, was expected to watch young Herman while the other children were at school. Grace reported, "On several occasions Herman ran away from Dorothy and went to school, running right down the center aisle to Dad. Sure enough, right on Herman's heels was Dorothy."[50]

According to local histories, schooling at Heath followed a traditional curriculum, emphasizing reading, writing, and arithmetic. Weekly music had been added in 1908 and weekly art in 1918. Spelling, geography, history, and science were regularly included, with all subjects being taught daily in time segments that varied from fifteen to forty minutes. Students studied penmanship and used the Palmer method beginning in 1910. It was not until 1927 that standardized tests measured student progress at the school. Physical education mostly consisted of games in the schoolyard. Grace Moyer recalled that her father was especially fond of skiing in Heath's deep snows, and after lunch during winter the children would go skiing or sledding.

When spring came, Golden Moyer was anxious to return to the southern plains. Years later, Catherine told her daughter Grace that Flora's friend Howard Robbins had "great plans for the children in our family" had Golden been content with life in the East.[51] On their way home, the Moyers visited New York City where they toured the Bronx Zoo and took their first subway ride, and Philadelphia where they saw the Liberty Bell. Then they camped on the banks of the Potomac for nearly a week and visited Washington, D.C. They shook the hand of the then-president, Calvin Coolidge, observed the House of Representatives in session, and visited the monuments and Bureau of Printing and Engraving. The family had a special tour of the Smithsonian Institution from their cousin, geologist David White—then associate curator of paleobotany at the Smithsonian and a member of the National Academy of Sciences. The Moyers also traveled to Mount Vernon by boat. On the way home they visited the Gettysburg battlefield, crossed the Mississippi River at St. Louis, and camped in the Arkansas Ozarks before returning to Oklahoma.

There is evidence that the Moyers returned sooner than originally anticipated because their farm was still rented upon their arrival in Oklahoma. The Moyers then lived for a time with Catherine's parents, Joseph and Jennie White, five miles from their farm home. Grace recollected that her family did not go back to their farm until the spring of 1928. Meanwhile, a new son, William ("Bill") was born to Catherine and Golden in Catherine's parents' home in January 1928. Their youngest son, Robert ("Bob") would arrive in 1930, the only child in the family to be born in a hospital. As an adult, Grace summed up the trip to Heath: "On returning to the windy prairie of northwest Oklahoma I am sure we all knew we had had a really 'fun' year. But only in looking back during the many subsequent years have we come to realize the great privilege and value afforded by our trip to Heath and our visit there."[52]

Caught in the problems that plagued farmers and ranchers on the southern plains, Golden Moyer was forced into bankruptcy in 1928. According to family lore, he eventually repaid all of his creditors save one—the person who was unwilling to wait a little longer for payment, thereby necessitating the bankruptcy filing.

In the years that followed, the Moyer family fortunes did not improve, however. A greater threat to their livelihood—and to others on the southern plains—appeared innocuously on January 21, 1932, in what seemed to be a relatively isolated event.

Around noon on that day a cloud ten thousand feet high appeared just outside Amarillo, Texas, some one hundred fifty miles southwest of Golden and Catherine Moyer's farm. The winds had been fierce all morning. Suddenly the sky turned brownish, then gray, as the cloud that defied description lumbered around the edge of the city. It wasn't a rain cloud, nor was it a cloud holding ice pellets. It wasn't a tornado. Observers said they had the feeling of being in a black blizzard, "with an edge of hard steel wool."[53] Weather bureau personnel were fascinated by the unusual cloud, and they wrote in their logs that it was "most spectacular."[54] When sunlight shone through its lighter edge, the cloud appeared greenish. After hovering over Amarillo, the cloud moved north up the Texas panhandle, toward Oklahoma.

Amarillo residents were witnessing the first of a series of dust storms in what is known on the southern plains as the Dirty Thirties. The worst duster—on Black Sunday, April 14, 1935—carried in one afternoon two times the amount of dirt that was dug to create the Panama Canal. In contrast, it took seven and one-half years to dig the canal.[55] Without warning, the Moyers found themselves in the midst of an area that would be called the Dust Bowl—where continual storms blew valuable topsoil, rendered the land unproductive, and choked people, animals, and communities. It was the greatest environmental disaster in the history of the United States.

Nature covered her face and wept.

From the late 1930s until the end of her life, Flora White had two groups of people with whom she felt a strong attachment—her family in Oklahoma, and her friends in the Heath colony. Her response to the Dust Bowl was to extend help to her Oklahoma family in ways that recalled Isaac Esty's kindness to the Whites during Flora's own girlhood. However, since she had limited means of support due to her own advanced age, she would have to rely on Heath friends for help and repay them with her loyalty.

NOTES

1. Edward Calver, *Heath, Massachusetts: A History and Guidebook*, 3rd ed. (Heath, MA: Heath Historical Society, 2009), 189.

2. Elisabeth Sifton, "The Serenity Prayer," *Yale Review* 86 (1998): 16.

3. "Cabot, Harold and Adeline," interviewed by Renee Garrelick, November 15, 1977, Renee Garrelick Oral History Program Collection, Concord Free Public Library. www.concordlibrary.org/scollect/fin_aids/OH_Texts/cabot.html.

4. "A Brief History of Trinity Church and Its Buildings," http://www.trinityconcord.org/history.shtml.

5. Miss Pickwick, "Girl about Town," *Daily Oklahoman*, February 9, 1941, C5.

6. Calver, *Heath, Massachusetts*, 15.

7. Newland Smith Jr., "Early Summer People in Heath," in *The Book of Heath: Bicentennial Essays*, ed. Susan B. Silvester (Ashfield, MA: Paideia Publishers, 1985), 141.

8. Elisabeth Sifton, *The Serenity Prayer: Faith and Politics in Times of Peace and War* (New York: W. W. Norton & Company, 2003).

9. Ibid., 18–21, 80.

10. Ibid., 23–24.

11. Ibid., 24.

12. Ibid., 19.

13. Sifton, "The Serenity Prayer," 17.

14. Betty G. Farrell, *Elite Families: Class and Power in Nineteenth-Century Boston* (Albany: State University of New York Press, 1993).

15. Sifton, *The Serenity Prayer*, 44.

16. Ibid.

17. Smith, "Early Summer People in Heath," 146.

18. Sarah Cushing Paine and Charles Henry Pope, *Paine Ancestry: The Family of Robert Treat Paine, Signer of the Declaration of Independence, Including Maternal Lines* (Boston: Printed for the Family, 1912), 319.

19. Calver, *Heath, Massachusetts*, 190.

20. Sifton, *The Serenity Prayer*, 45–46.

21. White, "Life Facts of Flora White and Family Recorded Mar. 18, 1939," Heath Historical Society, 16.

22. Sifton, *The Serenity Prayer*, 47.

23. Rev. Deacon Geraldine A. Swanson, "Deaconess Susan Trevor Knapp: A Pioneer of Women's Leadership in the Church," *The Episcopal New Yorker* (Spring 2011), 24–25.

24. Sifton, *The Serenity Prayer*, 45.

25. Ibid.

26. Calver, *Heath, Massachusetts*, 201. *Blue stocking* is a term used to describe an educated, intellectual woman.

27. Ibid., 199.

28. Smith, "Early Summer People in Heath," 140–153; Calver, *Heath, Massachusetts*, 196–205.

29. Calver, *Heath, Massachusetts*, 200.

30. Sifton, "The Serenity Prayer," 21–26.

31. Smith, "Early Summer People in Heath," 142.

32. Flora White, "Child Training and Child Education," (unpublished manuscript, n.d.), Flora White Papers, private collection, 9–10.

33. Calver, *Heath, Massachusetts*, 89.

34. White, "Life Facts," 8.

35. Flora White, "Light and Shadow" (Toronto: Columbian Music Publishers, Ltd., 1938); Flora White, "That Which Abides," in *The Poetry Digest: Annual Anthology of Verse for 1939* (New York, The Poetry Digest, 1939), 117; Mary A. White and Flora White, *Poems by Mary A. White and Flora White* (New York: Paebar, 1939).

36. Flora White's private papers at the time of her death included copies of her submissions that were published in *Unity* on May 31, 1923, September 28, 1931, July 23, 1934, and April 4, 1938.

37. Flora White, "A Year in India," *Springfield Republican* (Springfield, MA), August 10, 1931; Flora White, "Heath the General of George Washington, and Heath, the Town," *Greenfield Gazette and Courier* (Greenfield, MA), February 26, 1932, 3C.

38. Grace Moyer Share, "Notes on the Lives of Mary Abby and Flora White" (written in 1986). Flora White Papers, private collection, 4.

39. Timothy Egan, *The Worst Hard Time: The Untold Story of Those Who Survived the Great American Dust Bowl* (Boston: Mariner Books, 2006), 101.

40. Walter Prescott Webb, *The Great Plains* (Lincoln: University of Nebraska Press, 1931, 1959), 152–153.

41. Egan, *The Worst Hard Time*, 24–25.

42. Ibid., 57.

43. Ibid., 59.

44. Grace Moyer Share, "The Golden Moyer Family Spend the Winter of 1925–1926 in Heath, Massachusetts" (written in 1986). Flora White Papers, private collection, 1.

45. Ibid., 4.

46. Ibid.

47. Robert G. Ervin Jr. to Grace Moyer Share, 6 November, 1985, Flora White Papers, private collection.

48. Catherine Ervin, in discussion with author, August 10, 2003.

49. Flora White, "Child Training," 9–10.

50. Share, "The Golden Moyer Family," 5.

51. Grace Moyer Share, "The Summer of 1938" (written in 1986). Flora White Papers, private collection.

52. Share, "The Golden Moyer Family," 8.

53. Egan, *The Worst Hard Time*, 113.

54. Ibid.

55. Ibid., 8.

Chapter Eight

The Best of Her Generation

On April 19, 1935, Hugh Bennett walked into Room 333 of the Senate Office Building in Washington, D.C. As Director of the Soil Erosion Service established two years earlier under the U.S. Department of the Interior, he was one of the first people in Washington to recognize that the blowing dust on the southern plains was not just another natural disaster—like a tornado, hurricane, or flood—that required relief. Bennett suspected the dusters were caused by humans, and—while he could not stop the wind from blowing—he could try to change human behavior. His strategy was to influence Congress to create a permanent, well-funded agency to heal the land.

This was a change of tack on Bennett's part. When the dust storms began, he had stated, "Of all the countries in the world, we Americans have been the greatest destroyers of land of any race of people barbaric or civilized." Bennett further described what was happening on the southern plains as "sinister," and a sign of "our stupendous ignorance."[1] He was especially critical of how the government had encouraged exploitive farming by suggesting—through official bulletins and policies—that soil was a resource that could not be exhausted.

Five days after Black Sunday, Bennett was giving a new round of Senate testimony as the storm's detritus moved eastward. One year earlier, a southern plains dust storm had blanketed New York and Washington, attracting attention. In the aftermath of the newest duster, Bennett was monitoring the storm's movement. He thought that getting another taste of fresh plains soil would help people along the Atlantic seaboard understand that something had gone very wrong with the land. As he began his testimony with charts, maps, and a report on Black Sunday, the senators listened, and some appeared bored. Bennett reminded them that an inch of topsoil could blow away in an hour but it takes a thousand years to restore it. One senator who had been gazing out the window interrupted Bennett to remark, "It's getting dark outside." As senators went to the window, the sun over the Senate Office building disappeared, and dust from the southern plains once again covered the nation's capital. "This, gentlemen, is what I'm talking about," Bennett announced. "There goes Oklahoma."[2] Within a day, he had funding and a permanent agency to restore and sustain the soil.

THE SADDEST LAND

It was a monumental challenge. Journalist Ernie Pyle drove through the southern plains, calling the one hundred million acres comprising the Dust Bowl "this withering land of misery." He noted land that formerly had a farm on every quarter section was reduced to "nothing whatsoever" but "gray raw earth and few farmhouses and barns, sticking up from the dark gray sea like white cattle skeletons on the desert." Pyle wrote that it was "the saddest land I have ever seen."[3] For Flora White, the desolation of her relatives' Oklahoma farms recalled the human destruction of the fragile Berkshire ecosystem that had altered her own childhood.

The creation of the Bennett's Soil Conservation Service was not the only New Deal program to address conditions in the southern plains. Following his election, President Franklin Roosevelt declared that free-market agricultural economics had failed, as evidenced by the fact that the United States had produced more food than any nation in history; yet its farmers were being run off the land, penniless, while U.S. cities couldn't feed themselves. Roosevelt noted that the average farmer was earning only three hundred dollars a year, an 80 percent drop from the previous decade. As early as 1933, under the Agricultural Adjustment Act, the government had allocated acreage among individual farmers, encouraging them to take land out of production by paying subsidies raised by a tax on food processors. That same year the government paid farmers to plow under crops they had already planted, and to kill livestock they were raising.

As an adult, Bob Moyer (Catherine and Golden's youngest child and Flora's great-nephew) recalled that he was four or five when a "government man" came to the Moyer family farm for the purpose of eliminating weaker cows to drive up cattle prices. Wearing clothing that had likely been a cavalry uniform, the man arrived as previously scheduled, carrying a .22 rifle. Golden Moyer was silent as he led him to the livestock in pens surrounding the house. Surveying the animals, the government man first selected a small Jersey-Hereford cross that was thinner and weaker than the other cows. Bob was especially fond of that particular cow because she became paralyzed in calving; he and his brother Bill had nursed her back to heath so the cow could finally walk on her own. Bob recalled, "I saw the grim look of determination on . . . [the government man's] face and the pain on Dad's face. I stood frozen as the government man raised the .22, aimed right between those soft brown eyes, and shot." Golden Moyer walked toward the government man and said, "That's all. You're not going to shoot any more. I don't know how I'll do it, but I'll find or buy enough feed for my cows. Now leave." Bob added, "It took a lot of raw courage to make it through the depression. Looking back, I can see that both my parents were extremely courageous."[4]

Franklin Roosevelt also noted the courage of people like the Moyers. As the Great Plains lost population at a rate of ten thousand per month in what was the largest single exodus in U.S. history, the president took to the air waves. In his radio broadcast on September 6, 1936, Roosevelt encouraged people to hold on. He noted that "No cracked earth, no blistering sun, no burning wind, no grasshoppers are a permanent match for the indomitable American farmers and stockmen and their wives and children, who have carried on through desperate days, and inspire us with their self-reliance, their tenacity, and their courage."[5] Ten days earlier, the president had received a report titled *The Future of the Great Plains*, signed by Hugh Bennett and marked "personal and confidential." It stated that while the plains had suffered a severe drought, dry periods were a normal part of prairie life, going back eons. An enclosed map revealed that west of the ninety-eighth meridian (where the Moyers lived) twenty inches or less of rain fell annually—an amount insufficient to raise crops, regardless of the farming methods. The report concluded that the problem of the Great Plains was one of "[m]istaken public policies . . . a mistaken homesteading policy, the stimulation of war time demands which led to over cropping and over grazing, and encouragement of a system of agriculture which could not be both permanent and prosperous."[6] In perhaps its most damning indictment, the report stated, "The Homestead Act of 1862, limiting an individual holding to 160 acres, was on the western plains almost an obligatory act of poverty."[7] The report concluded by stating, "The situation is so serious that the Nation, for its own sake, cannot afford to allow the farmer to fail," adding "We endanger our democracy if we allow the Great Plains, or any other section of the country, to become an economic desert."[8]

Although Bennett was correct in linking the Homestead Act and other government policies to the environmental catastrophe known as the Dust Bowl, its antecedents go back to the European doctrine of *vacuum domicilium* that had shaped Anglo Americans' attitudes toward the land since their arrival in the New World. The doctrine held that people had a right to land if they "improved" it by growing crops or raising stock on it. After reading the report, Roosevelt went back to Bennett to discuss solutions to problems it highlighted and began—in one corner of Kansas—to rebuild the American grassland. The president wanted something more dramatic, however, and also initiated a program to plant trees to act as windbreakers, check erosion, and employ thousands of people.

Not everyone described the tenacity of southern plains farmers and ranchers as courageous. In Baltimore, H. L. Mencken—one of the most influential U.S. writers during the first half of the twentieth century—wrote a December 1936 article for *The American Mercury* titled "The Dole for Bogus Farmers." He argued that inhabitants of the Dust Bowl were not *real* farmers like those in Pennsylvania who requested no government assistance. Instead, Mencken said the plains farmers were land speculators "who went out on the wrong limb and got skinned."[9] Reflecting the twentieth-century eugenics movement, he wrote, "They are simply, by God's inscrutable will, inferior men," and argued that the solution to the problem of the Great Plains was to sterilize them.[10]

Flora White was one easterner who did not need a taste of topsoil to know there was an acute problem on the southern plains that demanded attention. She was in regular correspondence with her Oklahoma relatives—including her brother Joseph, his daughter Catherine, his son Charles, and Joseph's grandchildren—and was following their situation with great concern. Flora had a longstanding interest in agriculture, stimulated by her knowledge of the White family farm and Heath's own history of soil depletion through land clearance and overuse. In writing a history of the town, Calver would later observe that Heath began to experience decline in the 1830s—just as the last farm was "taken up and *improved*" [emphasis added].[11] As early as 1916, Flora White had helped to establish a local agricultural society, and she encouraged agricultural experimentation. In a characteristic act of agency, she sent her Oklahoma relatives trees to be planted on the windswept plains. White also shipped them used clothing of quality, provided by her friends. She offered advice, particularly in relation to the education of the Moyer children, some of whom had reached college age. For example, in a 1935 letter to Catherine Moyer, Flora recommended, "Do follow closely what Mr. Roosevelt is planning for the increased education of the youth. It may give an opportunity for Golden Jr. to go on with his college work. I do hate to have him deprived of it."[12]

EAST MEETS WEST

Flora White also made periodic train trips (over seventeen hundred miles each way) to Oklahoma where she visited her brother and his family and observed life on the southern plains firsthand. By 1937, Mary White had left Heath to enter a nursing home, and Flora was lonely—despite her large circle of friends. Over time, her tutoring had become "only occasional," and—apart from Mary—her brother Joseph, his children, and grandchildren were the people she considered to be family.[13]

When Flora White made a trip to Oklahoma in 1937, her brother had lost his wife Jennie to Hodgkin's disease one year earlier. As Jennie's health deteriorated, Flora had expressed deep regret that her brother's lot in life had not been easy. Her correspondence with Catherine seemed to recall his separation from the family during boyhood, loss of a leg through an accidental gunshot wound, death of his son at age eleven, and the fact that he was, at that time, losing his wife to a terminal illness:

> My heart aches so for your dear father. I think of him day and night and what lies before him. He is so sweet and so plucky—so self-eliminating—I can't bear to have him hurt. Life has always hurt him too much anyhow. I am sending you my letter to your father and mother which can go with whatever you get in the way of a token from me. [White enclosed a check.][14]

After his wife's death, Joseph White continued to live in northwest Oklahoma, residing on the farms of his daughter Catherine or his son Charles. During that period Joseph and Flora forged an even deeper bond as Flora lost Mary, her closest confidante, first to dementia, and then to death in 1938.

In May of that year, twenty-two-year-old Grace Moyer traveled by bus from Oklahoma to Massachusetts to spend the summer with her great-aunt Flora. Grace's reminiscences of that summer—her first trip east since 1926—provide insights into White's life during her final years.

White had sold Plover Hill in 1933 and, when Grace arrived, occupied the upstairs apartment of her Heath home. Another couple, George and Marion Peon, lived downstairs. According to one essay written for Heath's bicentennial, the White sisters had made prior arrangements for George Peon and his family to farm their land.[15] Calver notes that White credited certain "Heath Youths, Geo. Peon among them" for first suggesting the idea for an agricultural society.[16]

At Heath, Grace was impressed with the "many distinguished friends" Flora White entertained for dinner, assisted by her great-niece.[17] The guests included Reinhold and Ursula Niebuhr, Felix and Marion Frankfurter, Howard and Louise Robbins, and Angus and Kitty Dun. Each morning prior to having dinner guests, White raised the window of her kitchen and "called out her order to the vendor below."[18] The order typically included such items as calf's liver, lamb chops, sweetbread, oysters, clams, camembert, mushrooms, blueberries, and watercress. White's table was set with blue willow china, crystal, silver, and linen napkins. Grace recalled, "The meals were quite different from the meat, mashed potatoes, gravy, and pie served on the farm [in Oklahoma] to large groups of working men and boys. . . . My mind was saying 'Why use all of these dishes when a large plate, a knife, fork, and spoon would do?'"[19] Grace also reported that small talk was absent from the dinner conversation of White and her guests. "They talked philosophy," Grace stated.[20]

In addition to hosting dinners for Heath summer people, Grace and Flora accompanied Stanley and Florence Cummings of nearby Shelburne Falls, Massachusetts, on driving trips to Quebec and points of interest in western Massachusetts and southern Vermont. Born in Burma where his father was a missionary, Stanley Cummings was a graduate of Clark University and a former teacher; his wife Florence was a writer. During the course of the summer Flora and Grace also went sightseeing with Judge Francis Thompson of the Probate Court in Greenfield, Massachusetts.

Looking back on the summer half a century later, Grace wrote, "Aunt Flora was so good to me and did so much for me, yet her expectations of my abilities were often hard to live up to. A[unt] Flora would tell her friends that I did calculus for past time [*sic*], while to be exact I never did more calculus than my assignments."[21] (It was actually Flora's father, Joseph White II, who pursued calculus on his own.) Grace also wrote that Flora arranged for her great niece to have the lead in the annual play at Heath and also volunteered her to sing in a sextet at church. Given that Grace lacked training in both areas, she found the experiences to be stressful. Her reaction recalled the discomfort Grace's mother felt at Miss White's Home School because her background differed from that of her schoolmates who enjoyed class privilege.

After Mary White died in the autumn of 1938, Flora and her brother Joseph were free to spend winters together in Oklahoma. Because the deep snows and isolated location made the family farms unsuitable for a visit, the two siblings spent four winters together in Oklahoma City. Dean Howard Robbins, working with Bishop Thomas Casady of the Episcopal Diocese of Oklahoma, got permission for them to stay in a house that a church member vacated each winter. When Flora and Joseph were not together in Oklahoma, they corresponded—reminiscing about their childhood, sharing news, exchanging their own poetry, and sometimes acknowledging how their lives differed from one another. In one undated letter, written from Bucksteep Manor in Becket, Massachusetts, Flora included an explanatory note lest her brother think she was pretentious, writing "Don't let the above name [Bucksteep Manor] (predicated by a purely English owner) prejudice you as being snobbish. It does look as I admit but it was given to the church for diocesan use when the owners were no longer able to come here for a part of each year as had been their habit before the war."[22]

In a letter to Flora, Joseph enclosed a tribute he delivered at the funeral of a close Oklahoma neighbor and friend. He recalled the neighbor was "fair, square, honest and upright in all his dealings, never attempting to take advantage in any way, but almost invariably returning more than he received."

Joseph White remembered his friend's "tears of sympathy" at Jennie's death, adding, "No word was spoken but the clasp of his hand was more than spoken words."[23] Perhaps anticipating how Flora might have viewed the neighbor while he lived, Joseph volunteered to his sister that the deceased friend was "kind and willing but not exactly a Sunday School supt."[24]

DEAR COUSIN FLORA

During her trips to Oklahoma, Flora White received updates on happenings in Heath through her correspondence with a close friend and distant cousin, Robert Strong Woodward (1885–1957), a New England landscape painter. Although White's letters to Woodward are not extant, his letters to her reveal something about the nature of their friendship.

Long distance travel was not an option for Woodward, due to his unusual life circumstances. Woodward initially intended to be an engineer; however, a revolver accident at age twenty-one resulted in the paralysis of his lower limbs, extended hospitalizations, confinement to a wheelchair, and "a life-time necessity for a small retinue of nurses and attendants."[25] He developed a hobby of painting into his life's work. Having spent his early years living in a variety of locations, Woodward expressed no affinity for a particular place, save his grandfather's farm in the hill town of Buckland, Massachusetts, near Heath. In 1912, Woodward moved to the family farm in Buckland and began to make a modest living as an illustrator. Beginning in 1915, he set out to become a landscape artist. Because of his well-developed upper body strength, he was able to hitch his horse to his buggy and travel the dirt roads to paint local scenery. "I live in an isolated way," he explained. "And I'm not able to get at things. With me it's been local country, the local scenery I've cared for."[26]

Although Woodward's formal education in painting was limited to part of one year at the School of the Museum of Fine Arts in Boston, in 1919 he won the Hallgarten Prize for landscape at the National Academy of Design. His rural scenes of western Massachusetts and southern Vermont were exhibited regularly at the Vose Gallery of Boston and in regional museums. Many of Woodward's paintings were placed in the homes of wealthy clients of Los Angeles designer Harold Walter Grieve, who knew Woodward during his youth. Among the owners of Woodward's paintings were Hollywood screen actress Beulah Bondi; entertainers Jack Benny, George Burns, and Gracie Allen; poet Robert Frost; and Supreme Court justice Oliver Wendell Holmes Jr. In 1933 Woodward was the only New England artist invited to exhibit his work at the Century of Progress exhibit in Chicago.

Flora White was a strong supporter of Robert Strong Woodward's art. In 1935 she sent a reproduction of a Woodward painting to Vermont native

John Dewey. His response indicated an interest in seeing more samples of the artist's work in an exhibit at Macbeth's gallery in New York.[27] Her support continued when, beginning in 1937, Woodward maintained a studio in Heath, and the White sisters arranged showings of his paintings at their home. When, in 1939, White published a poem titled "That Which Abides" and dedicated it to Woodward, she described Life and Death each claiming half of his body, due to his partial paralysis. Even with limited choices, Woodward chose to pursue life-affirming activities through landscape painting.[28]

When Robert Strong Woodward acquired a 1936 Packard Phaeton, and customized the back seat so he could ride and paint outdoor scenery, "Cousin Flora" often accompanied him along with his chauffeur, a local boy named Mark Purinton, whom Woodward reportedly regarded as the son he never had. Purinton would later recall how, during White's final years, she was determined to enjoy a full life despite the physical limitations of aging. Purinton wrote:

> I had driven the big car up to her front door and she came out to enter the rear seat. I opened up the rear door and she grasped for the strap to help her enter, but was unable to get up onto the running board except with one foot. She turned, looked down at me and said: "Young man, put your hands on my rump and push." This I did, and she made it into the back seat. We went for another ride.[29]

Occasionally Woodward's letters to White offer a glimpse of the athletic woman who built a professional reputation developing female physique. Noting that the eighty-one-year-old White was taking tango and rumba lessons, Woodward cautioned his friend to mind her knees.[30] In several letters Woodward gave White a candid appraisal of his own health concerns,[31] as well as the challenges he faced in selling art in an uncertain world.[32] Woodward also urged White to take care of herself on her long trips to Oklahoma. By 1942 or 1943 she had opted for air travel, as documented in a letter Grace Moyer received from her younger sister, Dorothy. Writing from the East Coast, Dorothy Moyer reported, "Aunt Flora should be about to Okla. City by now. She was to take a plane from New York at 1:30 this afternoon and . . . [arrive in Oklahoma] in 8 hours." Dorothy added, "Gosh, wouldn't that be wonderous. If I just had $80 I'd fly home some week end."[33] In the same letter Dorothy confided, "Aunt F. didn't know it, but [White's friends] were going to have a Dr. check her over the day before she left. Mrs. Moors gave her $100 . . . [W]ouldn't it be wonderful to have friends like [that]."[34]

FRIENDLY PERSUASION

In White's yearning for family, she hoped that her great-niece Grace Moyer would live with her in the East, pursue graduate study, and follow in her professional footsteps. In a 1938 letter to Grace, White wrote:

> What would you think of Columbia University for your Ph.D.—You might get a Scholarship or Fellowship there—They have a lot of them—And maybe we could live together out there on Morningside Heights where we used to visit the Robbins so much—I have friends out there too—the Vanderbilts and others—Think it over and maybe something will open up.[35]

Ever the teacher, White couldn't resist correcting Grace's grammar in the same letter, adding, "Oh by the way—don't use the phrase 'get to see.' The 'get' is superfluous and is poor English. . . . Your brief note was a joy to receive though—in spite of the 'get.'"[36]

In her later years, Flora White was economically strapped.[37] However, she lived comfortably, due in part to her friends.[38] Ethel Moors likely gave White some level of financial assistance, and Angus Dun prepared her state and federal tax returns.[39] To achieve a manageable living environment while conserving funds, White relocated from her home in Heath to the Wayside Inn in nearby Buckland around 1940. The proximity of Buckland to Heath allowed her to keep up with the activities of the summer people. For example, she wrote to Grace, "Ethel Moors had me up at The Manse in Heath (you remember, my great-grandmother's residence—add two more greats for yourself)."[40]

White repaid her friends' kindness with loyalty. When, in 1941—as the likelihood of U.S. involvement in another world war increased—White's editor, John Haynes Holmes, discovered that his pacifist stand had incurred the opposition of the *Unity* editorial board. White wrote a letter to the board chairman in support of Holmes and cancelled her subscription.[41] Due to a combination of her own reading and experience, and the influence of Holmes and her Heath friends, White's late-in-life writings became more focused on the subject of race privilege. She criticized the British rule in India and Africa,[42] as well as the U.S. history of "lynchings, . . . discriminatory laws, dishonorable dealings with the American Indians, . . . [and the] massacre of Filipinos."[43] This time her work was published in her own name, as opposed to the male pen name under which "Zan Zoo" appeared. With an attention to race, class, and gender, White's desire for agency to gain "more life, and fuller" for her students, her family, and herself now had a universal application.

In January of 1942, White made arrangements for Holmes to receive all royalties from the sale of her novel, *Bloodroots in the Wake of Circum-*

stance.[44] (She began the book at the end of the nineteenth century and published it—against the advice of her friends—just six years before her death.) Holmes wrote a letter to White, stating he could not accept such generosity from a living author who justly deserved the royalties.[45] Ten weeks later Holmes wrote to thank White for her gift to his church, the Community Church on Park Avenue in New York. He added that apart from White's generosity, her personal friendship meant everything to him.[46]

During this period White also belonged to the American Civil Liberties Union (ACLU). A January 19, 1942 letter from Roger Baldwin—a well-known pacifist and ACLU Executive Director—thanked White for her note and her dues. Baldwin added that although the ACLU did not want her to make a financial sacrifice, his conversation with White underscored her commitment to the cause, and he appreciated the enthusiasm behind her donation.[47]

During the final years of her life, White's writing and publication efforts also reflected earlier endeavors and interests. In 1939 she published *Poems by Mary A. White and Flora White* and dedicated it to "our former pupils and our many friends."[48] Flora also wrote other poems that appeared in anthologies. Her frequent contributions to *Unity* included poetry and book reviews, as well as commentary. For example, White wrote an article about the disagreement between John Dewey and Robert Maynard Hutchins, president of the University of Chicago, on what constituted a true education. White felt that lay people should be participants in the dialogue.[49]

As the United States entered a new war, White's Oklahoma relatives had not yet recovered from the ravages of the Dust Bowl. By 1941 the dust still piled nearly to the tops of the fence posts. That summer Catherine Moyer's husband Golden was hospitalized, and he suffered a stroke the following year. He was confined to a wheelchair for the remainder of his life. In 1945, Catherine Moyer became a widow, and her sons continued to handle the family's farming and ranching operations.

Meanwhile, Flora White felt wartime losses on a personal level upon receiving news of the death of Army Lieutenant j.g. Henry Nichols ("Skip") Ervin, Bobby's brother and one of the boys she kept at Plover Hill. A member of the Harvard class of 1940, Skip's plane was lost in 1943 while he was fighting in the South Pacific. A scholarship in his memory—the Henry Nichols Ervin Scholarship—is annually given to a student at St. Mark's School in Southborough, Massachusetts.

In 1943, visiting cleric Reinhold Niebuhr uttered a simple prayer to a war-weary congregation of farmers and summer people at the Heath Union Church: "God, give us grace to accept with serenity the things that cannot be changed, courage to change the things that should be changed, and the wisdom to distinguish the one from the other."[50] Howard Robbins attended the service and thought Niebuhr's prayer should be included in material the

Federal Council of Churches was preparing for army chaplains. It appeared in the *Book of Prayers and Services for the Armed Forces, Prepared by the Commission on Worship of the FCC and the Christian Commission for Camp and Defense Communities.* With Niebuhr's permission, Alcoholics Anonymous began using the prayer at regular meetings, as part of a twelve-step program. Niebuhr never copyrighted it because—as his daughter Elisabeth Sifton explains—he assumed prayers were not private property and never would have envisioned them as a source of revenue. AA simplified the text to read, "God, grant me the serenity to accept the things I cannot change, the courage to change the things I can, and wisdom to know the difference."[51] The Serenity Prayer became widely duplicated and distributed throughout the world.

Although Flora White continued to carefully manage her physical fitness, her health began to decline as she aged, and she spent her last few years at the Parks Convalescent Home in Greenfield, Massachusetts. White's later correspondence suggests she had few regrets about foregoing marriage and children or founding a school to prepare young women "for higher education and for life."[52] When White was seventy-nine, she urged her great-niece Grace Moyer to challenge traditional gender roles and envision accomplishments beyond what she (Flora) had achieved. White wrote, "You know, Mrs. Dwight Morrow is taking President Neilson's place at Smith this year as he is retiring. She is a grand person and will I am sure make good while she is there. Maybe you are booked to become a college president Grace—who knows—And why not! You made a grand impression on everybody here."[53]

Perceiving that cultural differences between the East and West might deter Grace from moving, White looked for opportunities to mention young women who had successfully made the transition. In one letter to Grace, White wrote, "Did I tell you that there was a very able Oklahoma girl teaching in the Arms Academy at S[helburne] Falls? She is a graduate of the Katherine Gibbs School from which Ruthie Chapin graduated a year ago—The girl's name is Stewart—Her brother is a lawyer in Okla. City."[54]

Although Grace Moyer did not relocate to live with her great-aunt, in 1942 Grace's younger sister Dorothy began work as a research assistant at the Osborn Botanical Laboratory at Yale University. The proximity of New Haven, Connecticut, to Heath, Massachusetts, allowed Dorothy to visit White and meet her Heath friends. On one visit Dorothy was accompanied by her brother, Joe Moyer, who was in the Navy, stationed in North Carolina. He greeted White in uniform. By 1945 both Moyer sisters were working for the Parke-Davis Pharmaceutical Company in Detroit; they took the train to Greenfield, Massachusetts, where their Aunt Flora was living in the Parks Convalescent Home. It was the last time they saw her.

When Grace Moyer married Robert Share in 1945 and gave birth to their first child the following year, White sent a gracious note: "Congratulations &

Best Wishes from Aunt Flora who rejoices in this grand event. Much love to all three of you"[55]

After fracturing her hip from a fall at the convalescent home, Flora White died at Franklin County Public Hospital on February 14, 1948. Given her record of promoting the physical and intellectual development of young women, it is interesting that White's obituary complimented her by stating her educational work was praised by "men of note."[56]

Flora White's funeral was conducted at St. James Episcopal Church in Greenfield. Margaret Malone's son Dana served as a pall bearer, along with the Peons' son Donald. Lawrence Chapin was an honorary bearer, as was Angus Dun, who had presided over the funeral of President Franklin Roosevelt three years earlier. Due to the frozen ground, burial was delayed until after the spring thaw. On May 5, 1948, Flora White was interred beside her sister Mary at Heath's South Cemetery. The land was donated in 1771 by Colonel Jonathan White, Flora's great-great grandfather.

Following her aunt's death, Catherine Moyer received letters of condolence from Margaret Malone and Robert Strong Woodward. Malone eulogized the White sisters, noting that they were among the best of their generation and field of endeavor. She praised Flora for her generosity, fair-mindedness, loyalty, and courage, as well as for her excellent philosophy and well-informed liberalism.[57] On March 12, 1948, Robert Strong Woodward wrote to say how deeply he missed Cousin Flora.[58] Later Woodward wrote to describe her interment on a dark, misty day with a small number of people assembled for a ceremony that was at once sweet, sad—and beautiful.[59] Among the flowers was a tub of pansies sent by Flora's brother, Joseph. Woodward wrote that it was not practical for him to get out of the car for the service. However, he would continue to visit White's grave, located near the cemetery's roadside wall. He planned to periodically place a few of the native wildflowers there that had always delighted Cousin Flora.[60]

Robert Strong Woodward died in 1957. His young chauffeur, now Dr. Mark Purinton, maintains one of his studios and a website in his memory. Joseph White, Flora's brother, died in 1949 at the age of 92. His obituary included one of his poems, published in the 1939 edition of *Poetry Digest*.[61] The same volume featured a poem by Flora, who likely introduced him to the publication.[62]

NOTES

1. Timothy Egan, *The Worst Hard Time: The Untold Story of Those Who Survived the Great American Dust Bowl* (Boston: Mariner Books, 2006), 125.

2. Ibid., 228.

3. Ibid., 256.

4. Cliff Moyer, "More Than a Depression [as told by Robert Moyer]" in *Town of Gage History* (Gage, OK: Gage Chamber of Commerce, 1984), 66.

5. Egan, *The Worst Hard Time*, 269.

6. Ibid., 267.

7. Ibid., 268.

8. Ibid., 269.

9. H. L. Mencken, "The Dole for Bogus American Farmers," *The American Mercury*, (1936), 400, http://www.unz.org/Pub/AmMercury--1936dec-0400.

10. Ibid., 404.

11. Edward Calver, *Heath, Massachusetts: A History and Guidebook*, 3rd ed. (Heath, MA: Heath Historical Society), 182.

12. Flora White to Catherine White Moyer, 4 July 1935. Flora White Papers, private collection.

13. Flora White, "Life Facts of Flora White and Family Recorded Mar. 18, 1939," Heath Historical Society, 7.

14. Flora White to Catherine White Moyer, 14 February 1936. Flora White Papers, private collection.

15. Newland F. Smith Jr., "Early Summer People in Heath," in *The Book of Heath: Bicentennial Essays*, ed. Susan B. Silvester (Ashfield, MA: Paideia, 1985), 142.

16. Calver, *Heath, Massachusetts*, 189.

17. Grace Moyer Share, "The Summer of 1938" (unpublished manuscript, 1986). Flora White Papers, private collection, 2.

18. Ibid., 7–8.

19. Ibid.

20. Grace Moyer Share conversation with author, August 7, 2003.

21. Share, "The Summer of 1938," 2.

22. Flora White to Joseph White, 7 August 1943. Flora White Papers, private collection.

23. Joseph White, "A Tribute to the Memory of Charlie Pierce Presented at His Funeral Service December 29, 1938" (written in 1986). Flora White Papers, private collection.

24. Joseph White to Flora White, 5 August 1939. Flora White Papers, private collection.

25. Alastair Maitland, "Robert Strong Woodward in Heath," in *The Book of Heath: Bicentennial Essays*, ed. Susan B. Silvester (Ashfield, MA: Paideia, 1985), 161.

26. Ibid., 169.

27. John Dewey to Flora White, 20 February 1935. Flora White Papers, private collection.

28. Flora White, "That Which Abides," *Poems by Mary and Flora White* (New York: Paebar, 1939), 62–63.

29. Robert Strong Woodward, http://robertstrong woodward.com/Friends/Friendshtm.

30. Robert Strong Woodward to Flora White, 5 December 1941. Flora White Papers, private collection.

31. Robert Strong Woodward to Flora White, 18 November 1941. Flora White Papers, private collection.

32. Robert Strong Woodward to Flora White, 12 March 1942; Robert Strong Woodward to Flora White, 10 April 1942. Flora White Papers, private collection.

33. Dorothy Moyer to Grace Moyer, circa 1942–1943. Flora White Papers, private collection.

34. Ibid.

35. Flora White to Grace Moyer, 2 May 1940. Flora White Papers, private collection.

36. Ibid.

37. Calver, *Heath, Massachusetts*, 196.

38. Grace Moyer Share, "The Summer of 1938" (unpublished manuscript). Flora White Papers, private collection, 6–9.

39. Angus Dun to Flora White, 15 January 1941. Flora White Papers, private collection; Angus Dun to Flora White, 22 January 1942. Flora White Papers, private collection.

40. Flora White to Grace Moyer, 2 May 1940.

41. John Haynes Holmes to Flora White, 22 April 1941. Flora White Papers, private collection; John Haynes Holmes to Flora White, 29 April, 1941. Flora White Papers, private collection; William H. Holly to Flora White, 24 April, 1941. Flora White Papers, private collection.

42. Flora White, "India," *Unity*, January 1944.

43. Flora White, "Reply to Mr. Johnson," *Unity* 127 (7): 119.

44. Flora White, *Bloodroots in the Wake of Circumstance* (Kansas City, MO: Burton Publishing Company, 1942).

45. John Haynes Holmes to Flora White, 23 January 1942. Flora White Papers, private collection.

46. John Haynes Holmes to Flora White, 6 April 1942. Flora White Papers, private collection.

47. Roger Baldwin to Flora White, 19 January 1941. Flora White Papers, private collection.

48. Mary A. White and Flora White, *Poems by Mary A. White and Flora White* (New York: Paebar, 1939).

49. Flora White, "A Basic Necessity," *Unity*, December 2, 1940: 105.

50. Elisabeth Sifton, "The Serenity Prayer," *Yale Review* 86 (1998): 6.

51. "The Origin of Our Serenity Prayer," http://www.aahistory.com/prayer.html.

52. *Miss White's Home School*, 1906, 3.

53. Flora White to Grace Moyer, 15 October 1939. Flora White Papers, private collection.

54. Flora White to Grace Moyer, 2 May 1940.

55. Flora White to Grace Moyer Share and Bob Share, 1945, Flora White Papers, private collection.

56. "Writer, Educator, Miss White Dies," *Greenfield Gazette and Courier* (Greenfield, MA), February 16, 1948, 2.

57. Margaret Malone to Catherine White Moyer, 14 October 1948. Flora White Papers, private collection.

58. Robert Strong Woodward to Catherine White Moyer, 12 May 1948. Flora White Papers, private collection.

59. Robert Strong Woodward to Catherine White Moyer, 15 June 1948. Flora White Papers, private collection.

60. Ibid.

61. Joseph David White Obituary. Private collection; Joseph David White, "Voices," in *The Poetry Digest; Annual Anthology of Verse for 1939* (New York: The Poetry Digest, 1939), 118–119.

62. Flora White, "That Which Abides," in *The Poetry Digest; Annual Anthology of Verse for 1939* (New York: The Poetry Digest, 1939), 117.

Epilogue

In 2010, 706 people lived in Heath, Massachusetts, which still has the aura of a typical New England town. A plaque identifies the former home of Flora and Mary White, now a private residence. Plover Hill is also a private home. Over time, the forest has encroached on Heath's former fields, giving the town a wooded appearance. The scenery is still beautiful. The Heath Historical Society sells note cards depicting watercolors of town scenes; its webpage displays a photograph of "Center Schoolhouse in Winter" where three Moyer children studied under their father in 1925–1926.[1] The students are gone from Center School, which today houses school artifacts and a small library for genealogical and historical research. The current Heath Elementary School is a modern facility offering "Personalized learning in a unique rural environment."[2] It enrolls fifty-three children in grades prekindergarten through six.[3] Older students go to nearby Buckland to attend the Mohawk Trail Regional Middle School/High School.

The historic white clapboard sanctuary in the town center is the home of Heath Evangelical Union Church, an independent congregation that traces its roots to the 1892 merger of the town's Congregationalists, Methodists, and Baptists. The church has the distinction of housing an 1850 Opus 16 pipe organ—the oldest surviving instrument made by William A. Johnson, one of New England's foremost organ builders. With the support of neighboring communities, Heath residents raised funds for the instrument's restoration and, in 2013, celebrated its return to the church with an inaugural concert by Nathan Laube of the Eastman School of Music. Eighty-eight years earlier, the pipe organ made an impression on Golden Moyer Jr., who recalled it in a 1987 letter to his sister Grace.[4]

Myrifield, the house where Dr. Grace Wolcott offered occupational therapy to women patients, is today the location of a not-for-profit organization called the Myrifield Institute for Cognition and the Arts. It was founded in 2008 by professors from Case Western University, the University of Southern California, and Los Angeles College. The organization sponsors small gatherings of researchers from multiple disciplines who informally share their work and explore areas of collaboration between the cognitive sciences and the arts. Just as Myrifield evokes the collaborative spirit of Heath's early summer people, their influence is also felt in the lives of progressives who have chosen to reside at Heath into the twenty-first century. For example, a September 8, 2001, article in *The Los Angeles Times* announced the death of Presbyterian minister and theologian Robert McAfee Brown, who taught in the Pacific School of Religion at the University of California Berkeley.[5] Brown lived in Palo Alto but maintained a summer home in Heath, and—like Flora White—died in nearby Greenfield, Massachusetts, after a suffering a fall. A student of Reinhold Niebuhr's at Union Theological Seminary, Brown first came to Heath in the summer of 1943 to work on a farm; he then married and became a regular summer resident. He is remembered for initiating dialogue among religions and bringing liberation theology to the attention of mainstream Protestant churches.[6] In 1962, *Time* magazine called Brown—an official observer of the second Vatican Council—the "Catholics' favorite Protestant."[7] During his colorful life Brown was a freedom rider who went to jail during the Civil Rights Movement; he also protested the Vietnam War and nuclear weapons, evoking the pacifism of Heath residents who preceded him.

Although a number of Joseph White's progeny have visited Heath over the years, none have established residences there. Catherine Moyer remained in her Oklahoma farm home until the early 1950s; she then resided in Gage until her death in 1964. Today the children of Catherine's youngest son operate the Moyer Ranch in the area where she and Golden lived, and the old Moyer farm home remains in the family. Catherine's brother, Charles White, resided on his Oklahoma farm until his death in 1975. His home remains in the family, and the White Ranch is operated by his progeny. In 1941 Charles White was a founding member of the Board of Supervisors of the Ellis County Soil and Water Conservation District (later named the Ellis County Conservation District). He remained in that role for thirty years. Soil conservation districts, established throughout the United States, were Hugh Bennett's vision of a cooperative effort in which farmers entered into contracts to manage the land as a single, ecological unit. Today they are the only grassroots programs remaining from Roosevelt's New Deal. Although dusters returned to the southern plains during the 1950s, and droughts in 1974–1976 caused the soil to drift, the earth held much better than before. A major study in 2004 (comparing how farmers treated the land before and after the dusters of the 1930s) concluded that the conservation districts kept the soil from blowing.[8]

Joseph White's grandchildren, whom Flora was anxious to educate, chose fields of study (engineering, medicine, the sciences, animal husbandry) that reflected a Western practicality over the English literature and philosophy that she enjoyed during adolescence and young adulthood. Golden Jr. and Joe Moyer became engineers for oil companies; Herman became a physician. Although G. Stanley Hall predicted that child study would become the pre-eminent "women's science," Grace and Dorothy studied sciences dominated by men.[9] During World War II, Grace taught physics to Army Air Corps cadets. As a research assistant at Yale, Dorothy co-authored journal articles on vitamin deficiencies and sources, and then did vitamin research at Parke-Davis. The three youngest grandchildren—Bill, Bob, and Joe White—all became successful ranchers in northwest Oklahoma. Dorothy and Joe White served on local school boards, and Bill was an aide to a U.S. Congressman from Oklahoma. Two grandsons (Bob and Joe Moyer) served in the U.S. Navy.

The youngest and last surviving grandchild—Joseph Brintain White—died in Oklahoma in 2005. Today, next to the farm home where he grew up, a tall evergreen is the sole survivor of a group of trees Flora sent to family members on the southern plains many years ago. Demonstrating agency in a land threatened by drought, White's relatives helped the tree survive by nourishing it with dish water. Flora would have admired their life-affirming act as well as the tree's resilience, as evidenced by the remarks she first made at the Buffalo meeting of the NEA and later published in the *Sloyd Bulletin*:

> I have noticed in certain countries beyond the tropics trees that have impressed me with their grandeur and vigor; and then some morning I have gone forth and found them lying in the dust with helpless, upturned roots, wind-blown. Sun and shower have fondled them. With no obstacles to overcome, no winters to resist, no rocks to upturn, they had put forth a rank, showy, ineffective verdure—a growth in appearance but not in strength.
> We want no windblown characters.[10]

As Elisabeth Sifton observed, "character was everything" to Heath people.[11]

Flora White's desire to obtain "more life, and fuller" for her students, her relatives, her friends, and herself—and ultimately for all of humanity—can be seen in an ongoing effort to achieve agency. After experiencing childhood poverty that restricted her opportunities, she promoted the education of children with an eye to their own needs and desires. When scientific and medical authorities claimed that women were intellectually and physically limited, White developed her own capabilities while founding a school that pushed young women far beyond the gender restrictions of the time. When an environmental and economic catastrophe threatened the futures of her great-nieces and great-nephews, she offered assistance that recalled Isaac Esty's kindness when she was a girl in Amherst. When global imperialism limited the life options of people of color, she drew on her writing ability to call attention to the problem. Even when aging diminished her capacity, White continued to challenge herself—mentally and physically—through individual effort and interactions with stimulating and accomplished people.

Perhaps Flora White's final act of agency was to leave documents that would tell her life story, specifying that they be entrusted to her brother and his progeny. At the time of her death in 1948 there was little scholarly interest in women's history. However, the changing role of women (which White helped to bring about), and the willingness of friends at Heath and relatives in Oklahoma to safeguard her papers for many decades, resulted in new areas of scholarly inquiry in which her papers were beneficial. Time proved her right, and Flora White's papers eventually set the record straight on her own contributions, as well as those of other women.

In looking back at Flora White's experience from a twenty-first century perspective, it is important to note that she first rebelled against the status quo as a teacher in a public school system during a period of rapid industrialization. In the late nineteenth and early twentieth centuries, educational reforms reflecting Frederick W. Taylor's scientific management produced what Joel Spring calls "an increased sense of powerlessness [i.e., a lack of agency] among many teachers." Spring added that the system justified "the traditional educational harem of female schoolteachers ruled by male administrators," adding, "Within the hierarchal structure of the new corporate model, teachers were at the bottom of the chain of command."[12] White's response was to leave public education and found her own school, first at Springfield and then at Concord.

Spring contends that today, in the wake of the 2001 passage of the federal legislation known as the No Child Left Behind Act, public schools are increasingly engaged in developing standards to track student and teacher progress using the latest technology, thereby running the risk of reducing human beings to statistical data. He notes that such practices seem to evoke the scientific management of a century ago, in which teachers felt powerless. Other scholars have reported that new educational reforms are eroding teacher agency, a critical factor in student learning.[13] This trend is occurring in a teaching force that is—as in White's day—overwhelmingly female.[14]

Flora White's story should be considered, in part, as a cautionary note. She would remind us, as she reminded NEA members in 1896, that education should be life-enhancing, not life-restricting—underscoring her point by adding, "I don't believe we can get beyond that."

NOTES

1. "Heath Historical Society," http://www.townofheath.org?page_ids2127.

2. "Mohawk/Hawlemont School Districts: Heath Elementary School" http://Mohawkschools.org/heath.php.

3. "Heath Elementary" School and District Profiles. Massachusetts Department of Elementary and Secondary Education, 2015.

4. Golden Moyer Jr. to Grace Moyer Share, 10 March 1987, Flora White Papers, private collection.

5. Dennis McLellan, "Robert Brown, 81; Championed Liberation Theology," *Los Angeles Times*, September 8, 2001.

6. Liberation theology is a political movement in Roman Catholic theology that interprets the teachings of Jesus in relation to liberation from unjust economic, political, or social conditions.

7. McLellan, "Robert Brown," September 8, 2001.

8. Timothy Egan, *The Worst Hard Time: The Untold Story of Those Who Survived the Great American Dust Bowl* (Boston: Mariner, 2006), 311.

9. Dorothy Ross, *G. Stanley Hall The Psychologist as Prophet* (Chicago: University of Chicago Press, 1972), 260.

10. Flora White, "Physical Effects of Sloyd," *Sloyd Bulletin* 2 (1899): 9–10.

11. Elisabeth Sifton, *The Serenity Prayer: Faith and Politics in Times of Peace and War* (New York: W. W. Norton & Company, 2001), 19.

12. Joel Spring, *The American School: A Global Context from the Puritans to the Obama Era* (New York: McGraw-Hill, 2011), 300.

13. Sue Lasky, "A Sociocultural Approach to Understanding Teacher Identity, Agency, and Professional Vulnerability in a Context of Secondary School Reform," *Teaching and Teacher Education* 21 (2005): 899–916; Mark Priestley et al., "Teacher Agency in Curriculum Making: Agents of Change and Spaces for Manoeuvre," *Curriculum Inquiry* 42 (2012): 191–214; Lauren Anderson, "Embedded, Emboldened, and (Net)Working for Change: Support-Seeking and Teacher Agency in Urban, High-Needs Schools," *Harvard Educational Review* 80 (2010): 541–573.

14. In 2014 *The New York Times* reported that that over 75 percent of all U.S. teachers in kindergarten through high school are women. See Motoko Rich, "Why Don't More Men Go into Teaching?," *New York Times*, September 6, 2004.

Appendix

FAMILY RELATIONSHIPS: A NOTE ON SOURCES AND METHODOLOGY

The telling of Flora White's story would be incomplete without a discussion of my family connection to her, the sources that relationship allowed me to access, and my approach to utilizing them. Although I never knew Flora White, she was my maternal grandmother's aunt, and in many ways I bene-fited from that relationship. After her death, White's papers were sent to her brother Joseph (my great-grandfather) who lived on a farm in Oklahoma. Because my relatives were "savers" who stored her papers for nearly the next half century, I became the grateful recipient of rich primary source material including personal correspondence, lectures, photographs, and poetry that had never before been examined by scholars. Given the difficulty of finding historical materials on women of White's era, this was no small advantage.

Yet the familial relationship with White also presented challenges as I examined her life during her retirement, especially from the 1920s until her death when relatives I had known and loved—my mother, grandmother, aunts, and uncles—became actors in her story. Some, including my grand-mother and mother, lived with Flora White for a year; most kept in contact with her through correspondence or her yearly extended stays in Oklahoma. All of my family members gratefully acknowledged the material and emo-tional support she gave them through the Dust Bowl years. As I ventured beyond her career as a progressive educator to examine new sources, I inevi-tably encountered evidence of personal insecurities, economic hardships, and strained family relations of which I had been unaware. I began to second-guess my decisions about which details to include and exclude as I made new discoveries about people with whom I had enjoyed a close relationship. I also developed a growing discomfort with that fact that my connection to White had been closer in time than I previously acknowledged. As I pored through old correspondence, I understood that family members who welcomed me into the world were, in the same time frame, responding to letters of condolence following White's interment. Despite my best attempts at detachment, Flora White's life story was becoming *personal*. Throughout this process, fellow biographers and colleagues urged me to explore this familial relationship to determine where *I* fit into the telling of Flora White's life.

A COMFORT ZONE

When I began my research on White, I was confident of my ability to avoid the trap described by biographer Lynda Anderson Smith, who warned that "[f]ascination and over-identification with the subject, combined with a desire to please" leads to distortion and destroys impartiality. She urged biographers to mitigate "fascination with reason, . . . [and balance] subjectivity with objectivity" in their work.[1] Since I had never known White—and my relatives who knew her were deceased—I believed I could write her life story in an evenhanded manner. My initial plan seemed to bear fruit. In a careful study of the available primary and secondary sources, I learned that White had founded a school based on the principles of Organic Education a decade before Marietta Johnson established the Organic School at Fairhope, Alabama. This finding challenged views of current scholars, reflected in a 2013 dissertation from the University of Amsterdam that claimed, "only one reformer—Marietta Johnson of Fairhope, Alabama—dared to found a school, its core curriculum sailing under the flag of [Charles Hanford] Henderson's organic education."[2] I also learned that White had made a bold and very critical statement on the status of schooling when she presented a paper at the 1896 meeting of the National Education Association (NEA). According to Kate Rousmaniere, women teachers were strongly discouraged from speaking in that NEA meeting. I found that White challenged the prevailing medical and scientific views of her day by championing the intellectual and physical capabilities of women. Her school alumnae included the dean of Wellesley College as well as graduates who were prominent in the arts and community service.

My expectation of an evenhanded study of Flora White was heightened by the fact that she became my biographical subject largely by happenstance. During the summer of 1994, my daughter Sarah traveled from our home in St. Louis to attend a theater program for high school students in Boston. Since Sarah was interested in several colleges and universities in the Northeast, she, my husband Jim, and I planned a whirlwind driving tour of campuses following the theater program's conclusion. One planned stop was

Williams College, located in Williamstown in a remote area of northwest Massachusetts. I had never been to that part of the state but noticed on the map that our route would take us within a couple of miles of the small village of Heath where my mother's forebearers, the Whites, lived for nearly two hundred years. My mother was not an Easterner, having been born and nurtured to adulthood on the High Plains of western Oklahoma. However, as a young child she lived with her family at Heath for one school year in the home of her great-aunt, Flora. After college graduation my mother was employed in Connecticut for two years, and she reestablished her relationship with White. As Jim, Sarah, and I rode down Massachusetts Highway 2 toward Williamstown, I pondered my family history and asked that they indulge my curiosity by making a quick right turn toward Heath. As we climbed the hill to the small village, I promised the stay would be a short one.

With its classic town center and isolated eighteenth-century farm homes, Heath appeared to have changed very little over the years. One of the houses had a plaque indicating that Flora White had lived there. Intrigued, I inquired at the small post office, the only official-looking building that appeared to be open. After introducing myself and revealing my relationship to White, I asked the postal employee if she knew anyone in town who might be able to shed additional light on my forebearer. She listed to me, silently nodded her head, and made a phone call. Within minutes, Pegge Howland appeared. As president of the Heath Historical Society, she gave us a tour of the Heath town center and sold me several of the society's books that contained information on White. As we toured, a man who resided in the town center told Jim that Flora and her sister Mary "blew into the town like a hurricane."[3] Howland added that White had raised some eyebrows by leading her female students in calisthenics on the town green at a time when women were discouraged from physical activity. As we departed from Heath, I concluded that there was more to be discovered about Flora White as an educator and woman who challenged gender stereotypes. My daughter Sarah decided to go to Yale, and I did not return to northwest Massachusetts for seventeen years. My next trip to Heath, however, was in the role of biographical researcher. I renewed my acquaintance with Pegge Howland and learned that she and her husband David had purchased Flora White's home where my mother had lived. Pegge graciously gave me a tour.

In growing up, I learned through family lore that Flora White had a private school for girls in Concord, Massachusetts. I also knew that my maternal grandmother (White's niece) had attended the school for one year. However, even as an adult, I knew nothing about White's relationship to progressive education, and I am fairly certain my relatives were unaware of this connection as well. Instead, they communicated that Aunt Flora was a colorful personality who was connected to important people. Although the 1994 visit to Heath piqued my curiosity, I had limited opportunity in which to pursue her life story due to my full-time employment as a school district administrator. In 2004, I accepted a tenure-track position at a state university in Illinois and focused my interest in finding primary and secondary sources on White's life. My faculty appointment was in the Department of Educational Leadership, so my initial goal was to explore White's role as a woman leader in the formative period of progressive education. Since the topic had little to do with anyone I knew or had known, I was in my comfort zone.

PRODDED BY BIOGRAPHICAL THEORISTS

Still, I found it necessary to distinguish my work in historical biography from that of a genealogist. In reading *The Challenge of Feminist Biography*, I noted with interest Elisabeth Israels Perry's essay on her subject, Belle Moskowitz (1877–1933), her paternal grandmother. Perry had never known Moskowitz, who died six years before Perry was born. The distance between writer and subject was more pronounced by the fact that Perry's parents divorced when she was a baby. She spent her childhood largely with her mother and had no memory of her father ever talking about *his* mother. Perry eventually learned that Moskowitz was "almost a family secret," even though she organized the women's vote for New York Governor Al Smith and was the only woman on the executive committee of the Democratic National Committee. When Perry's colleagues questioned whether she could maintain scholarly detachment in studying her paternal grandmother, Perry protested that she had never "loved" Moskowitz "in the way one loves a grandmother," adding, "I'm a historian, not a hagiographer."[4]

While there were similarities between Perry's situation and my own study of White, there were also important differences. For example, Perry learned very early that Moskowitz had thrown away all of her papers, making the search for primary sources very difficult. Perry had to contextualize large portions of Moskowitz's life, thereby avoiding the mistake of affording her undue importance in historical events. Eventually Perry "hit a delicious find" when she opened a file on water power from Al Smith's post-1929 papers and discovered fifteen letters from Moskowitz to Smith from the mid-1920s, none of which dealt with water power.[5] In weighing the benefits and liabilities of writing about a relative, Perry acknowledged that her relationship to Moskowitz had given her access to places that were closed to others. At the same time, Perry made discoveries about family members that "disturbed" her, and she "fretted over which to use."[6]

Flora White's sources were easier to locate than those of Belle Moskowitz. Through the generosity of my late aunt, Florence Oetken Moyer, I became the grateful recipient of an archive that contained many of Flora White's primary sources. It includes two caches of letters White wrote to her mother and sister Mary while teaching in the Cape Colony in southern Africa in 1885 to 1887, and during her study in Sweden in the summer of 1891.[7] This correspondence was supplemented by two letters White wrote to the president of the alumni association at Westfield State College (her alma mater), as well as correspondence she sent to Oklahoma to Catherine White Moyer (White's niece) and Grace Moyer Share (White's great-niece) during the 1930s and 1940s. In 1986, Share penned her recollections of the summer of 1938 when she traveled from Oklahoma to Massachusetts for an extended stay with her great aunt Flora. These reminiscences are now part of the archive, as are reflections of Catherine White Moyer's two oldest children (Golden and Grace) on their experiences living in the White sisters' home in Heath in 1925–1926. Also included is a collection of letters White received from her friend, New England landscape artist Robert Strong Woodward, and from her brother Joseph. There are copies of informational booklets from White's school, her published articles, and drafts of speeches she presented to professional audiences. There are also several White family histories situated in Massachusetts and in England before the Puritan migration of the 1630s. Although not part of the collection I inherited, the voices of White's former students provide an important supplement to the information in her school bulletins. Their interview transcripts, compiled during the 1970s, are available online through the Renee Garrelick Oral History Program Collection of the Concord Free Public Library. They are supplemented by a taped interview of White's former student Dorothy Winsor Bisbee, which her grandson, Rick Zamore, also conducted in the 1970s.

In addition to having access to these materials, I was fortunate to experience my own "delicious find" when I returned to Heath in 2011. Seeking information on Flora's parents, I discovered a booklet that the Heath Historical Society had attributed to an unknown White family member. Clearly hand written by my biographical subject, it was titled, " Life Facts of Flora White and Family Recorded Mar. 18, 1939." The booklet gave a detailed, first-person description of White's family members and friends as well as her educational experiences, professional activities, religious involvement, writing and travels, and real estate purchases. What she chose to include and exclude in this document was revealing. At the time of writing, Flora's brother Joseph was her only surviving sibling. His name appears at the top of a listing of "Family & Friends" followed by "His daughter Catherine" and the names of her seven children. (The fourth child, Dorothy, was my mother.) In addition, Flora listed her brother's son, Charles, and his son, also living in Oklahoma. Even though White's oldest sister Emma had ten children, Flora made it clear that Emma had moved to Washington State many years earlier. The relationship was apparently not a close one, and Emma's children and grandchildren were not listed. Finding this document confirmed the importance of my close family members to Flora White, and therefore to me, her biographer. The point was underscored by a note she left in her personal papers indicating they were intended for the use of her brother Joseph, his children, and grandchildren.

WORKING THE HYPHEN

In "Necessary Betrayals: Reflections on Biographical Work on a Racist Ancestor," Lucy E. Bailey offers insight on challenges scholars face in writing about deceased family members. She cites Michelle Fine's use of the term, "working the hyphen," noting that the hyphen symbolizes ways in which researchers are linked with the people they study. Fine states that some researchers tend to romanticize the links and affinities between researchers and subjects; others undertheorize the relationships; still others grapple with the methodological possibilities and interpretive pitfalls that such relationships present for biographical inquiry. Dismissing the possibility that researchers can be neutral, Fine writes that, regardless of how researchers are linked to their subjects, the attachments should be considered an important part of qualitative work. Citing a cultural tendency to romanticize bloodlines that raises challenging methodological issues, Bailey notes that biographers might easily glorify ancestors' accomplishments at the expense of critical questions, avoid offending family members during interviews, worry about which family secrets to include and hide, or deliberate on how to negotiate such matters with relatives. Researchers may also struggle with the question of "how to bear the ethical dilemma of championing particular aspects of a life and remaining silent on others that present the subject in a richer, more human, and yet, less favorable light."[8] As I mused over Bailey's cautionary note, I tried to base my decisions to include or exclude information on whether it was important to understanding Flora White. I therefore chose to include some information that might be embarrassing (a relative's bankruptcy) while excluding a relative's medical history that was less pertinent.

AN ASSESSMENT

When Elisabeth Israels Perry pondered her relationship with Belle Moskowitz, she concluded, "On the whole, the ledger of my kinship to my subject is more positive than negative." Perry reported she had never been close to her father, and learning about his family gave her "a certain peace" about their relationship. Writing about Moskowitz's role in the history of feminism also made Perry closer to her daughter. Finally, the familial connection prodded Perry to "see the project through" when she encountered obstacles and became discouraged.[9]

I think my familial relationship to Flora White also falls on the positive side of the ledger. It gave me access to rare primary sources on women's history that might otherwise have been lost through the passing of genera- tions. While locating women's biographical sources can prove challenging, discovering sources on *women teachers* is especially difficult, according to Alison Prentice and Marjorie R. Theobald. They note that the "recovery and interpretation of...the hidden, private world of female teachers presents for- midable methodological problems," not the least of which is that "sources are scarce and widely scattered."[10]

Family connections also allowed me, in Bailey's words, to make White "more human" by acknowledging information that might put her in a "less favorable light." For example, White believed, following a tradition going back to Rousseau, that teachers should not attempt to mold their pupils according to the teachers' preconceived ends. Yet both my grandmother (who attended Flora's Concord school) and my aunt (who spent the summer of 1938 with Flora) felt "pushed" by White to meet her high academic and social standards. The combination of Flora's early poverty following the death of her father, the intellectual climate of Heath, and the poverty of her Oklahoma relatives in the Dust Bowl caused her to place a premium on education as a means of exercising agency to improve one's position. She was very proud of the accomplishments of her ancestors and reminded her relatives (and perhaps herself) that they came from good stock. In my re- search, I learned that, as an adult, my grandmother questioned Flora's em- phasis on family ancestry.[11] I concluded that Grandmother was ambivalent on the subject when relatives reported she routinely took the family history volumes with her to the cellar when seeking shelter from tornadoes.

My biographical research convinced me that Flora White's narrative was not only situated in New England, and was closer to my own experience than I had realized. Veering off Highway 2 was an important turn in the road of my own life story, and my own self-awareness.

NOTES

1. Lynda Anderson Smith, "The Biographer's Relationship with Her Subject," in *Writing Educational Biography: Explorations in Qualitative Research*, ed. Craig Kridel (New York and London: Garland, 1998), 200.

2. Jeroen F. Staring. "Midwives of Progressive Education: The Bureau of Education Ex- periments 1916–1919," PhD diss., University of Amsterdam, 2013, 26.

3. James Morice, in discussion with author, September 22, 2014.

4. Elizabeth Israels Perry, "From Belle Moskowitz to Women's History," in *The Challenge of Feminist Biography*, ed. Sara Alpern et al. (Urbana and Chicago: University of Illinois Press, 1992), 95.

5. Ibid., 86.

6. Ibid., 95.

7. I am using "archive" loosely to describe a collection of documents I received from my relatives, Florence Moyer, Grace Moyer Share, and Sara Kennedy.

8. Lucy E. Bailey, "Necessary Betrayals: Reflections on Biographical Work on a Racist Ancestor," in *Life Stories: Exploring Issues in Educational History through Biography*, eds. Linda C. Morice and Laurel Puchner, 254–264 (Charlotte, NC: Information Age).

9. Perry, "From Belle Moskowitz to Women's History," 95.

10. Alison Prentice and Marjorie R. Theobald, eds., *Women Who Taught: Perspectives on the History of Women and Teaching* (Toronto: University of Toronto Press, 1991), 9.

11. Catherine White Moyer to Joseph White, December 5, 1941 (private collection).

Acknowledgments

In writing *Flora White: In the Vanguard of Gender Equity*, I had the support of many people who helped locate, preserve, and contextualize primary sources on White's life. I am also deeply indebted to the individuals who contributed their editorial and technical expertise to the book.

Deserving special mention are my aunts, Florence Oetken Moyer and Grace Moyer Share, who recognized the importance of White's documents for future generations and took steps to preserve the material during the last years of their lives. Aunt Florence maintained Flora White's personal papers, which she inherited upon the death of her husband Golden Moyer Jr., the oldest of Joseph White's grandchildren. Aunt Grace preserved the letters she received from Flora, and wrote recollections of her experiences with the White sisters in 1924–1925 and 1938. Both aunts gave me their papers at a time when I was beginning a tenure-track position in educational leadership at Southern Illinois University Edwardsville (SIUE). Sensing the documents' potential contribution to educational history and women's history, I made Flora White's life story a major focus of my research. Other family members—including Sara Kennedy, Brinda White, Joy White, Koral Moyer, Kenneth Moyer, and Kris-Ann Moyer—also provided important sources and information that helped humanize my biographical subject and establish the focus of her initiatives.

These family sources were amplified by material furnished by librarians, archivists, and members of local historical societies, and by the relatives of one of White's former students. A key contributor was Pegge Howland of the Heath (MA) Historical Society, who introduced me to several local histories during my 1994 visit to the town. When I returned in 2010, she helped me research the society's archives and, with her husband David Howland, gave me a tour of their home—the White sisters' former residence where Cathe-

193

rine and Golden Moyer and their five children also lived in 1924–1925. Other Massachusetts residents made important contributions to the book. The Howlands' neighbor Robert Viarengo—current owner of Plover Hill—graciously offered me photographs and information on his property. In Boston, law librarian Eva Murphy researched the 1851 legislative record of Flora's father, Joseph White II. Karen Canary, archives assistant at the Ely Library at Westfield (MA) State University, furnished primary and secondary sources on Flora White's normal school experience. Michele Plourde-Barker, archivist at the Springfield (MA) history museum, located the White sisters' residences and schools during their early teaching careers. Rick Teller, archivist at the Williston Northampton School, provided information and insights on former headmaster Archibald Galbraith, a student and friend of Flora White. In addition, John Bisbee—a Vermont resident whose mother, Dorothy Winsor Bisbee, attended White's Concord school—shared a recording of her 1970s interview, conducted by her grandson, Rick Zamore. In consultation with his niece Dorothy Bisbee, John also sent me information related to his mother's papers in the Schlesinger Library at Harvard. In addition to these contributions, the staff of the SIUE Lovejoy Library helped me contextualize primary documents by locating key secondary sources. They also gave me an opportunity to receive feedback on my work from the SIUE community by inviting me to give the annual "Focus on Faculty Research" talk in 2010. The title was "Writing Educational Biography: Flora White, 1860–1948."

Presentations of my early work on Flora White also occurred at the annual meetings of scholarly societies—the International Society for Educational Biography, the Society of Philosophy and History of Education, the Conference on the Status of Research on Girls and Women, the Gender in Education Conference, the History of Education Society UK, the Australia and New Zealand History of Education Society, the AERA Biographical and Documentary Research Special Interest Group, and the Society for the Study of Curriculum History. Aside from providing important spaces for me to receive comments from other scholars, many of my conference presentations eventually found their way into peer-reviewed journals where I received helpful suggestions from editors. These journals included *Gender and Education, History of Education, History of Education Review, Educational Studies, Vitae Scholasticae, Journal of Historical Biography,* and *Journal of Philosophy and History of Education.*

Apart from the formal feedback I received from academics, I was fortunate to benefit from their comments on my work in one-on-one conversations and small-group discussions. I greatly appreciate the insights provided by David Greenhaw, president of Eden Theological Seminary, and by a group of professors from universities throughout the St. Louis metropolitan area. Named the Bi-state Action Research Collaborative (ARC), this group reviews and discusses a range of qualitative research in the field of education, presented each month by a different author. Among the ARC participants, several professors (Laurel Puchner, Owen Van den Burg, Jane Zeni, and Ann Taylor) deserve recognition for their substantive feedback on my research over an extended period. One additional member of the group—Louis M. Smith, professor emeritus at Washington University in St. Louis—offered me wise counsel, both at ARC meetings and during a twelve-month sabbatical that I took in 2013–2014, with the generous support of the administration and board of trustees of Southern Illinois University.

Dr. Smith's biographical work is well recognized. In dedicating *Writing Educational Biography: Explorations in Qualitative Research*, Craig Kridel noted that Smith's research "portrays the scholar's love and enthusiasm for the adventure of biography."[1] That enthusiasm was always apparent during ARC discussions. I found it to be of particular benefit when, during my sabbatical, Smith agreed to meet with me monthly to discuss each chapter draft of *Flora White: In the Vanguard of Gender Equity*. These monthly exchanges with Lou over coffee and lunch remain some of my most pleasurable memories in writing the book.

Finally, *Flora White: In the Vanguard of Gender Equity* was enhanced by the technical skills of a number of persons who lent their expertise to the project. They include professional indexer Robert Swanson, former SIUE graduate student Shana Nygard, photographer Donald Morice, and members of the editorial, design, production, and marketing teams at Lexington Books—especially Brian Hill (acquisitions editor for history), his assistant editor Eric Kuntzman, and Caitlin Bean (assistant editor/production). Their importance to me is summed up by the eminent biographer Nigel Hamilton, who wrote, "If you do not publish, you cannot be a biographer."[2] I was fortunate to have Lexington's support at every stage of the book's creation—from the acceptance of my proposal through the final printing of *Flora White: In the Vanguard of Gender Equity*.

In reflecting on the meaning of these contributions, I am drawn to Barbara Finkelstein's essay, "Revealing Human Agency: The Uses of Biography in the Study of Educational History." Finkelstein noted that the significance of a biography of a little-known figure like Flora White goes far beyond chronicling the facts of her life. Rather, the biography is important because it "reveals the relative power of individuals to stabilize or transform the determinacies of cultural tradition, political arrangements, economic forms, social circumstances and educational processes into new possibilities."[3] Finkelstein gives, I believe, an apt description of the effects of Flora White's quest for agency. I hope that readers and contributors alike gain insight and inspiration from her experience in the pages of *Flora White: In the Vanguard of Gender Equity*.

Portions of this book previously appeared in:

Morice, Linda C. "Flora White (1860–1948): New Woman, Stark Choice." *Educational Studies* 45 (2009): 478–495.

Morice, Linda C. "A 'Marked Success': Physical Activity in Miss White's School." *Gender and Education* 20 (2008): 325–334.

Morice, Linda C. "A 'Marked Success': Physical Activity in Miss White's School." In *Gender Balance and Gender Bias in Education*, edited by Deirdre Raftery and Maryann Valiulis, 21–30. London: Routledge, 2011.

Morice, Linda C. "A Place Called Home: Educational Reform in a Concord, Massachusetts School, 1897–1914." *History of Education* 41 (2012): 437–456. The journal can be accessed at http://www.tandfonline.com.

Morice, Linda C. "Balancing Work and Intellectual Activity: Boston's Sloyd Training School." *History of Education Review* 38 (2009): 56–68.

Morice, Linda C. "Rediscovering a Biographical Subject: Moving from the Public to the Private Sphere in the Life of Progressive Educator Flora White, 1860–1948." *Journal of Historical Biography* 11 (2012): 41–69.

Morice, Linda C. "Revisiting Schools of Tomorrow: Lessons from Educational Biography." *Vitae Scholasticae* 32 (2015): 5–18.

Morice, Linda C. "The Progressive Legacy of Flora White," *Vitae Scholasticae* 22 (2005): 57–74.

NOTES

1. Craig Kridel, ed. *Writing Educational Biography: Explorations in Qualitative Research* (New York: Garland, 1998).

2. Nigel Hamilton, *How to Do Biography: A Primer* (Cambridge: Harvard University Press, 2008), 344.

3. Barbara Finkelstein, "Revealing Human Agency: The Uses of Biography in the Study of Educational History," in *Writing Educational Biography: Explorations in Qualitative Research*, ed. Craig Kridel (New York: Garland, 1998), 46.

Bibliography

"Abramson, August." *The Jewish Encyclopedia.* http://www.ljewishencyclopedia.com/articles/621-abramson.

"Address at the Funeral of Mr. Joseph White, Heath. Oct. 18, 1861." Flora White Papers. Private collection.

Adler, Felix. "Education and Character," *School Journal,* November 3, 1894.

Alden, Lyman P. "The Shady Side of the 'Placing-Out System.'" In *The Social Welfare Forum: Official Proceedings.* Boston: George H. Ellis, 1885.

Aldridge, Jerry, and Lois McFayden Christiansen. *Stealing from the Mother: The Marginalization of Women in Education and Psychology from 1900–2010.* Lanham, MD: Rowman & Littlefield Education, 2013.

Alpern, Sara et al., ed. *The Challenge of Feminist Biography: Writing the Lives of Modern American Women.* Urbana and Chicago: University of Illinois Press, 1992.

Amato, Paul R., and Shelley Irving. "Historical Trends in Divorce in the United States." In *Handbook of Divorce and Relationship Dissolution,* edited by Mark A. Fine and John H. Harvey. New York and London: Routledge, 2006.

Anderson, Lauren. "Embedded, Emboldened, and (Net) Working for Change: Support-Seeking and Teacher Agency in Urban, High-Needs Schools." *Harvard Educational Review* 80 (2010): 541–573.

Anderson, Virginia De John. "Migrants and Motives: Religion and the Settlement of New England, 1630–1640." *New England Quarterly* 58 (1985): 339–383.

"Babcock, Elizabeth D." Interview by Renee Garrelick, May 16, 1977, Renee Garrelick Oral History Program Collection, Concord Free Public Library. www.concordlibrary.org/scollect/fin_aids/OH_Texts/babcock.html.

Bailey, Lucy E. "Necessary Betrayals: Reflections on Biographical Work on a Racist Ancestor." In *Life Stories: Exploring Issues in Educational History Through Biography,* edited by Linda C. Morice and Laurel Puchner, 253–272. Charlotte, NC: Information Age, 2014.

_____. "Engendering Curriculum History: Some Methodological Musings." *Journal of Philosophy and History of Education* 65 (2015): xv–xxx.

Baldwin, Roger, to Flora White. 19 January 1941. Flora White Papers. Private collection.

"Balliet, Thomas Minard." *Biographical Dictionary of American Educators,* vol. 1, 81–82. Westport, CT: Greenwood Press, 1978.

Bascom, John. "The Life of Joseph White, with Tributes of Friends." In *Lancaster, Mass., Heath, Mass., Joseph White.* Privately printed, n.d. Private collection.

Basnett, Susan. "Travel Writing and Gender." In *The Cambridge Companion to Travel Writing,* edited by Peter Hulme and Tim Youngs, 225–241. Cambridge: Cambridge University Press, 2002.

Bean, William G. "Puritan Versus Celt, 1850–1860." *The New England Quarterly* 7 (1934): 70–89.

Bijon, Beatrice, and Gerard Gacon, eds. *In Between Two Worlds: Narratives by Female Explorers and Travellers, 1850–1945*. New York: Peter Lang, 2009.

Billington, Ray Allen. *America's Frontier Heritage*. New York: Holt, Rinehart and Winston, 1966.

Bisbee, Dorothy. Email message to John Bisbee, February 29, 2016.

Bisbee, Dorothy Winsor. Interview by Rick Zamore, circa 1970.

Blanchard, Joseph N. "A Sermon in Memory of E. Winchester Donald, D. D. LL. D. Late Rector of Trinity Church, Boston, Preached in Trinity Church Sunday Afternoon, November 20, 1904." Boston: Printed for Trinity Church, 1905.

Blanton, Casey. *Travel Writing: The Self and the World*. New York: Routledge, 2002.

Blunt, Alison. *Travel, Gender and Imperialism: Mary Kingsley and West Africa*. New York: Guilford Press, 1994.

Bolin, Paul E. "The Massachusetts Drawing Act of 1870: Industrial Mandate or Democratic Maneuver?" In *Framing the Past: Essays on Art Education*, edited by Donald Soucy and Mary Ann Stankiewicz, 59–68. Reston, VA: National Art Education Association, 1990.

Bremer, Francis. *The Puritan Experiment: New England Society from Bradford to Edwards*. New York: St. Martin's Press, 1976.

"A Brief History of Trinity Church and Its Buildings." Trinity Episcopal Church. http://www.trinityconcord.org/history.shtml.

Brown, George Allen. "Memoir: Marietta Johnson and the School of Organic Education." In *Marietta Johnson, 30 Years with an Idea*, x–xv. University, AL: University of Alabama Press, 1974.

Brown, Kathleen M. "Pivotal Points: History, Development, and Promise of the Principalship." In *The SAGE Handbook of Educational Leadership*, edited by Fenwick W. English, 81–108. Los Angeles: SAGE Publications, 2011.

Brown, Robert T. *The Rise and Fall of the People's Colleges: The Westfield Normal School, 1839–1914*. Westfield, MA: Institute for Massachusetts Studies, Westfield State College, 1988.

"Cabot, Harold and Adeline" Interview by Renee Garrelick, November 15, 1977, Renee Garrelick Oral History Program Collection, Concord Free Public Library. www.concordlibrary.org/scollect/fin_aids/OH_Texts/cabot.html.

Caine, Barbara. *Biography and History*. New York: Palgrave Macmillan, 2010.

Callahan, Raymond E. *Education and the Cult of Efficiency: A Study of Social Forces That Have Shaped the Administration of Public Schools*. Chicago: University of Chicago Press, 1962.

Calver, Edward. *Heath, Massachusetts: A History and Guidebook*. Heath, MA: Heath Historical Society, 2009.

Clark, Christopher. *The Roots of Rural Capitalism: Western Massachusetts, 1780–1860*. Ithaca, NY: Cornell University Press, 1990.

"Clark, Gladys." Interview by Renee Garrelick, April 12, 1981, Renee Garrelick Oral History Program Collection, Concord Free Public Library. www.concordlibrary.org/scollect/fin_aids/OH_clark.html.

Clarke, John R. "Margaret Fisher: An American Modernist," *Woman's Art Journal* 24 (2003): 11–16.

Cleverley, John, and D. C. Phillips. *Visions of Childhood: Influential Models from Locke to Spock*. New York: Teachers College, Columbia University, 1986.

Clifford, Geraldine Joncich. "The Historical Recovery of Edyth Astrid Ferris." In *Writing Educational Biography: Explorations in Qualitative Research*, edited by Craig Kridel, 147–215. New York and London: Garland Publishing, 1995..

Comings, S. H. *Industrial and Vocational Education: Universal and Self Sustaining*. Boston: Christopher Publishing House, 1915.

Concord, Massachusetts: American History through Literature. http://www.endnotes.com/american-history-literature-literature.concord-massachusetts.

Cremin, Lawrence A. Preface to Charles E. Strickland and Charles O. Burgess, *Health, Growth and Heredity: G. Stanley Hall on Natural Education.* New York: Teachers College Press, 1965.

————. *The Transformation of the School: Progressivism in American Education, 1876–1957.* New York: Alfred A. Knopf, 1969.

Dewey, John, to Flora White. 5 August 1939. Flora White Papers. Private collection.

Dewey, John, and Evelyn Dewey. *Schools of Tomorrow.* New York: E. P. Dutton, 1915, 1943, 1962.

Derounian-Stodala, Kathryn Zabelle. "Captivity, Liberty and Early American Consciousness." In *Early American Literature* 43 (2008): 715–724.

Diehl, Lesley. "The Paradox of G. Stanley Hall: Foe of Coeducation and Educator of Women." *American Psychologist* 41 (1986): 868–878.

Donovan, Mary S. *A Different Call: Women's Ministries in the Episcopal Church, 1850–1920.* Wilton, CT: Morehouse-Barlow, 1986.

Duff, Sarah Emily. "Head, Heart and Hand: The Huguenot Seminary and the Construction of Middle Class Afrikaner Femininity." Master's thesis. University of Stellenbosch, 2006.

Dun, Angus. Unpublished correspondence. Flora White Papers. Private collection.

Eaton, William Edward, ed. *Shaping the Superintendency: A Reexamination of Callahan and The Cult of Efficiency.* New York: Teachers College Press, 1990. www.concordlibrary.org/scollect/fin_aids/OH_Texts/richardson.html.

"Educational Survey." *School and Home Education,* October 1915.

"Educators' Conference at Plymouth." *New York Times,* July 15, 1894.

Edwards, Davis. "Founder of Organic Education Tells of New School." *New York Times,* March 16, 1913.

Egan, Timothy. *The Worst Hard Time: The Untold Story of Those Who Survived the Great American Dust Bowl.* Boston: Mariner Books, 2006.

Elphick, Richard, and Rodney Davenport, eds. *Christianity in South Africa: A Political, Social, and Cultural History.* Cape Town: Creda Press, 1997.

Emerson, Ralph Waldo. "Concord Hymn, 1837." In *Early Poems of Ralph Waldo Emerson.* New York: Thomas Y. Crowell, 1899.

Ervin, Robert Jr. to Grace Moyer Share. 6 November 1985. Flora White Papers. Private collection.

"Erving—Early Settlement: Extracted from Louis H. Everts, 1879. *History of the Connecticut Valley in Massachusetts,* vol. II." http://www.franklincountyhistory.com/erving/everts/03html.

Evans, Sara M. *Born for Liberty.* New York: The Free Press, 1989.

Everett, Dianne. "Gage." Oklahoma Historical Society. http://digital.librarry.okstate.edu/encyclopedia/entries/G.GA009.html.

Eyestone, June E. "The Influence of Swedish Sloyd and Its Interpreters on American Art Education." *Studies in Art Instruction: A Journal of Issues and Research,* 34 (1992): 28–38.

Fallace, Thomas, and Victoria Fantozzi. "A Century of John and Evelyn Dewey's *Schools of Tomorrow:* Rousseau, Recorded Knowledge, and Race in the Philosopher's Most Problematic Text." *Educational Studies* 5 (2015): 129–152.

Farrell, Betty G. *Elite Families: Class and Power in Nineteenth-Century Boston.* Albany: State University of New York Press, 1993.

Field, Eugene. *A Little Book of Western Verse.* New York: C. Scribner, 1892.

The Final Account of Harriet M. White, Administratix of the Estate of Joseph White, Late of Heath. Flora White Papers. Private collection.

Finkelstein, Barbara. "Revealing Human Agency: The Uses of Biography in the Study of Educational History." In *Writing Educational Biography: Explorations in Qualitative Research,* edited by Craig Kridel, 45–60. New York: Garland Publishing, 1968.

Foner, Eric. *Free Soil, Free Labor, Free Men: The Ideology of the Republican Party Before the Civil War.* Oxford and New York: Oxford University Press, 1995.

Fortmiller, Hubert C. Jr. *Find the Promise: Middlesex School, 1901–2001.* Concord, MA: Middlesex School, 2003.

"Transactions of the Forty-first Annual Meeting of the Alumnae Association of the Woman's Medical College of Pennsylvania." Philadelphia: Alumnae Association of the Woman's Medical College of Pennsylvania, 1916, 35.

Franklin B. Sanborn Papers, Georgetown University.

Franzosa, Susan Douglas. "'Schools Yet-to-Be:' Recovering the Work of Nineteenth Century Women in Early Childhood Education," *Vitae Scholasticae* 32 (2015): 5–24.

Galbraith, Archibald V. *Some Objectives of the Endowed Preparatory School.* East Hampton, MA: Williston Academy, 1967.

Gardner, Eugene Clarence. *Springfield Present and Prospectives: The City of Homes.* Springfield, MA: Pond and Campbell, 1905.

George, Henry. *Progress and Poverty: An Inquiry into the Causes of Industrial Depressions, and of Increase of Want with Increase of Wealth.* New York: W. J. Lavell, 1879.

Glasscock, Jean. *Wellesley College, 1875–1975: A Century of Women.* Wellesley, MA: Wellesley College, 1975.

"Grace Wolcott, M.D." *Boston Medical and Surgical Journal,* 173 (1915): 791–792.

Grossberg, Michael. "Who Gets the Child? Custody, Guardianship and the Rise of Judicial Patriarchy in Nineteenth-Century America." *Feminist Studies* 9 (1983): 235–260.

Guild, Edward P. *Centennial History of Heath, Massachusetts.* Boston: Advertiser Publishing Company, 1885.

Gutek, Gerald L., and Patricia A. Gutek. *Bringing Montessori to America: S. S. McClure, Maria Montessori, and the Campaign to Publicize Montessori Education.* Tuscaloosa, AL: University of Alabama Press, 2016.

Hall, G. Stanley. *Adolescence: Its Psychology and Its Relations to Physiology, Anthropology, Sociology, Sex, Crime, Religion and Education.* New York: D. Appleton Company, 1904, 1907, 1915.

Hamilton, Nigel. *How to Do Biography: A Primer.* Cambridge: Harvard University Press, 2008.

Hansot, Elisabeth, and David Tyack. *The Dream Deferred: A Golden Age for Women School Administrators.* Stanford, CA: Institute for Research on Educational Finance and Governance, School of Education, Stanford University, 1981.

Hargreaves, Jennifer, and Patricia Vertinsky, eds. *Physical Culture, Power, and the Body Beautiful.* New York: Routledge, 2007.

Harvard Class of 1877, Seventh Report. Cambridge, MA: Harvard, 1917.

"Heath Elementary." School and District Profiles. Massachusetts Department of Elementary and Secondary Education, 2015.

Heath, George. "Zan Zoo." *Harper's New Monthly Magazine* 83 (1891): 345–355.

"Heath Historical Society." http://www.townofheath.org?page_ids2127.

"Heath—The Church of Christ in Heath: Extracted from Louis H. Everts, 1879." *History of the Connecticut Valley in Massachusetts,* vol. 2. http://www.franklincountyhistory.com/heath/everts/13.html.

Henderson, Charles Hanford. "The Aim of Modern Education." *Appleton's Popular Science Monthly* (1896).

———. *Education and the Larger Life.* Boston and New York: Houghton Mifflin, 1904.

———. *What Is It to Be Educated?* New York: Houghton Mifflin, 1914.

Hendry, Petra Munro. *Engendering Curriculum History.* New York and London: Routledge, 2011.

Henry, Sarah, and Mary A. Williams. *North Bennet Street School: A Short History, 1885–1985.* Boston: Chadis Printing, 1987.

"Here and There." *Posse Gymnasium Journal* 3 (1895): 10.

Herndon, Ruth Wallis, and John E. Murray, eds. *Children Bound to Labor: The Pauper Apprentice System in Early America.* New York: Cornell University Press, 2009.

History Proceedings of the Pocumtuck Valley Memorial Association, vol. II. Deerfield, MA: Pocumtuck Valley Memorial Association, 1898.

Hoffman, Norma. "Pauline Agassiz Shaw, 1841–1917: A Forgotten Visionary." *AFFILIA* 15 (2000): 300–368.

Holly, William H. to Flora White. 22 April 1941. Flora White Papers. Private collection.

Holmes, John Haynes. Unpublished correspondence. Flora White Papers. Private collection.
"'Homelike' School Assn. To Meet Here." *Washington Times*, April 8, 1920.
Howells, William Dean, and Henry Miller, eds. *The Heart of Childhood*. New York: Harper & Brothers, 1906.
Invoice of the Estate of Joseph White, Deceased. Flora White Papers. Private collection.
James, William. *Principles of Psychology with Introduction by George A. Miller*. Cambridge: Harvard University Press,1983. First published in 1890 by Henry Holt and Company.
———. *Talks to Teachers on Psychology: And to Students on Some of Life's Ideals with Introduction by Gerald E. Myers* (1983). Cambridge: Harvard University Press. First published in 1899 by Henry Holt and Company.
Jarvis, Edward. *Traditions and Reminiscences of Concord, Massachusetts, 1779–1878*. Concord, MA: Library Corporation, Concord Free Public Library, 1993.
Jasanoff, Maya. *Liberty's Exiles: American Loyalists in a Revolutionary World*. New York: Vintage Press, 2012.
Johnson, Marietta. *30 Years with an Idea*. University, AL: University of Alabama Press, 1974.
Joseph and Jennie White Obituaries. Private collection.
Josiah Davis Store. 50/52 Belknap Street, *Survey of Historical and Architectural Resources, Concord, Massachusetts*, vol. 1, form 94. Boston: Massachusetts Historical Commission, 1994.
Katz, Michael B. *The Irony of Early School Reform: Educational Innovation in Mid-Nineteenth Century Massachusetts*. New York: Teachers College, Columbia University, 2001.
———. *The Undeserving Poor: America's Enduring Confrontation with Poverty*. Oxford: Oxford University Press, 2013.
Keegan, John. *Fields of Battle: The Wars for North America*. New York: Vintage Books, 1995.
Keeling, Drew. "Transatlantic Shipping Cartels and Migration between Europe and America, 1800–1914." In *Essays in Economic and Business History* 17 (2012): 195–213.
Kenealy, Arabella K. "Woman as an Athlete, 1899." In *Out of the Bleachers: Writings on Women and Sport*, edited by Stephanie L. Twin, 35–51. Old Westbury, NY: Feminist Press, 1979.
Kliebard, Herbert M. *The Struggle for the American Curriculum, 1893–1958*. New York and London: Routledge, 1989.
Kridel, Craig, ed. *Writing Educational Biography: Explorations in Qualitative Research*. New York: Garland, 1998.
"La Jolla Woman Takes Own Life." *San Diego Union*, February 19, 1935.
Larsson, Gustaf. "Letter to Sloyd Graduates." *Sloyd Bulletin* 2 (March 1899): 4.
———. *Sloyd*. Gustaf Larsson, 1902.
Lasky, Sue. "A Sociocultural Approach to Understanding Teacher Identity, Agency, and Professional Vulnerability in a Context of Secondary School Reform." *Teaching and Teacher Education* 21 (2005): 899–916.
Lazeron, Marvin. "Urban Reform and the Schools: Kindergartens in Massachusetts, 1870–1915." *History of Education Quarterly* 11 (1971): 115–142.
"Letter from Mrs. Sarah J. Hastings Nichols." In *Heath, Mass. Centennial*, edited by Edward P. Guild. 125. Boston: Advertiser Publishing Co., August 19, 1885.
Lockwood, John H. *Western Massachusetts: A History, 1636–1925*. www.ebooksread.com/authors-eng/john-h-john-hoyt-lockwood/western-massachusetts-a-history-1636–1925-volume-3-kco.shtml.
Longfellow, Henry Wadsworth. *The Song of Hiawatha: An Epic Poem*. Chicago: M. A. Donahue, 1898.
"Looking Back over Centuries White Family First Mentioned in 1333." *The Franklin Press and Shelburne Falls News*, May 2, 1929, 1–3.
"Magazine Tells of Marietta Johnson, Visionary." *UA News*, January 2, 2001.
Maher, Francis. "John Dewey, Progressive Education and Feminist Pedagogies: Issues of Gender and Authority." In *Feminist Engagements: Reading, Resisting, and Revisioning Male Theorists in Education and Cultural Studies*, edited by Kathleen Weiler, 13–32. New York: Routledge, 2001.

Maitland, Alastair. "Robert Strong Woodward in Heath." In *The Book of Heath: Bicentennial Essays*, edited by Susan B. Silvester, 159–171. Ashfield, MA: Paideia, 1985.

Malone, Margaret. Unpublished correspondence. Flora White Papers. Private collection.

Mandell, David. *King Philip's War: Colonial Expansion, Native Resistance, and the End of Indian Sovereignty*. Baltimore: Johns Hopkins University Press, 2010.

Martin, Jane Roland. "Excluding Women from the Educational Realm." *Harvard Educational Review* 52 (1982): 133–148.

Mason, Mary Ann. *From the Father's Property to Children's Rights*. New York: Columbia University Press, 1994.

Massachusetts Vital Records, 1841–1910. "May 22, 1856: The Caning of Senator Charles Sumner." United States Senate http://www.senate.gov/artandhistory/history/minute/The_ Caning_of_Senator Charles_Sumner.htm.

McFarland, Philip. *A History of Concord Academy*. Concord, MA: Concord Academy, 1986.

McKay, Ernest. "Henry Wilson and the Coalition of 1851." *The New England Quarterly* 36 (1963): 338–357.

McLellan, Dennis. "Robert Brown, 81; Championed Liberation Theology." *Los Angeles Times*, September 8, 2001.

Melvin, A. Gordon. *Education: A History*. New York: John Day, 1946.

Menken, H. L. "The Dole for Bogus American Farmers." In *The American Mercury*, December 1936: 400–407. http://www.unz.org/Pub/AmMercury-1936dec0400.

Miller, Spencer Jr. "Address by Spencer Miller Jr.: An Interpretation of Its Founding in 1785 Upon the One Hundred and Fiftieth Anniversary." In *Sesquicentennial Anniversary of the Town of Heath, Massachusetts*, edited by Howard Chandler Robbins, 19–23. Heath, MA: Heath Historical Society, 1935.

Miss White's Home School, Concord, MA: 1900.

Miss White's Home School, Concord, MA: 1906.

"Mohawk/Hawlemont School Districts: Heath Elementary." http://mohawkschools.org/ heath.php.

Mosteller-Timbes, Cynthia. "Marietta Johnson School of Organic Education." *Encyclopedia of Alabama*. www.encyclopediaofalabama.org/article/h-1863.

Moyer, Catherine to Joseph White. 5 December 1941. Flora White Papers. Private collection.

Moyer, Cliff. "More Than a Depression [as told by Robert Moyer]." In *Town of Gage History*, 65–66. Gage, OK: Gage Chamber of Commerce, 1984.

Moyer, Diana. "The Gendered Boundaries of Child-Centred Education: Elsie Ripley Clapp and the History of US Progressive Education." *Gender and Education* 21 (2009): 531–547.

Moyer, Dorothy, to Grace Moyer, circa 1942–1943. Flora White Papers. Private collection.

Moyer, Golden Jr. "White, Joseph David." *Our Ellis County Heritage: 1885–1974*, vol. 1., 493. Gage, OK: Ellis County Historical Society, 1974.

———. Letter to Grace Moyer Share. 19 March 1987. Flora White Papers. Private collection.

New Hampshire Technology Education Curriculum Guide. New Hampshire Technology Education Association, 2001.

New York Herald. April 7, 1860.

Newman, Joseph W. "Experimental School, Experimental Community: The Marietta Johnson School of Organic Education in Fairhope Alabama." In *"Schools of Tomorrow," Schools of Today: What, Happened to Progressive Education*, edited by Susan F. Semel and Alan R. Sadovnik, 67–102. New York: Peter Lang, 1999.

———. "Marietta Johnson and the Organic School." In *Founding Mothers and Others: Women Educational Leaders during the Progressive Era*, edited by Alan R. Sadovnik and Susan F. Semel, 19–36. New York: Palgrave, 2002.

Nichols, Guild. "North End History: Boston's First Neighborhood." www.northendboston.com.

Novick, Carla, M.D., "Polydacytly of the Foot." *Medscape Reference: Drugs, Diseases & Procedures*. http://emedicine.com/article/1260255-overview#a0199.

"Obituary: Grace Wolcott, M.D." *Boston Medical and Surgical Journal*, 173 (1915): 791.

O'Donnell, Laurel. "Christ Church Parish—Springfield, Mass.—Rev. John Cotton Brooks.http://www.hampdencountyhistory.com/springfield/christchurch/cc069.html.

"Old Strong House (1744)." Historic Buildings of Massachusetts. http://mass. historicbuildingsct.com.

"The Origin of Our Serenity Prayer." http://www.aahistory.com/prayer.html.

Paine, Sarah Cushing, and Charles Henry Pope, eds. *Paine Ancestry: The Family of Robert Treat Paine, Signer of the Declaration of Independence.* Boston: Printed for the Family, 1912.

Paul, Sherman, ed. *Walden and Civil Disobedience by Henry David Thoreau.* Boston: Houghton Mifflin, 1960.

Pauline Agassiz Shaw: Tributes Paid Her Memory at the Memorial Service Held on Easter Sunday, April 8, 1917 at Faneuil Hall. Boston: Privately printed.

Perlmann, Joel, and Robert A. Margo. *Women's Work: American Schoolteachers, 1650–1920.* Chicago: University of Chicago Press, 2001.

Perry, Arthur. "The Life of Joseph White, with Its Historic Antecedents." *Lancaster, Mass., Heath Mass., Joseph White.* Privately printed, n.d. Private collection.

Perry, Elisabeth Israels. "From Belle Moskowitz to Women's History." In *The Challenge of Feminist Biography: Writing the Lives of Modern American Women,* edited by Sara Alpern et al., 79–96. Urbana and Chicago: University of Illinois Press, 1992.

Philpott, A. J. "Mary O. Abbott's Sculptures on Exhibition in Concord." *Boston Sunday Globe,* May 29, 1930.

Pickwick, Miss. "Girl about Town." *Daily Oklahoman.* February 9. 1941.

Plourde-Barker, Michele to Linda C. Morice. 24 August 2004. Private collection.

Plover Hill Camp for Girls in Charge of the Misses White. Boston: Todd Printer, 1907.

"Poetess, Educator Lives Quietly in Retirement." *Greenfield Gazette and Courier,* July 14, 1947.

The Poetry Digest: Annual Anthology of Verse for 1939, 117. New York: The Poetry Digest, 1939.

Porterfield, Amanda. *Mary Lyon and the Mount Holyoke Missionaries.* Oxford: Oxford University Press, 1997.

Pratt, John Winsor, and Richard Jay Zecklauser. "The Fair and Efficient Division of the Winsor Family Silver," *Management Science* 36 (1900): 1293–1301.

Prentice, Alison, and Marjorie Theobald, eds. *Women Who Taught: Perspectives on the History of Women and Teaching.* Toronto: University of Toronto Press, 1991.

Priestley, Mark et al. "Teacher Agency in Curriculum Making: Agents of Change and Spaces for Manoeuvre." *Curriculum Inquiry* 42 (2012): 191–214.

"Professor Dewey's Report on the Fairhope Experiment in Organic Education." *John Dewey: The Middle Works, 1899–1924,* vol. 7, 387–389. Carbondale and Edwardsville, IL: Southern Illinois University Press, 1979.

Radner, Joan N., and Susan S. Lanser. "Strategies of Coding in Women's Culture." In *Feminist Messages: Coding in Women's Culture,* edited by Joan Newton Radner, 1–30. Urbana and Chicago: University of Illinois Press.

Reese, William J. "The Origins of Progressive Education." *History of Education Quarterly* 41 (2001): 1–24.

Reitz, Conrad. "The Tragic Genius of Eugene Marais," 1980. http://www.caans~acaen.ca/ Journal/issues_online/Issue_II_I_1980b/Reitz.pdf.

Rich, Mokoto. "Why Don't More Men Go into Teaching?" *New York Times,* September 6, 2004.

"Richardson, Lawrence Eaton." Interviewed by Renee Garrelick, January 19, 1978, Renee Garrelick Oral History Program Collection, Concord Free Public Library. www. concordlibrary.org/scollect/fin_aids/OH_Texts/richardson.html

Robbins, Howard Chandler. "The Church of Christ in Heath." In *Sesquicentennial Anniversary of the Town of Heath, Massachusetts,* edited by Howard Chandler Robbins, 138–144. Heath, MA: Heath Historical Society, 1935.

Robert, Dana L. *American Women in Mission: A Social History of Their Thought and Practice.* Macon, GA: Mercer University Press, 1996.

Rodgers, Daniel T. "Socializing Middle-Class Children: Institutions, Fables, and Work Values in Nineteenth-Century America." *Journal of Social History* 13 (1980): 354–367.

Roos, Isaac to Flora White. 16 June 1887. Flora White Papers. Private collection.

Ross, Dorothy. *G. Stanley Hall, The Psychologist and Prophet.* Chicago: University of Chicago Press, 1972.

Rousmaniere, Kate. *Citizen Teacher: The Life and Leadership of Margaret Haley.* Albany, NY: State University of New York Press, 2005.

Rowlandson, Mary. *The Sovereignty and Goodness of God: Being a Narrative of the Captivity and Restoration of Mrs. Mary Rowlandson.* Cambridge: Samuel Green, 1682. In Almira Larkin White, *Descendants of John White, 1638–1900,* vol. 1. Haverhill, MA: Chase Brothers Printers, 1900.

Rugg, Harold, and Ann Shumaker. *The Child-Centered School.* New York: Arno Press and *The New York Times,* 1969.

Sadovnik, Alan R., and Susan F. Semel, eds. *Founding Mothers and Others: Women Educational Leaders during the Progressive Era.* New York: Palgrave, 2002.

Salomon, Otto. *The Theory of Educational Sloyd,* Boston: Silver Burdett, 1900.

Sanneh, Lamin. "Christian Missions and the Western Guilt Complex." *The Christian Century,* 8 (1987): 331–334.

Sargent, Porter E. *The Handbook of Private Schools.* Boston: Porter E. Sargent, 1918.

Schriber, Mary Suzanne. *Writing Home: American Women Abroad, 1830–1920.* Charlottesville, VA: University Press of Virginia, 1997.

Scott, Harriet M., and Gertrude Buck. *Organic Education: A Manual for Teachers in Primary and Grammar Grades.* Boston: D. C. Heath, 1897, 1899.

Seigfried, Charlene Haddock. *Feminist Interpretations of John Dewey.* University Park, PA: The Pennsylvania State University Press, 2002.

Semel, Susan F., and Alan R. Sadovnik, eds. *"Schools of Tomorrow," Schools of Today: What Happened to Progressive Education.* New York: Peter Lang, 1999.

Share, Grace Moyer. "Identification of People" (written in 1986). Flora White Papers. Private collection.

———. "Notes on the Lives of Mary Abby and Flora White" (written in 1986). Flora White Papers. Private collection.

———. "The Golden Moyer Family Spend the Winter of 1925–26 in Heath, Massachusetts" (written in 1986). Flora White Papers. Private collection.

———. "The Summer of 1938" (written in 1986). Flora White Papers. Private collection.

Sharp, James Clement. *John Cotton Brooks.* Cambridge: Harvard University, 1909.

Sifton, Elisabeth. "The Serenity Prayer." *Yale Review* 86 (1998): 16–65.

———. *The Serenity Prayer: Faith and Politics in Times of Peace and War.* New York: W. W. Norton & Company, 2003.

Sklar, Kathryn Kish. *Catharine Beecher: A Study in American Domesticity.* New Haven: Yale University Press, 1976.

Smith, Louis M. "Adventuring as Biographers: A Chronicle of a Difficult Ten-Day Week," *Vitae Scholasticae* 31 (2014): 5–22.

Smith, Lynda Anderson. "The Biographer's Relationship with Her Subject." In *Writing Educational Biography: Explorations in Qualitative Research,* edited by Craig Kridel, 195–200. New York: Garland, 1998.

Smith, Newland F. Jr. "Early Summer People in Heath." In *The Book of Heath: Bicentennial Essays,* edited by Susan B. Silvester, 140–158. Ashfield, MA: Paideia Publishers, 1985.

Smith-Rosenberg, Carroll, and Charles Rosenberg. "The Female Animal: Medical and Biological Views on Woman and Her Role in Nineteenth Century America." *Journal of American History* 60 (1973): 332–356.

Spring, Joel. *The American School: A Global Context from the Puritans to the Obama Era.* New York: McGraw-Hill, 2011.

"Springfield History." http://www.quadrangle.org/springfield-history.htm.

Staring, Jeroen F. "Midwives of Progressive Education: The Bureau of Educational Experiments 1916–1919," PhD diss., University of Amsterdam, 2013.

Stocks, Arthur. "Buffalo and Its Attractions." *The School Review* 4 (1896): 494–511.

Stow, Doug. "Nääs: Placing the Hands at the Center of Education." *Woodwork* (2008): 60–63.

Stow, Sarah D. Locke. *History of Mount Holyoke Seminary, South Hadley, Mass: During Its First Half Century, 1837–1887*. New York: Russell Sage Foundation, 1992.

Swanson, Rev. Deacon Geraldine A. "Deaconess Susan Travor Knapp: A Pioneer of Women's Leadership in the Church," *The Episcopal New Yorker*, Spring 2011, 24–25.

Sweeney, Kevin. "Rum, Romanism, Representation, and Reform: Coalition Politics in Massachusetts, 1847–1853." *Civil War History* 22 (1976): 116–137.

Tanner, Pearle. "Heath and Its Families." In *Sesquicentennial Anniversary of the Town of Heath, Massachusetts, 1785–1935*, edited by Howard Chandler Robbins, 53–61. Heath, MA: Heath Historical Society, 1935.

Taylor, Frederick W. *The Principles of Scientific Management*. New York: Harper and Row, 1911.

"Tenth Generation." Ancestry of Ralph J. Turner. rockcreekexperiment.com.

Thompson, John H. "Historical Address." In *Centennial History of Heath, Massachusetts*, edited by Edward P. Guild. Boston: Advertiser Publishing Company, 1885.

Thompson, Leonard. *A History of South Africa*. New Haven and London: Yale University Press, 2000.

Thorbjornsson, Hans. "Otto Salomon (1849–1907)." *Prospects: The Quarterly Review of Comparative Education* 23 (1994): 1–11.

———. "Swedish Educational Sloyd: An International Success." *Tidskrift* (2006): 10–34.

Thoreau, Henry David. *Walden and Civil Disobedience*, edited by Paul Sherman. Boston: Houghton Mifflin, 1960.

Toulouse, Teresa A. *The Captain's Position: Female Narrative, Male Identity, and Royal Authority in Colonial New England*. Philadelphia: University of Pennsylvania Press, 2007.

Twin, Stephanie L. "Women and Sport." In *Sport in America: New Historical Perspectives*, edited by Donald Spivey, 193–217. Westport, CT: Greenwood Press, 1985.

Tyack, David B. *The One Best System: A History of American Urban Education*. Cambridge, MA: Harvard University Press, 1974.

Tyack, David, and Elisabeth Hansot. *Managers of Virtue: Public School Leadership in America, 1820–1980*. New York: Basic Books, 1982.

———. *Learning Together: A History of Coeducation in American Public Schools*. New York: Russell Sage Foundation, 1992.

U.S. Bureau of Education. "A Statement of the Theory of Education in the United States of America as Approved by Many Leading Educators," Washington, D.C.: U.S. Government Printing Office, 1874.

U.S. Census. Franklin County, Massachusetts, 1860.

Urban, Wayne J., and Jennings L. Wagoner Jr. *American Education: A History*. New York and London: Routledge, 2009.

Van Breda, John to Flora White. 15 June 1887. Flora White Papers. Private collection.

Vertinsky, Patricia A. *The Eternally Wounded Woman: Women, Doctors, and Exercise in the Late Nineteenth Century*. Urbana and Chicago: University of Illinois Press, 1994.

Webb, Walter Prescott. *The Great Plains*. Lincoln: University of Nebraska Press, 1931, 1959.

Weiler, Kathleen, "The Historiography of Gender and Progressive Education in the United States," *Paedagogica Historica* 42 (2006), 161–176.

Weis, Doctor Frederick Lewis. "Lancaster's Part in the Founding of Heath." In *Sesquicentennial Anniversary of the Town of Heath*, edited by Howard Chandler Robbins, 30–36. Heath, MA: Heath Historical Society, 1935.

White, Almira Larkin. *Genealogy of the Descendants of John White*, vol. I. Haverhill, MA: The Chase Press, 1900.

White, David to Joseph White II. 12 March 1851. Flora White Papers. Private collection.

White, Flora. "Light and Shadow." Toronto: Columbian Music Publishers, Ltd., 1938.

———. "Life Facts of Flora White and Family Recorded Mar. 18, 1939." Heath Historical Society.

———. "That Which Abides." In *The Poetry Digest: Annual Anthology of Verse for 1939*. New York: The Poetry Digest, 1939, 117.

———. Letter to Anne Halfpenny. 17 June 1940. Westfield State University.

———. "A Basic Necessity." *Unity*, December 2, 1940.

———. "Reply to Mr. Johnson." *Unity* 127 (1941): 119.

———. *Bloodroots in the Wake of Circumstance.* Kansas City, MO: Burton, 1942.

———. Letter to Joseph White, 7 August 1943. Flora White Papers. Private collection.

———. "India." *Unity,* January 1944.

———. "Child Training and Child Education." n.d. Unpublished lecture. Flora White Papers. Private collection.

———. "Growth and Education." n.d. Unpublished lecture. Flora White Papers. Private collection.

———. Unpublished correspondence. Flora White Papers. Private collection.

White, Flora J. "Physical Effects of Sloyd." Paper presented at the annual meeting of the National Education Association, Buffalo, New York, 1896.

———. "Physical Effects of Sloyd." *Sloyd Bulletin* 2 (1899): 5–10.

———. "The Boers of South Africa in Their Social Relations." *Journal of Social Science* 38 (1901): 177–188.

White, Joseph David. "Voices." *The Poetry Digest: Annual Anthology of Verse for 1939,* 118–119. New York: The Poetry Digest, 1939.

White, Mary A., and Flora White. *Poems by Mary A. White and Flora White.* New York: Paebar, 1939.

White, Joseph. n.d. Unpublished manuscripts. Flora White Papers. Private collection.

———. Letter to Flora White, 5 August 1939. Flora White Papers. Private collection.

Whittaker, David J. *The Impact and Legacy of Educational Sloyd.* London and New White, York: Routledge, 2014.

Woodward, Robert Strong. http://robertstrongwoodward. com/Friends/Friendshtm.

———. Unpublished correspondence. Flora White Papers. Private collection.

Worden, Nigel. *Slavery in Dutch South Africa.* Cambridge: Cambridge University Press, 2010.

"Writer, Educator Miss White Dies." *Greenfield Gazette and Courier,* February 16, 1948.

Zamore, Rick, circa 1970. Interview of Dorothy Winsor Bisbee. Private collection.

Index

Abbot, Mary Ogden, 135, 136
Abbott, Grafton St. Loe, 135
Abbott, Mary Adams, 135
Abramson, August, 88–89, 91
A. Bronson Alcott: His Life and Philosophy
   (Sanborn and Harris), 114
ACLU. *See* American Civil Liberties
   Union
Adler, Felix, 144n5
*Adolescence: Its Psychology and Its
   Relation to Physiology, Anthropology,
   Sociology, Sex, Crime, Religion and
   Education* (Hall), 132
Afrikaners, 64–65, 65–66
Agassiz, Louis, 44, 104
Agricultural Adjustment Act, 166
Alcoholics Anonymous, 175
Alcott, Amos Bronson, 114
Alcott, Louisa May, 114, 115, 135
Alden, Henry Mills, 2, 74
Alden, Lyman P., 29
Aldridge, Jerry, 128
Algonquin tribes, 14, 15, 17, 116
American Board of Commissioners for
   Foreign Missions, 59
American Civil Liberties Union (ACLU),
   3, 155, 174
American Psychological Association, 85
American Revolution, 17, 18, 24, 28, 105,
   113, 134

American Social Science Association, 65,
   68, 114
Amherst, Massachusetts, 30, 31
Amherst History Museum, 32
"Amour," 94
Anderson, Virginia De John, 13
Andover Theological Seminary, 31, 50

Babcock, Elizabeth Darling, 121, 131, 136
Bagley, William C., 127
Bailey, Lucy E., 5–6, 190, 191
Ball, Myrtle Anne, 130
Balliet, Thomas, 49, 116
Bassnett, Susan, 73
Beecher, Catharine, 50–51
Bennett, Hugh, 165–166, 166, 167,
   167–168, 180
Bennett's Soil Conservation Service, 166
Berg, Hjalmar, 93
Bijon, Beatrice, 58, 61
Billington, Ray Allen, 33n4
biographer: "adventuring" experiences of
   Massachusetts and Oklahoma as, 4;
   Bailey's cautionary note to, 190;
   "delicious find" of, 189–190;
   evenhanded study by, 186–187; family
   connection of, 185, 191; Heath tour of,
   187; learning through family lore of,
   187–188; on locating women's
   biographical sources, 191; Perry
   situation similarities with, 188;

207

About the Author

Linda C. Morice is Professor Emerita of Educational Leadership at Southern Illinois University Edwardsville. Her research focuses on educational history, women's history, and educational biography. She is co-editor, with Laurel Puchner, of *Life Stories: Exploring Issues in Educational History through Biography* (2014). Morice has also published articles in a number of academic journals, including (among others) *Gender and Education, History of Education, History of Education Review,* and *Educational Studies.*

9 781498 542388